WHICH WAY AHEAD?

Canada after Wage and Price Control

DOUG AULD, JACK CARR, LOUIS CHRISTOFIDES,
TOM COURCHENE, JAMES W. DEAN, JOHN FLOYD,
HERB GRUBEL, JOHN HELLIWELL, STEPHAN KALISKI,
DAVID LAIDLER, RICHARD LIPSEY, MICHAEL PARKIN,
SIMON REISMAN, GRANT REUBER, MICHAEL WALKER

The Fraser Institute

The Fraser Institute is an independent Canadian economic and social research and educational organization. It has as its objective the redirection of public attention to the role of competitive markets in providing for the well-being of Canadians. Where markets work, the Institute's interest lies in trying to discover prospects for improvement. Where markets do not work, its interest lies in finding the reasons. Where competitive markets have been replaced by government control, the interest of the Institute lies in documenting objectively the nature of the improvement or deterioration resulting from government intervention.

The work of the Institute is assisted by an Editorial Advisory Board which includes:

The Fraser Institute is a national, federally-chartered, non-profit organization financed by the sale of its publications and the contributions of its members.

*Orders for publications and membership enquiries
should be addressed to:*

THE FRASER INSTITUTE
626 Bute Street
Vancouver, British Columbia
Canada V6E 3M1

Telephone (604) 688-0221

WHICH WAY AHEAD?

WHICH WAY AHEAD?

Canada after Wage and Price Control

Contributors include
THOMAS COURCHENE, RICHARD LIPSEY, SIMON REISMAN;
MICHAEL WALKER (Editor)

THE FRASER INSTITUTE
1977

Canadian Cataloguing in Publication Data
Main entry under title:
Which way ahead?

　　Includes the text of the Government of Canada's
working paper: The way ahead : a framework for
discussion.
　　ISBN 0-88975-010-6
　　1. Wage-price policy—Canada—Addresses, essays,
lectures. 2. Canada—Economic policy—Addresses,
essays, lectures.　I. Walker, Michael, 1945-
II. Courchene, Thomas J., 1940-　　　III. Lipsey,
Richard G., 1928-　　　IV. Reisman, Simon, 1919-
V. Canada. The way ahead : a framework for
discussion.　VI. Fraser Institute, Vancouver, B.C.
HC120.W24W45　　331.2′1′01　　C77-002096-8

First published April, 1977 by the Fraser Institute.

Contents

PART I — THE PAST AS PROLOGUE

CONTROLS: THE GREAT FALLACY

Simon S. Reisman

WAGE-PRICE CONTROLS: HOW TO DO A LOT OF HARM BY TRYING TO DO A LITTLE GOOD

Richard G. Lipsey

ARE WAGE AND PRICE CONTROLS WORKING?
Michael Walker

PART II — ABOUT TURN: CANADA AFTER CONTROLS

THE ECONOMY WITHOUT CONTROLS
Grant L. Reuber

UNWINDING WAGE AND PRICE CONTROLS
David E. W. Laidler and Michael Parkin

CONTROL AND DECONTROL
Richard G. Lipsey

DECONTROL: THE SPECIAL CASE OF RENTS
Michael Walker

POST-CONTROLS AND THE PUBLIC SECTOR

Thomas J. Courchene

PART III — WHICH WAY AHEAD?

THE WAY AHEAD: A PROMISE UNFULFILLED
Douglas A. L. Auld

COMMENTS ON *THE WAY AHEAD: A FRAMEWORK FOR DISCUSSION*
Jack Carr

THOUGHTS ON *THE WAY AHEAD*
Louis N. Christofides

THE CASE FOR CONTINUED CONTROLS (AND OTHER HERESIES)
James W. Dean

THE WAY AHEAD: A COMMENT ON *THE FRAMEWORK FOR DISCUSSION*

John E. Floyd

MAKING REALISTIC CHOICES ON *THE WAY AHEAD*

Herbert G. Grubel

THE WAY AHEAD: SMALL IF NOT BEAUTIFUL

John F. Helliwell

COMMENTS ON THE WORKING PAPER: *THE WAY AHEAD: A FRAMEWORK FOR DISCUSSION*

Stephan F. Kaliski

APPENDIX

THE WAY AHEAD: A FRAMEWORK FOR DISCUSSION

Government of Canada, October, 1976

WHICH WAY AHEAD?

Canada after Wage and Price Control

Preface

In April 1976 the Fraser Institute published a book entitled *The Illusion of Wage and Price Control*. At that time there was widespread support in the business community for the "nasty tho' necessary" anti-inflation controls programme of the government — though sober reconsiderations were underway. At the same time, organized labour was vehemently objecting to the policy and poking its collective finger in the general direction of the government's eye. All in all, Canadians were in the process of re-examining their romance with controls. In the period since October 1975, when the controls programme was launched and the Anti-Inflation Board (AIB) was established, public support for the programme has deteriorated steadily. In October 1975, 70 per cent of Canadians were in favour of price controls while some 54 per cent favoured wage controls. By April 1976, only 58 per cent of those surveyed by the Canadian Institute of Public Opinion favoured controls and by September 1976, only 44 per cent were in favour. The business community, often caught between the jaws of government controls and the unions, is less persuaded now of the virtues of the controls programme and several business groups have publically withdrawn their support. Union objection has evolved from vehement (the constitutionality hearing before the Supreme Court) to militant (the attempted, though hardly successful, 'day of protest').

In the face of this growing general opposition the federal government has nonetheless stood firm — at least up to the point of this writing. Meanwhile, much consideration is being given, both publicly and privately, to the prospective state of Canadian society in the post-controls period. The musings of the Prime Minister about the death of the market and the necessity to view the world along Galbraithian lines have gained considerable notoriety and prompted a hostile reaction in the community at large.

In October 1976, the government released a document entitled *The Way Ahead* which outlines the "principles and strategies" underlying "the economic and social directions the government intends to take after controls end." A document sufficiently vague to say everything and nothing about the intentions of the government, *The Way Ahead* nevertheless merits the careful attention of concerned Canadians.†

The current juncture

The purpose of this Fraser Institute publication is to draw together some important views that are pertinent to the current debate — views on the controls programme and its effectiveness as well as on the policies required in the future.

---

†Editor's Note: For reader convenience we have reproduced *The Way Ahead* as an appendix.

THE PAST AS PROLOGUE

In Part One of the book, the first two essays by prominent Canadian scholars deal with the reasons why controls should be abandoned. In the case of Mr. Simon Reisman, former Federal Deputy Minister of Finance, the views are those of one who supported controls as a short-term measure but who is discomforted by the implications of long-term controls. In Reisman's view, we should now declare victory and get out of controls before the side-effects outweigh whatever advantage may have been gained. In the course of his remarks, Mr. Reisman considers at length, and dismisses, the Galbraithian view of the economy and the policy of continued controls that stems from it.

Reisman's view

Although Mr. Reisman is adamant that general controls should go he is less confident that the public sector should be free of them. In fact, he specifically suggests that a review committee be established to set the rates of remuneration in those areas of the public sector that provide an essential service and where, as a consequence, work stoppages should not be permitted. In his view, a system like this is necessary to ensure the maintenance of essential public services while at the same time ensuring the equitable treatment of public employees and the elimination of a potentially dangerous source of renewed inflationary pressure.

Lipsey on controls

Professor Richard Lipsey provides an overview of the reasons why controls should be avoided. In his discussion he is concerned with controls as a socio-political phenomenon as well as an economic policy. Professor Lipsey's unique insights are flavoured by a concern that, like a lad who has had his way with a lass, governments having once tried controls, will resort to them intermittently in the future. Lipsey concludes:

> "If this does happen, then the time for alarm will already have passed. If these forces for repetition are to be resisted, and the long-term consequences are not to occur, then an appreciation of the long-term effects of repeated controls policies are needed in Canada now."

Are controls working?

There is no disputing the fact that during the period since controls were adopted, the inflation rate in Canada has fallen. The question is, *what fraction of this decline can properly be attributed to the controls programme?* Although it will never be possible to answer this question precisely, it is possible and necessary to make some estimate. In this spirit, I have, in my short essay at the end of Part One, used the forecasts that were made of Canadian economic performance on the eve of controls to estimate what would have happened *without controls*. On the basis of these forecasts and adjustments made necessary by changes in the exchange rate, I estimate that fully eight-tenths of the actual fall in the consumer price index during 1976 would have occurred without controls.

If, in addition to this, one makes some allowance for the effects of the contractionary monetary policy being pursued by the Bank of Canada, it seems highly unlikely that the anti-inflation programme could have been responsible for more than a few tenths of one per cent of the total reduction in the inflation rate. By all accounts, not a very substantial "pay-off" from such a substantial effort.

ABOUT TURN: CANADA AFTER CONTROLS

Part Two of the book is concerned specifically with the Canadian economy after controls. *It deals with what is likely to happen and with what should happen.* In the lead essay in this Part, Professor Grant L. Reuber provides constructive criticism of current government policy as well as an outline of the specific areas that should receive priority in the current policy debate.

Reuber on structural changes

The general policy direction advocated by Professor Reuber is one designed to re-establish "the credibility and integrity of longer-term monetary and fiscal policies through demonstrated performance." This would involve a continuing tight monetary stance and a combination of tax cuts, for both persons and business, and a reduction in government spending. Business tax cuts could come in the form of inflation accounting which Professor Reuber regards as a desirable structural reform in any case. Reuber's view is that current spending restraints by government have been "marginal and conventional" and that more determined efforts in this regard are required. A particular concern of his is that whatever "breathing space" has been provided by the AIB may be wasted since "no significant policy modification seems in the offing" and "the recent government policy paper entitled *The Way Ahead* . . . may easily be interpreted as providing further evidence of government uncertainty and confusion."

Professor Reuber suggests that special attention be given to a number of specific structural problems — among them, food policy, competition and trade policy, the income support system and inter-governmental cost-sharing programmes. In his view "the main structural changes in the domestic economy since 1970 have emanated from government policies" and the task ahead is to redesign "these policies in a way which gives higher priority to efficiency and economic growth." In concluding, Reuber notes that this "will require a high degree of political skill and courage, perhaps unprecedented since World War II."

Laidler and Parkin on decontrol

The second essay in Part Two, by Professors Laidler and Parkin, is concerned with the process of decontrol. Having considered the extent to which the recent decline in the rate of inflation can be attributed to controls, the authors conclude that it would be wise to wind up the programme as soon as possible. Laidler and Parkin bring to their analysis a depth of experience with controls (in the U.K.) that few Canadian analysts have. In the absence of much hard information about the Canadian scene, their informed judgments as to what the experience of other countries teaches is invaluable.

Having concluded that controls should go, the authors proceed to consider a variety of decontrol strategies. The most important feature of such strategies in their view, is "that the measures adopted . . . should not lead economic agents to expect a renewed bout of inflation." Two basic sorts of strategy are considered: "gradual decontrol and abrupt decontrol."

Under the gradual decontrol strategy, three different alternatives are considered. The first, the fadeout option, would involve the phasing out of controls by simply reducing the rigour with which they are enforced. This strategy, pursued on several occasions in the U.K. (1968-1970 and early 1974) by a government doubtful of its own political position, would have the effect of shifting more of the burden of controls onto the most law-abiding and socially responsible members of the population. As with controls in general, lax enforcement would, in effect, punish those who comply and reward those who don't. Aside from its obvious inequities, this strategy has the effect of encouraging a contempt for the law and increasing uncertainty as to the government's ultimate intentions. It is also the authors' view that this sort of decontrol scheme "has made a major contribution to creating the impression that Britain is, at present *ungovernable.*" On balance, lax enforcement does not appear to be a promising route to follow.

The second phase-out option would involve the decontrol of those sectors for which controls are already redundant — i.e., those sectors where wages and salaries are already conforming to the expectations that policy makers had for the programme. In the view of Laidler and Parkin, this policy option would only be a desirable way to proceed if the controls were smoothing the transition to lower rates of inflation. It is their opinion, however, "that controls are by now making the adjustment rougher than need be . . ." and that ". . . adverse consequences would persist wherever controls were left in place."

The most serious objection to sectoral decontrol "is the very impossibility of conducting the search for such areas in any objective fashion." For example, "are the levels of profits in a particular industry within the guidelines because they are at the maximum level market conditions will permit or because firms in that industry are complying with regulations? Are wage settlements in a particular industry in excess of the guidelines because of market forces, or because of a tacit agreement between employers and employees to make allowances for a roll-back in their initial bargain?"

In the absence of an objective criterion, controls might well come off, as in the fadeout option, "in a haphazard fashion with perhaps the political influence of specific groups playing a bigger role than economic criteria in deciding who was first to be decontrolled."

The third phased-decontrol strategy considered by Laidler and Parkin would involve removal of controls from either wages or profits and subsequent removal of remaining controls. The authors are not hopeful about this option either, largely because of the social and political strife that would undoubtedly accompany it. Thus, they are led by the elimination of alternatives to the view that the best strategy would be a quick removal of the controls.

In defending their choice of a quick removal the authors point out that, their preference notwithstanding, there may be some optimal strategy that would ease the adjustment back to the market. However, given the current lack of information about the economy it could only be by pure chance that any gradual decontrol plan selected made matters better instead of worse.

Lipsey on present dangers

In his second essay in the volume, Professor R.G. Lipsey discusses some real and, in his view, popularly imagined aspects of the Canadian economy before, during, and after controls. In setting the scene for his remarks Professor Lipsey records "four well-established facts."

1. World inflationary pressures in the 1970's have been due to excessive world demand for goods and services resulting from large increases in money supplies on a global basis.

2. Governments cannot permanently determine the price level by wage-price controls.

3. Even though wage and price controls can temporarily slow down inflation, the magnitude of their effect is unlikely to be greater than one to two percentage points.

4. The only respectable argument for temporary wage and price controls is that they may reduce inflationary expectations.

Having noted the facts, Professor Lipsey launches an attack against "one of the mightiest and most unreasonable myths now current in Canada." The myth, based on Galbraith's theory that inflation is caused by monopoly elements in our society, is "that by increasing competitiveness, the government can make the economy significantly less inflation-prone." Lipsey maintains that both the majority of economists who reject Galbraithian analysis and the minority who accept it would "agree that the main plank of the government's long term anti-inflation policy — increasing the degree of competitiveness in the Canadian economy — bears no relation to inflation one way or the other."

In discussing the process of decontrol, Professor Lipsey points out that controls should properly be viewed as an exercise in 'sympathetic magic.' Like the rituals of old designed to bring on events such as the Spring Thaw, the magic must be worked at precisely the right time. Thus, Lipsey advises, "the government must carefully choose the moment — the first possible time during the next two years — when the inflation rate is nearly as low as might reasonably be expected given world conditions, and when preferably the rate is currently falling. The government must then remove the controls, and it might be best to do this in a sudden surprise operation with no transitional period."

The latter parts of Lipsey's paper deal with the economy after controls and the possibility that controls will be reinstituted. In considering the post-controls economy he challenges another myth that the government has tried to create: "that a new society or a new social order would be prepared during the controls period and instituted when the controls were terminated." Lipsey sees this development as highly unlikely and in any event unnecessary and potentially dangerous to the Canadian standard of living.

"The main problem in the post-controls world . . . will be to avoid a lapse back into a further bout of controls." Lipsey cites three reasons why this may happen: 1. disillusionment when the promised new socio-economic order does not materialize; 2. government expectations that controls are the best way of fighting inflation; 3. the monetarists are seriously discredited by an inflationary surge not *initiated* by excessive printing of money.

In Lipsey's view, we must not permit ourselves to lapse into further bouts of controls. "The British experience charts our course to disaster if we wish to sail this way . . . I can think of no easier way to seriously curtail the free enterprise system in Canada and bring about the onset of the Corporate State that Professor Galbraith thinks we already have than to engage in a series of bouts of wage-price controls . . . The very survival of our free enterprise economy requires that we educate public opinion to be hostile to any attempt to try controls again and again, and again . . ."

The special case of rents

My essay in Part Two considers the special case of rents. Rent controls were in force in several provinces (Quebec and B.C.) and pending in several others before the AIB was announced. The implied perception that rents are somehow different than other prices would be enough to suggest that rent decontrol deserves special attention. An additional reason is the fact that, unlike general wage and price controls, rent controls are notoriously long lived and tend quickly to become institutionalized.

In my essay, I provide an analysis of the economic and political factors that produce rent control type policies. The two key aspects of the process are seen to be the perennial lack of up to date information and the existence of members of the community for whom the cost of basic accommodation is a significant problem.

A decontrol strategy for rents can only be permanently successful if it removes the underlying factors responsible for the adoption of controls. The plight of disadvantaged tenants can only properly be dealt with via an income supplement scheme and this, together with a public information programme, is the principal element in our decontrol scheme. The second element relates to the dearth of current information about housing markets and the extent to which market adjustment is impinging upon the budgets of the whole community. It is suggested that monies currently being expended on rent control enforcement be re-deployed in monitoring housing conditions and consumer expenditures more closely.

In the course of the essay, I have also dealt with the economic and political effects of decontrol. It is estimated that the average percentage increase in rents recorded after controls are abandoned is unlikely to exceed 18 per cent and in the particular case of Vancouver is unlikely to exceed 15 per cent.

The evidence on the political consequences of decontrol is slim owing to the very lack of instances where decontrol has been tried. Evidence from the U.S. indicates that even in the face of fairly large increases in rents after decontrol the electoral ramifications for those opting for rent decontrol may be insignificant.

Courchene on the public sector

Although all of the authors in this volume, save one, are in favour of removing general wage and price controls, there is a similar agreement that controls should remain on the public sector. The final paper in Part Two, by Professor Thomas J. Courchene, presents a complete statement of this viewpoint and provides a critical focal point for the way ahead.

Problem 1 - Government deficits

In his paper, Professor Courchene considers four ways in which the public sector contributed to the present inflation and presents suggestions of ways in which, in the future, public sector behaviour should be modified. Having established that excessive monetary expansion was responsible for recent inflation rates in Canada, Professor Courchene points out that federal government deficits have been one of the chief causes of monetary growth. Although there is no necessary relationship between federal government deficits and the rate at which the Bank of Canada prints money, in the past there has been such a relationship. "Viewed in this light, federal deficits did contribute directly to the inflationary process."

Recommendations

Professor Courchene reflects the opinions of a large and growing number of observers in suggesting that future success in coping with inflationary potential will be determined to a large degree by governments' success in reducing their deficits. If there were no deficits, the pressure upon the Bank of Canada to print more money would be eliminated. The amount of money created could then be determined by the long-range objective of eliminating inflation.

Throughout his discussion of the inflationary impact of the activities of the public sector, Professor Courchene's analysis keeps leading him back to the fundamental importance of reducing the size of the deficit. In some sense the rest of his paper deals with the measures that must be adopted if the objective of smaller deficits is to be achieved. Courchene notes that a principal cause of the large deficits has been the generous salary settlements awarded to civil servants in recent times and not exclusively to the automatic operation of programmes like the unemployment insurance fund. (Although he also points out that this programme is the most generous in the world.)

Problem 2 - Growth in the public sector

In analyzing the inflationary effect of government, Courchene identifies three sorts of influences. *First*, there is the overall increase in demand for resources by government spending activity. This causes the overall demand for labour, equipment and materials to be higher than it would have been and hence raises prices. *Secondly*, the increase in the share of taxes out of gross incomes necessary to finance public sector growth (from 30% to 40% in the last decade) has had a disincentive effect on people and caused a reduction from trend in potential output growth and productivity. In addition to the disincentive effect, much of the tax money extracted has served to redirect funds away from productive investment toward current consumption — especially in the form of income transfers. *The third way* in which government creates the potential for inflation is the fact that many of the services supplied by government are apparently not considered to be valuable by Canadians. In setting their after-tax wage targets, Canadians are tending less and less to acknowledge that they receive services for the taxes they pay. An increase in taxes therefore produces an increase in wage demands so that the after-tax position is protected. If people felt that they were receiving value for the taxes they paid they would not be as anxious to ensure that their after-tax purchasing power was rising as quickly. Of course, unless there is an expansionary monetary policy the additional wage claims produced by a concern for after-tax incomes would not be inflationary. (This point is discussed by several of the authors.)

Recommendations for control of public sector growth

In reflecting on the impact of the Anti-Inflation Board (AIB) on the growth of the public sector, Professor Courchene finds it amazing that the AIB was not empowered even to recommend on ways in which the public sector ought to be regulated. He nevertheless feels that the anti-inflation programme has indirectly set in motion a process that will have an effect on the growth of government. The fact of controls has focused public attention more acutely on matters economic and on the fact that the government sector is expanding so rapidly. The fact that government expenditure is expanding considerably faster than the rate permitted in the wage guidelines has tended to put government programmes in the public eye — especially new programmes or expansion of old ones. In the long term this must have an effect on public sector growth.

One of the effects of this new awareness seems to be a growing challenge to the notion that governments are inherently better than the private sector at providing certain services. The post office is perhaps an excellent example of this.

In putting forward recommendations for the control of public sector growth, Professor Courchene focuses attention on remedies to improve the efficiency of the public sector as it is. In other words, how can the process of government be altered so as to get the job done with less cost?

Fiscal responsibility

The first area considered is the fact that currently there is a maldistribution of revenue and expenditure responsibility. That is, the government incurring the expense for programmes is often not the one responsible for raising the revenues. For example, in cost-sharing programmes (health, welfare and higher education) the provincial governments incurred the costs while the federal government provided half the revenue. The fact that the provinces were accordingly spending "50 cent dollars" could not have helped the problem of controlling expenditure growth. The recently negotiated changes in this arrangement doubtless are an acknowledgement of the problem and will be beneficial in its solution.

The same sort of issue arises with respect to provincial-municipal financial arrangements — particularly in regard to school board negotiations with teachers. In Courchene's view "...in order to get a handle on government expenditure growth it is essential that those economic units responsible for generating expenditure growth are also responsible for finding the revenue required to finance the projects. To fail to adopt this simple and basic principle is essentially to invite severe resource misallocation and in the longer term to contribute to loss of control over the growth of the public sector."

A matter of incentives

"The basic problem is that there do not exist adequate definitions of just what constitutes *output* in many areas of the public sector. This being the case it is not surprising that there are often no incentives for cost effectiveness."

"...success in the bureaucracy is often linked to being able to obtain and spend the largest possible budgetary allotment."

"...government departments are often run on the basis of being alloted *real* inputs, i.e. so much physical office space, so many employees at a particular classification level, etc. If...the...dollar prices of these items rise, the budget is simply expanded to accommodate the acquisition of these real inputs."

The attack against the problem of government efficiency should include the introduction of "market-oriented incentives," more reliance on "cash budgets" and "zero-base budgeting" ('where each year *all* of a department's or agency's activities come up for review and not merely any new activities'). However, in Professor Courchene's view one of the greatest roadblocks to prescribing cures is the lack of a thorough understanding of what motivates government agents and agencies. "Introducing market-type incentives into a bureaucratic process only makes sense to the extent that the actors involved...will respond to these incentives." Courchene cites and summarizes some of the work of Professor D. Hartle on this point.

Hartle, a former secretary of the Federal Treasury Board in Ottawa, essentially views the budgetary process as a complex game between four teams of players — the politicians, the senior bureaucrats, the media and the lobbyists. His is what might be termed a 'conspiratorial' view of the budgeting process. ". . . senior bureaucrats have about as much power to reward and punish ministers as ministers have to reward and punish senior officials." It follows that ministers do not often find it expedient to harass senior bureaucrats by cutting their budgets to the point where present employees must be laid off.

It is Courchene's view that Hartle's preliminary work is the first step in an essential effort to discover exactly how the budget process works. Having discovered how it works, we will be in a much better position to formulate incentives to make it work more efficiently.

Incentives for users

"There is another aspect of this incentive issue that is also contributing significantly to the mushrooming of the public sector, and that is the lack of incentives to economize on the services provided by governments. Health care is probably the best example."

The overall solution to this problem would be to, in some way, 'charge for service,' while at the same time not imposing unfair costs on low income groups in the economy. "Deterrent fees" are at least partially effective in preventing undue waste but they are regressive. "One intriguing alternative [in the case of medical services] . . . would be to increase the medical exemption allowable for income tax purposes and allow the taxpayer to benefit from any excess of this exemption over the actual medical expenses he/she generates."

Bankruptcy of tradition

Courchene, along with several other of the authors, views the current unemployment situation in Canada, at least in part, as a direct consequence of past government policies. It is his view that in the past governments have responded to unemployment by expanding the size of the government sector.

"Yet increasing the size of the government sector is as likely to be the cause of higher unemployment as the remedy to be used to control it. To a substantial degree, Canada's transfer system has now built into it significant work-disincentive elements which have made unemployment at the same time a more desirable and less costly (in terms of foregone income) way of life." As a consequence, "it is no longer appropriate to define full employment in terms of an unemployment rate in the 3% to 4% range. A figure near 6 per cent is probably more reasonable." One of the consequences of this is that ".. any attempt to restore rates of unemployment to the 4% level are bound to be highly inflationary. If the 4% range or thereabouts continues to be the ultimate target for government policy, it becomes increasingly important to introduce structural reform which would serve to reduce the degree to which Canadians find spells of unemployment to be a desirable alternative to employment." This ".. would entail *less*, not more, government spending." Courchene goes on to note that past approaches involving increased government spending have usually produced an increase in unemployment. In other words, they have contributed more to the problem than to the solution.

Problem 3 - Indexation

While acknowledging the benefits of indexing in helping to smooth the timing of wage adjustments in the private sector, Professor Courchene is of the view that in the recent Canadian context public sector indexing has itself been a source of inflationary pressure. The inflationary pressure has arisen as a result of Ottawa's attempts to offset, via indexing, changes in real incomes occasioned by a change in world prices for a variety of primary products. The indexing of a variety of government transfer payments and the attempt to insulate Canadian consumers from the effects of higher world prices for oil helped produce a situation where ". . . individual Canadians came to believe that one and all had the right to ensure that his/her income kept abreast of the rise in the cost of living irrespective of the march of economic events."

In a broader context, indexation of a sort has been applied with respect to regional income disparities. The Department of Regional Economic Expansion has been the principal tool of this more generalized indexing. Although "Canadians appear to have accepted the fact that a considerable effort toward combatting regional economic disparities is essential to national unity," it is nevertheless true that, "complete indexation is not possible without totally jamming the allocative mechanisms." For example, "no amount of federal transfers to the Maritime provinces . . . is going to offset the fact that Alberta's relative economic position within Confederation has been enhanced substantially as a result of the oil crisis."

Recommendations on indexing

"As far as the post-controls period is concerned, the message . . . is rather straightforward. Large and rapid changes in relative prices of many commodities have occurred in the recent past and this situation is likely to continue. These price shifts often usher in corresponding changes in the distributions of political and economic power both within and between nations. Where these disturbances are perceived as longer term in nature, governments should recognize that to attempt to index these changes fully is bound to be at the same time very inflationary and very disruptive of efficient allocation of resources. Social justice may require partial indexation or even full indexation for selected groups of persons, but attempts to do more than this will provide inappropriate expectations for the rest of the country to attempt to imitate."

Problem 4 - Collective bargaining in the public sector

On the eve of controls in the fall of 1975, the rate of wage increase in the public sector had risen to 18% per year as compared to 14% in the private sector. There was even some speculation at this time that the AIB was created specifically to control public sector wage increases. The fourth area that Professor Courchene has identified as a source of public sector inflationary pressure is the *process* of bargaining in the public service.

He points out that not only was the actual rate of wage increase greater in the public sector, but also the indexing of public servants' pensions pushed the value of the wage-benefit package to inordinate levels. "One estimate suggested that an equivalent pension scheme for the private sector would, extrapolating conditions prevailing in 1975, require contributions in the neighbourhood of 16-20% on the part of both employers and employees."

In the presence of this example in the public sector and given the expansionary tone set by monetary policy, "whatever incentive the private sector may have had to resist wage demands was effectively eliminated. Bereft of any economic base, wage behaviour . . . becomes a matter of expectations and political or social clout." On the basis of his analysis, Courchene concludes that "the most serious challenge to the successful removal of controls may well come from public sector wage developments." In Courchene's view, the problem with public sector wage settlements arises for two reasons: *(A)* because of the peculiar nature of the government as employer and *(B)* because of the unusual position of government employees in collective bargaining.

The government as employer

Several attributes of governments make them particularly vulnerable to wage demands. *First of all*, they are not constrained by the necessity to produce their output at a profit. *Secondly*, in a growing economy — given our tax structure — the government does not even have to change tax *rates* to acquire the revenue necessary to finance increased wage costs. *Thirdly*, in the case of the federal government, even when the government cannot meet its cash requirements from tax revenues it has access to the printing press and captive markets for its debt. (The latter owing to the various regulations to which the chartered banks are subject.) *Fourth*, obligations of the federal government like those incurred in its present pension agreement do not significantly impinge on the government's current cash position.

Civil servants as employees

The most outstanding difference between civil servants and private sector employees as wage bargainers is that civil servants bargain from a position of job security. A consequence of this is that the size of the wage settlement achieved by civil servants has no effect on the probability that they will become unemployed or be employed fewer hours. Therefore, civil servants have no "work pattern" repercussion incentives to moderate their wage demands. A 20 per cent wage increase in the public sector will lead to a 20 per cent increase in annual income — that this is not so in the private sector is amply demonstrated by the substantial layoffs and terminations in the private sector during the past two years.

Third party implications

In the case of private sector strikes, except in rare instances, the cost of the strike falls on the employers and the employees. (If General Motors were strikebound for six months the consumer could simply switch to competing automobile makers. Hence, the consumers' burden would be negligible.) In the case of public sector strikes the public is, in effect, used as a whipping boy — there being, by definition, no substitute for public services. (Nor, in the main, can they be stockpiled as can most private sector output.) As a consequence, great pressure is put on the government to settle the strike and to do so quickly.

In Professor Courchene's opinion the third party implications of public sector work stoppages is a "fairly powerful argument against the right to strike in the public sector." At the very least, "if strikes are allowed . . . third parties should have some recourse in law to demand compensation from government and striking labour for the breaking of the implicit 'social contract' of continuous provision of the public services."

Arbitration in the civil service

Since the 1960's, either the government or the employees in a federal civil service labour negotiation have had the right to call for binding arbitration. As a consequence of the fact that arbitration has meant "applying previous settlements in one area of the public service to another area," wage gains in one area are and have been quickly passed along to other areas. "Compulsory arbitration then becomes the vehicle for unions with little or no inherent market power to share in the rewards of the wage leader. This process also applies to the provincial level as well. For example, it only takes one school board settlement in Ontario to set the target for the remaining boards."

Recommendations

"The first recommendation is that controls be taken off the private sector before they are taken off the public sector." This recommendation follows from the fact that restrictive monetary policy — the only anti-inflation policy thus far adopted by the government — will affect the private sector but will not affect the public sector.

While public sector controls based on actual private sector wage increases would suffice in the short run, Courchene is of the opinion that more substantive changes have to be made in the long term. As far as a permanent arrangement in the area of vital services is concerned, Courchene finds attractive the suggestion of Mr. Reisman, discussed earlier in the Preface. In the "less essential" areas, strikes should be permitted but arbitration of the *final offer* variety should be adopted. (By this scheme the team of arbitrators would be required to select *in whole* one or other of the final offers of management or labour.)

"Finally, the time may be ripe for some degree of *privatization* of activities currently in the government sector or some methods of compensating *third parties* to any public sector strike so that collective bargaining in the public sector introduces some potential costs that impact on both sides in the case of a strike."

"In summary, in the enterprise system that characterizes our economy, consideration of productivity and profits should dominate wage determination. The role for the public sector is to ensure that its employees receive remuneration packages that match those in the private sector. The proposals in this section are designed to ensure that in the post-controls period the public sector not be allowed once again to resume its position as the wage leader in the economy. *The future of the private sector, let alone the concern over a re-spiralling of inflation, surely rests upon this proposition.*"

THE WAY AHEAD

In October 1976, the federal government, in response to requests from "many groups and individuals," released a document entitled *The Way Ahead.* The document was intended, in the words of the government, "to outlin[e] the economic and social directions the government intends to take after controls end." It . . . "outlines these principles and strategies and provides a context for further consultation."

In some sense, this document is one of the most important economic documents that the current government has released. It is apparently meant to be a statement of how the government views its role in the moulding of the future. As a consequence, it deserves the careful consideration of all concerned Canadians.

In keeping with its mandate to improve public awareness and understanding of the key economic and social issues confronting Canadians, the Fraser Institute invited, in addition to the authors of Parts One and Two, twelve prominent Canadian academics to comment on *The Way Ahead.* Given the pressure of other commitments, only eight were able to respond. The purpose of Part Three of the book is to present the views of those who prepared contributions. Since these essays are in the nature of informed commentaries on a government document, they have not been subjected to the Institute's normal editorial review process. However, for the benefit of the reader, I have inserted notes where this was thought necessary. In the remainder of this introduction I have, without implying that all of the commentators are of a single mind, summarized the basic thrust of the reviews.

The government and inflation

There is expressed in most of the essays the sentiment that *The Way Ahead* reflects a certain confusion on the part of its authors. In fact, the apparent confusion and ambiguity is severe enough that one reviewer remarked "as far as outlining future government economic policy is concerned it would have been better if *The Way Ahead* had never been written " (Carr). One of the most disturbing aspects of this confusion is the failure to acknowledge the essential and necessary role of government in the inflationary process. In their assessment of the causes of inflation the authors of *The Way Ahead* have identified a range of events and activities that are involved in the inflation process without indicating which of them is most important - if any. This eclecticism is attacked by most of the reviewers and one of them remarks that the position of the authors of the document "amounts to a virtual abdication of any responsibility with respect to control of inflation " (Christofides).

In a sense it is not surprising that governments deny the responsibility for inflation and attempt to blame it on market failure, greed and the weather. However, if the government's true understanding of the inflation process is adequately reflected in *the document* then the way ahead could well indeed be a rocky road. There is no acknowledgement of the fact that unless the government permits inflation to occur via increases in the money supply, inflation cannot occur: no acknowledgement of the fact that "inflation is always and everywhere a monetary phenomenon" (Carr). While the government may publicly deny responsibility in its formulation of policy it should realize that:

a. "inflation is caused by excess monetary expansion and can be eliminated only by bringing the money supply under control,

b.   if inflation is to be controlled the Bank of Canada must give the rate of monetary expansion precedence over all other policy targets, and

c.   unless the government is willing to borrow extensively from the general public, it must keep its budget under control.

Recognition of these facts of life is an absolute prerequisite to sensible discussion of Canada's policy options in the post-control period " (Floyd).

Government understanding of basic economics

Another disturbing feature of *the document*, according to several Fraser Institute authors, is the apparent failure on the part of the government authors to realize the difference between the *level* of all prices and the *relationship between* prices (Carr, Floyd, Auld). Increased scarcity of particular commodities (oil, gas, coffee, etc.) causes the price of these products to rise *relatively* faster than the prices of other products. However, these price rises in themselves will not cause the level of all prices to rise. A rise in oil prices, for example, is a signal to consumers and producers that a higher *proportion* of a given total income must be allocated to oil if the supply of oil is to be maintained. Since what is involved here is a reallocation of real resources, less income is available to be spent on other things and the prices of everything else will, in due course, rise *relatively* less.

The rise in oil prices accordingly affects the size of the slice of a given income pie that must go to the oil sector but has no effect on the size of the pie. If the government wants to create the illusion that we don't have to make this adjustment in our expenditures, it can do so by creating a bigger pie in dollar terms. That is, by printing more money it can cause the price of everything to rise and the fact that a larger real slice must go to the oil sector will, for a time, be hidden in the inflationary haze.

While such camouflage may be expedient for political purposes, it must not be allowed to obscure the fact that the oil price rise in itself is not inflationary. In particular, it is critical that this sort of thinking not be permitted to permeate policy making in the future as it obviously has in the past.

In the post-controls period it is very likely that there will be bursts of wage increases. These wage increases should be viewed as *relative* 'price' changes and although "there will be a great temptation to accommodate these wage increases through monetary expansion, this must be resisted " (Auld).

The new trade-off

Many of the reviewers were concerned more about what was not in *the document* than with what it contained. Among the things that it does not contain is a recognition of the fact that Canada is in the process of a new sort of trade-off. This trade-off involves the rate of unemployment and economic growth on the one hand and the provision of public goods and income equality on the other. Policies to increase the provision of public goods and services lower the potential growth rate by increasing current consumption at the expense of investment in productive capital. Minimum wage laws, unemployment insurance benefits and other labour market policies have raised the minimum unemployment rate attainable.

> "... the trade-off between income equality and public goods on the one hand and unemployment and growth on the other is an unpleasant but unavoidable fact of life. This fact needs to be explained to the people of Canada and responsible politicians of all parties must refrain from promising to deliver the impossible. The public and political debate should shift instead to the discussion of the nature of the trade-off and how far the people of Canada want to go on it " (Grubel).

This issue of a new sort of trade-off is raised by several authors in this volume, both in connection with what *can be* accomplished on the road ahead and *how* this should be done. The message for policy makers is that some existing policies mitigate against the achievement of some policy goals - high growth, low unemployment, stable prices - and the attempt to avoid this fact could produce a disastrous situation. For example, as Professor Courchene notes in the second Part, the decision to maintain a minimum wage and the highest unemployment benefits in the world may well mean that Canada is stuck with a "full employment" unemployment rate of, say, 6 per cent. Attempts to reduce the unemployment rate below this level would produce a permanently higher and increasing rate of inflation. Unless, of course, we choose to remove the policies responsible for the high unemployment rate.

Similarly, the increasing tax burden implied by the expansion of the public sector may well reduce incentives to the point that we are doomed to low and falling rates of productivity growth.

In other words, we as a nation have to adjust our expectations about the performance of policy to be consistent with policy choices that have already been made. What is involved here is not a repudiation of minimum wage laws, the unemployment insurance programme, health and welfare legislation, etc. but rather an acknowledgement of what they imply. It might well be that once this is realized Canadians would like to revise their opinions on some of these programmes. This is a separate issue but one upon which policy makers should dwell in their thinking about the way ahead. The relevant questions to ask in connection with these issues are discussed by Professor Doug Auld in his review as well as by Professors Courchene and Grubel.

The Canadian dollar

Another issue that apparently escaped the attention of the authors of *The Way Ahead* is the fact that Canada is a relatively small economic entity embedded in a world-wide trade and financial system. As a direct consequence, the policy choices that Canada can make are, to some extent, circumscribed. The implications of the necessity to reckon in "world trade terms" are investigated at length by Professor John Floyd. From his analysis it would appear that in the past there has been relatively little attempt in Canada to buck the world tide of inflation. Rather, Canadian monetary policy has been so executed as to produce in Canada an inflation rate compatible with stability of the exchange rate. In terms of the future, it is Floyd's view that, "if the choice is for a politically determined exchange rate, there is no need to discuss anti-inflation policy further." Since the matter is not discussed in *The Way Ahead* it is difficult to know what one should infer about the government's attitude.

Market power - market failure

There is almost unanimous rejection of the proposition advanced by *the document* that market power and/or market failure has been or can be a cause of inflation. The one dissenting voice, Professor James W. Dean, argues that the problem with *The Way Ahead* is that it is not radical enough in its view of the causes of inflation. In fact, it is Dean's view that because market power produces a setting in which inflation is likely to occur, wage and price controls of some sort ought to be retained. (However, Dean admits that inflation in this case is the result of expansionary government policies pursued because of the threat of the unemployment that he says would otherwise occur.)

In the view of Professor Stephan Kaliski, the only convincing example of the potential inflationary effects of market power produced in *The Way Ahead* is the process of public sector pay determination. In Kaliski's view, "surely here, if anywhere, there is crying need for 'mechanisms' and 'structures' to be put in place before the present controls expire and a particular responsibility upon governments to develop them."

The Fraser Institute has been pleased to support the work of the authors and is publishing their views in the public interest. However, owing to the independence of the authors, the views expressed by them may or may not conform severally or collectively with those of the members of the Institute.

PART I

the past
as prologue

Controls:
The Great Fallacy

SIMON S. REISMAN

*Former Federal Deputy Minister of Finance
Chairman, Reisman & Grandy Ltd.*

THE AUTHOR

Simon S. Reisman was born in 1919 in Montreal. He received a B.A. degree from McGill University, and postgraduate degrees in Economics from McGill (1942) and the London School of Economics (1945). Recently retired, he has had a distinguished career with the Government of Canada, including positions as Deputy Minister of Finance, Secretary of the Treasury Board, and Deputy Minister for the Department of Industry, Trade and Commerce. In 1975, he received the Government General's Prize for Outstanding Public Service for Canada.

At present, Mr. Reisman heads his own firm, Reisman and Grandy Limited. He is also a Visiting Professor at the University of Toronto, a Member of the Board of Governors of Carleton University and a Member of the Advisory Council of the School of Business, University of Western Ontario.

Controls:
The Great Fallacy

SIMON S. REISMAN*

Former Federal Deputy Minister of Finance
Chairman, Reisman & Grandy Ltd.

I. INTRODUCTION - ON GALBRAITH AND GADFLIES

In one of his early books of more than 20 years ago, John Kenneth Galbraith predicted the future would bring no let up in public controversy over economic issues. Economists should find that encouraging, he noted, since much of their income and most of their prestige is derived from this source.

As it turned out, his forecast was quite accurate. Of course, he has contributed with considerable relish and no little humour to maintaining that controversy - whether by expounding unorthodox views to explain why American capitalism performed "quite brilliantly" during the first post-war decade, or postulating new personal theories to explain why it has faltered in the past decade.

Professor Galbraith has been aided and abetted in his theories by the series of upheavals that have racked the industrial nations, in recent years; disturbances that have raised major questions about the soundness of our economic system. For my part, I welcome the developing debate on this issue because I consider it of fundamental importance to determine what went wrong with the system if we are to restore economic health and maintain it in the future.

*An earlier version of this paper was delivered at a *Financial Post* conference in Toronto, October, 1976.

History makes it clear that the pillars of past conventional wisdom were sometimes built on sand. In challenging the conventional wisdom of the present, Professor Galbraith performs a useful service for he compels us to take a fresh look at what are the basic principles governing the operation of a modern industrial economy.

II. ECONOMIC THEORIES

As a starting point for this reappraisal, it is necessary to go back to the 1930's when the Great Depression destroyed an economic doctrine accepted as gospel for more than a century. Say's "Law," which broadly held that over time the economy would automatically maintain its equilibrium at full employment, proved to be fallacious.

Keynes' contribution

With his brilliant work, "The General Theory of Employment, Interest and Money," John Maynard Keynes revolutionized economic thinking. He dethroned Say's Law and its basic theorem that equilibrating mechanisms in the market would ensure that savings and capital investment remained in balance, thus maintaining aggregate demand in line with productive capacity. Lord Keynes demonstrated how and why savings and investment could get out of line for an uncomfortably prolonged period, leading either to a sustained decline in aggregate demand, output and employment; or to the generation of demand in excess of productive capacity and a consequent price inflation.

To remedy this serious defect in the system, Keynes advocated that the state intervene to maintain stability. If productive resources were under employed, the government would expand aggregate demand by increasing the availability of credit at favourable interest rates and/or reduce taxes and increase government spending. If, on the contrary, demand was pressing too hard on available capacity, the process would be reversed.

Following the Second World War, governments of virtually all the industrial nations accepted a large measure of responsibility for maintaining reasonably full employment and relatively stable prices. Implicitly or explicitly, they undertook to do so largely through application of the monetary and fiscal policies proposed by Lord Keynes.

New trouble?

For a good many years following the war, these policies worked reasonably well in avoiding extreme economic disturbances in most of the industrial world. The central question that arises then is why have we experienced the more severe economic gyrations and particularly the prolonged inflation of more recent years? Is there some fundamental defect in the accepted view of how the system operates? Have the essential elements of the system itself changed? Are we, as the Prime Minister suggested in a speech to the Canadian Club of Ottawa, January, 1976 living in "a new economic era" which precludes even a modified free market system from dealing with the problems of inflation and unemployment? Professor Galbraith's response to these questions is a resounding "yes."

On a previous occasion, I gave a rather lengthy paper on Professor Galbraith's conception of the forces that govern a modern industrial economy. I will not reproduce it here. But I would like to comment briefly on those concepts that are of particular relevance to the issue of wage and price control.

Galbraithian cosmology

In Galbraith's view, the private sector of the economy is made up of two quite distinct parts. One sector, described as the "market system," consists of many relatively small enterprises - 12 million in the United States - which are largely subject to competitive forces and function in accordance with neo-classical economic theories. The other sector, which he calls the "planning system," is made up of a limited number of very large, mature corporations which dominate the industrial heartland of the economy. In the United States, these corporations - variously estimated by him to number anywhere from 500 to 2,000 - are said to account for around one-half of all the goods and services produced in the private area of the economy.

The vast size of these corporations and the oligopolistic power which they wield are determined by a number of compelling forces. Size and market power are essential to develop the complex technologies that are the hallmark of the "planning system." In Galbraith's view, they are essential to free this controlling group of corporations from the constraints and uncertainties of competition and enable them to exercise the control over costs, prices, labour and materials that is a prerequisite for the implementation of planning and the minimization of risks. They provide the means of dominating the consumer and the market sector of the economy and of transforming government into their compliant hand-maiden.

A matter of motives

The giant corporations are controlled by a vast sub-group of technocrats, rather than by shareholders, boards of directors or the executive management. This techno-structure is not intent on the maximization of profits; it is concerned with the minimization of risk and the generation of some minimum level of earnings sufficient to forestall interference from outside sources - such as shareholders - and provide sufficient funds to finance new capital investment. The strongest motivating force is growth of sales and output because that is the source of the greatest potential reward for the technocrats.

Professor Galbraith does not suggest that the giant corporations seek to exploit the consumer by charging excessively high prices. On the contrary, they pass along to the consumer the very considerable benefits derived from their technological prowess because that is consonant with their goal of avoiding outside interference and increasing the growth of sales.

The wage-price spiral

There is, it seems, only one fatal flaw in the ability of the large corporations to control costs and prices. In the face of demands from their unions for substantial wage increases, they would rather yield than fight, secure in the knowledge that they can readily pass along increased wage costs to the consumer through increased prices. Increased prices in turn lead in time to new union demands for increased wages. Thus a perpetual cost-price spiral gets generated.

Fatal flaws?

In Professor Galbraith's view, monetary and fiscal policies are no longer adequate to maintain reasonable stability of output, prices and employment because the giant corporations and the satellite labour unions spawned by them operate largely outside the competitive forces through which these policies have their impact. These corporations march to a different drummer. Monetary restrictions have little effect because of their own large internal financial resources. Reductions in government expenditures hardly affect them because defence outlays remain largely untouched. A decline in aggregate demand may force a temporary reduction in output and an increase in unemployment, but it will have little impact on moderating increases in wages and prices.

It is by this line of reasoning, as I understand it, that Professor Galbraith arrives at the conclusion that the only means of ensuring reasonable price stability and reasonably full employment is through the adoption by the state of permanent controls over prices and wages to govern the behaviour of the giant corporations and their unions.

The bone of contention

I do not accept Galbraith's description of our economic system or his analysis of the way it functions. Therefore, I do not accept his prescription of permanent controls which is based on that analysis.

All the available evidence indicates that the giant corporations - however defined - which exercise a measure of market power occupy a considerably smaller area of the economy than Professor Galbraith suggests, no more than one-quarter at best.

Nor is there any evidence that the degree of corporate concentration - and hence of oligopolistic power - has increased significantly over the past several decades in either the United States or Canada and thereby altered the basic structure of the economy.

More importantly, neither Galbraith nor anyone else has presented theoretical or empirical evidence to support his thesis that the large corporations are virtually immune from the forces of competition. Undoubtedly some of them possess a greater measure of discretionary power to influence costs and prices than smaller enterprises. The difference is more one of degree and of timing, than of basic operating conditions in the market-place. If anything, the performance and fortunes of the large corporations in recent years in many countries and industries contradict Professor Galbraith's assertions.

Unanswered questions

In the Galbraithian model, there are no definable upper limits on the wage demands of the large unions, no upper limits on the size of wage increases the large corporations are prepared to accept, and no upper limits on the price increases that can be passed along to a pliant consumer. If we accepted that model we would be asking ourselves today *why inflation has not led inevitably to hyper-inflation.* We would have to explain *why it is that wage costs in this country have for several years now been rising at roughly twice the rate of those in the United States, where the giant corporations are much more commonplace.* We would have to explain *why inflation is more virulent in Britain and France than in the United States or in Germany.* We would have to explain *why inflation has been more severe in some recent periods than in others.* Galbraith's analysis does not provide an answer to these questions.

The view of the consumer as a mere pawn in the hands of the giant corporation does not ring true intuitively, nor is it supported by any empirical evidence. There are many instances, some quite spectacular, of the consumer resisting new products or higher product prices.[†]

My view

In my judgment, a significant degree of competition continues to exist domestically within and between most

---

[†]Editor's Note: For a discussion of this point see Assar Lindbeck, *The Political Economy of the New Left,* 1970 (Harper & Row, 1972).

oligopolistic industries in Canada and the United States. This is an important constraint on prices and wages.

In a great many of these industries, domestic competition is strongly reinforced by foreign competition. Professor Galbraith pictures foreign competition as being virtually non-existent in relation to the large dominant corporations. In his world, foreign multinational corporations respect the pricing and other restrictive practices of the domestic oligopoly in whose market they are operating. But this picture does not square at all with the facts as we know them or indeed with his acknowledgement that many multinational corporations - particularly those in the United States - have been forced to develop productive facilities in low-wage countries abroad in order to meet price competition of foreign producers in their own home market and in third markets.

In short, I do not believe there have been fundamental changes in the structure of the economic system over recent decades. I do not believe there has been a significant increase in concentration and market power. I do not believe the large corporations and their workers have somehow become exempt from the forces of competition.

III. THE SOURCE OF CURRENT DIFFICULTIES

Why then have we seen such a lengthy and disruptive period of inflation, even in the face of unemployment statistics that are high by historical standards?

While a number of special factors have been at play nationally and internationally, the root cause, in my judgment, has been the failure of the industrial nations severally and collectively to maintain sound economic management through the proper use of fiscal and monetary policy. In his book on *American Capitalism* a quarter-century ago, Professor Galbraith rightly warned of the critical danger that fear of political unpopularity would deter governments from imposing the measures of restraint necessary to keep the growth of aggregate demand within reasonable bounds. That danger has come to pass.

U.S. roots

We have to look back a decade and a half to trace how and why events unfolded as they did. The U.S. Presidential election of 1960 brought a Democratic Administration to power that was for the first time openly committed to application of Keynesian economic policies. The New Economists making up that Administration were strongly confident of their ability to operate the U.S. economy very close to the limits of its productive capacity without generating undue inflationary pressures, an objective that was to be reinforced by voluntary price and wage guideposts.

The U.S. economy subsequently experienced a strong resurgence under the stimulus of expansionary measures. Professor Galbraith undoubtedly reflected a consensus view when he told an interviewer for U.S. News and World Report in the spring of 1966 that the business cycle had been "substantially tamed," with the price-wage guideposts providing particular cause for hope that inflation would be "less of a problem in the future than in the past."

In fact, the U.S. economy was already poised on the brink of an inflationary outburst. It did not take long to establish the ill-founded nature of President Johnson's assurance to Congress in January 1966 that the United States could press ahead with his Great Society programs, meet its massively increasing commitments in Vietnam, and still prevent the outbreak of a "destructive price-wage spiral."

The resulting boom and inflation created by the U.S. decision to opt for both guns and butter had a substantial impact on many other industrial nations, particularly Canada. One consequence of these developments was an accelerating increase in the chronic U.S. balance of payments deficit with the rest of the world progressively undermining the foundations of the existing international monetary system.

Global manifestations

The long economic upsurge of the 1960's came to a halt at the turn of the decade as the industrial nations moved to contain the inflationary forces it had unleashed. But political pressures soon developed for a resumption of the good times so many people had come to enjoy and expect. During the early 1970's, country after country moved to inject renewed stimulus into their economies. This was reinforced on the monetary side by the efforts of a number of nations to forestall long overdue revaluation of their currencies.

By 1973, the cumulative effect of the expansionary measures adopted by individual countries was a global economic boom that touched off massive increases in the prices of many industrial raw materials - a process that was further aggravated by hoarding and speculation. Coincidental crop failures around the world and the four-fold increase in international oil prices compounded the problem, but they were not the basic cause of the rampant inflation sweeping around the globe.

The fact that inflation receded only slowly after the world plunged from economic boom into the worst recession of the post-war period is by no means evidence, as has been suggested, that the system is "out of joint." It is not surprising after nearly a decade of rising costs and prices that expectations of continuing inflation should have become deeply embedded in the economic system and the psychology of people everywhere.

Canadian causes

As a major trading nation, Canada was particularly vulnerable to the impact of these global forces. But there were also some developments in this country which contributed to the creation of additional, domestically-generated inflationary pressures.

Government spending

One of those factors was a massive increase in government spending. Between 1965 and 1975, the share of government expenditures in total national output jumped from 30 per cent to 43 per cent with a corresponding increase in the level of government revenue to finance it.

Unemployment insurance changes

A second inflationary factor was the far-reaching revision of the unemployment insurance system in 1971, which established the most generous and open-handed benefit provisions to be found anywhere in the world. These changes had a two-fold impact. They added substantially to federal government expenditures. And, perhaps even more importantly, they had the effect of drawing hundreds of thousands of marginal, secondary workers into a labour force that was already growing considerably more rapidly than that of any other industrial nation.

This heavy influx of workers of course had an adverse impact on unemployment levels. In 1972, average unemployment rose to 6.3 per cent from 5.4 per cent the previous year, creating the illusion of an economy in which considerable slack continued to exist. Strong political pressures for the injection of further stimulus into the economy were applied to a minority government in a precarious parliamentary position. In reality, the economy was already growing strongly and operating very close to the limits of productive capacity. In 1972, real GNP rose by 5.9 per cent and the following year it rose by 7.2 per cent. The resulting response of Canadian economic policy to the pressures for further stimulus added a strong domestic impetus to the inflationary pressures surging in from abroad.

Public sector unionization

A third important factor was the rapid spread of unionization throughout the public sector after collective bargaining rights were extended to federal employees by the Public Service Staff Relations Act of 1967. According to the Labour Department's annual survey, "Working Conditions in Canada," the proportion of public administration employees covered by collective bargaining agreements - excluding local firemen and policemen - rose from around 25 per cent in 1965 to 95 per cent last year.

Substantial pay increases subsequently won by some highly militant unions in the public sector have unquestionably played a powerful role as pace-setters for workers in every part of the economy, contributing to the much faster increase of wages and salaries generally in Canada than in the United States over the last several years.

The recession in Canada was much less severe than in the United States and consequently acted as a less effective brake on inflationary forces. Following the lead of public service unions, workers in the private sector continued to press for substantial wage and salary increases notwithstanding the fact that in doing so they were only worsening the already serious erosion of Canada's international competitive position that had been under way since the early 1970's and jeopardizing both present and future employment.

IV. CONTROLS BUT NOT FOREVER

So by early 1975 it was becoming increasingly apparent that Canada was being driven to the brink of crisis by the unrestrained inflationary pressures rebounding through the economy. Following my departure from the public service I was among those who urged the adoption of mandatory price and wage controls. I advocated this course because we had reached the point where monetary and fiscal policies acting alone could only have been effective in curbing inflation at very heavy cost in terms of lost output and employment.

I said then and repeat now that controls should only be imposed for a limited time and for a limited purpose, as a temporary supplement to demand management policy. In *Economics and the Public Purpose*, Galbraith said: "fiscal policy remains essential for maintaining a general balance between demand and supply. No modern development makes this policy - or the resulting balance between aggregate demand and supply - less important." Had he included a reference to the critical role of a sound monetary policy, I could have endorsed this quotation.

Controls can provide time in which to re-establish sound monetary and fiscal policies. They establish a political framework in which governments can constrain wage pressures from their own large and growing public service unions. And they impart a form of shock treatment for the inflationary psychosis that has contributed to the spiral of costs and prices.

15

If controls are to do any good at all in helping to restore price stability much depends on public confidence and support, and the skill of the government in the design and administration of the programme. I regret to say that the current Canadian experiment with peace-time wage and price control seems to lack these essential elements. Much confusion surrounded their introduction, and great uncertainty surrounds their administration. (For example, a year after their announcement, the regulations affecting prices and profits remained to be determined.) In the circumstances the benefits to be obtained from their use are likely to be quite limited and we have probably exhausted their potential.

Controls must go

It is essential that the controls be removed without long delay. As the months go by, they produce an ever-diminishing return in restraining inflation and ever-growing costs in hampering the growth of output and capital investment.

I am confident that once proper fiscal, monetary and other policies are effectively in place, costs and prices in the private sector will be effectively contained by the forces of competition - particularly as the reality of Canada's deteriorating competitive position becomes more starkly evident.

Proposals for public sector pay

I am far less confident, however, about the prospects for maintaining stability in the public sector after controls are removed. Certain unions in the public sector are able to exercise considerable bargaining power particularly where essential public services are involved. With the lifting of controls, these unions could once again act as pace-setters for other parts of the public sector and the private sector as well.

Much of the present militancy in certain public sector unions stems from resentment over past failures of governments to keep pay standards in line with those in the private sector before collective bargaining was established. Too often when governments decided to economize public service wages were the easiest target.

I believe that a new approach to remuneration in essential public services is needed. Consideration should be given to establishment of a tripartite body composed of representatives of government, labour and the public. This body would be charged with responsibility for identifying those areas of the government sector where prolonged work stoppages cannot be tolerated because of the resulting damage to the public interest.

At the outset, annual increases in remuneration in such services should be geared to the rise in national industrial wages or some other appropriate yardstick. Maintenance of this approach over any extended time, however, would fail to take account of relative changes in pay scales required to reflect the changing needs of society. To provide for these necessary adjustments, I would propose that this same tripartite body periodically review relative pay scales, establishing as objective tests as possible to determine whether changes should be made on the basis of such factors as supply and demand inside and outside the public sector and compensation levels for comparable employment in private industry. As I see it, an approach of the nature I have outlined is necessary to ensure equitable treatment of the public employees involved, maintenance of essential public services, and elimination of this potentially dangerous source of renewed inflationary pressure.

V. GROWTH AND FREEDOM . . . THE WAY AHEAD

Before concluding, I shall comment briefly on the thesis that stable and sustained growth can only be achieved by the imposition of permanent controls.

History tells us that wherever and whenever wage and price controls have been used for any sustained period they gradually disintegrate in the face of growing efforts to circumvent them. History also tells us that governments, in the mistaken belief that controls are a substitute for fundamental economic policy, fail to apply the necessary fiscal and monetary discipline and the controls break under the strain of excessive demand pressures. I believe controls will prove unsustainable in Canada as it becomes increasingly evident that, by distorting the allocation of resources, they are stifling production, employment and productivity, retarding technological development, and depressing the standard of living.

More important than the damage to economic efficiency is the loss of freedom which a control system entails. Over the years we have witnessed increasing state encroachment in many aspects of society. The complexity of modern living makes a larger and more ubiquitous state inevitable in certain respects. But none of these, I contend, touches the lives of ordinary people in so fundamental a manner as wage and price controls - if maintained beyond a relatively short period. Their permanent use would deliver a vital blow to the very innards of our free society. Indeed, the ultimate result would, in my view, be an authoritarian political system ruled by force.

The instinctive sense of ordinary citizens feeling that their basic freedom was being challenged explains, more than anything else, why Canadians across this land felt uneasy about the Prime Minister's 1975 year-end comments prognosticating more state regulation of the economic process. I am confident that as long as Canadians retain their political freedom they will not accept such an outcome to the current debate, indeed they must not.

Perhaps the case against perpetual controls was most succinctly put by a certain Harvard professor nearly 25 years ago:

"Although little cited, even by conservatives, administrative considerations now provide capitalism with by far its strongest defence against detailed interference with business decisions. To put the matter bluntly, in a parliamentary democracy with a high standard of living there is no administratively acceptable alternative to the decision-making mechanisms of capitalism. No method of comparable effectiveness is available to decentralize authority over final decisions."

I am convinced that when he wrote those words Professor Galbraith got it right the first time. Despite all its imperfections, I am not aware of any alternative to the market system that can serve our economic interests without threatening our personal freedom. What is required of governments is that they establish and maintain an environment in which the market may best perform its essential function.

Wage-Price Controls: How to do a Little Harm by Trying to do a Little Good

RICHARD G. LIPSEY

Sir Edward Peacock Professor of Economics
Queen's University

THE AUTHOR

Richard G. Lipsey was born in British Columbia in 1928. He was educated at Victoria College and the University of British Columbia, and did graduate work at the University of Toronto and the London School of Economics. He received his Ph.D. from the University of London in 1957. Dr. Lipsey is presently Sir Edward Peacock Professor of Economics at Queen's University, Kingston. He has held many posts in the academic and public sectors, including a chair in economics at the London School of Economics, the chairmanship of the Department of Economics at the University of Essex, member of the council of Britain's National Institute of Economic and Social Research (London), and panel member for the Policy Analysis Group of the federal Department of Consumer and Corporate Affairs.

Professor Lipsey is author of several textbooks, including *Economics: An Introductory Analysis* (with P.O. Steiner) which has had four American and two Canadian editions and has also been translated into Spanish and French. His latest book is *Mathematical Economics: Methods and Applications* (with G.C. Archibald), published by Harper & Row. He has contributed many articles to learned journals, including *The Review of Economic Studies, Economica, The Banker, Lloyds Bank Review,* the *American Economic Review,* and the *Canadian Journal of Economics.*

Wage-Price Controls:
How to do a Little Harm
by Trying to do a Little Good

RICHARD G. LIPSEY*

Sir Edward Peacock Professor of Economics
Queen's University

I. INTRODUCTION

Every economic policy has costs and benefits. A rational approach to policy requires that we try to estimate the magnitudes of each, using the best analytical techniques at our command and drawing on historical experience wherever possible. It is especially important to look beyond the direct and immediate effects since, in any policy, the long-run balance of costs and benefits may differ greatly from the short-run balance.

The themes of this paper are that both theoretical reasoning and historical experience teach three important lessons concerning wage-price controls. *First*, the benefits they yield are entirely of a temporary nature; and even these benefits are almost negligibly small. *Second*, the policy of attempting to contain inflation by wage-price controls is unlikely, when it has been tried once, to be confined to situations of extraordinary economic crises. It is more likely to be resorted to frequently, increasing in its degree of severity with each subsequent application, until it threatens to become a permanent and serious feature of the economy.

*A revised version of Remarks delivered to a Symposium on Canadian Wage-Price Controls at the Annual Meetings of the Canadian Economics Association, Quebec City, June 1976. I am grateful to Professor Scott Gordon for detailed comments and suggestions. Reprinted with permission from *Canadian Public Policy*, Winter 1977, pages 1-13.

Third, the indirect and long-term effects of wage-price controls are almost totally on the cost rather than on the benefit side. The effects on the economy are almost always harmful, and the political consequences on the organization of society are potentially disastrous. This leads me to the general conclusion that wage-price controls should be opposed under virtually all peace-time circumstances since they produce at best small and transitory short-term benefits in return for large and persistent long-run costs.

II. THE SHORT-TERM EFFECTS OF CONTROLS

Wage-price controls do not have a permanent effect on the price level

Arguments that controls can be used to defend the 'integrity of the dollar' imply that they can permanently affect the price level. Controls represent an attempt to determine the price level by legislation. A wealth of well-tested economic theory shows that such attempts are doomed to long-term failure. Wage-price controls that are removed after two or three years are followed by bursts of inflation that take the price level to where it would have been given the values of the relevant economic variables had the controls never existed. Can any economist, for example, doubt that the Canadian price level in 1952 was determined by the relevant economic variables in 1952 and was independent of any temporary depressing pressures exerted by war-time wage-price controls?

Controls can delay an inflation

What wage-price controls can do, if they are tough enough, is to rearrange the inflation rate in time, changing somewhat the time path by which we move from one price level to another. In some circumstances such as wars and balance of payments crises it is useful to postpone an inflation temporarily. If, however, the goal of policy is to protect the purchasing power of money, such postponement is of little value. Once the controls are removed the price level will soon reach the level it would have attained had the controls never existed.

Even the transitory effects of wage-price controls are surprisingly small. The best estimate from the experiments that have been made many times in other countries is that a complete wage-price freeze can temporarily slow down the rate of inflation by about two percentage points (for example, the rate of inflation will be eight per cent per year where it would have been ten per cent); that a looser form of controls similar to the ones now existing in Canada can accomplish about a one percentage point reduction; while controls of lesser severity accomplish nothing.[1]

Wage-price controls could reduce inflationary expectations

If the government wishes to slow down the rate of inflation by reducing the rate of monetary expansion, some serious problems can arise until people learn what is happening and revise downwards their expectations of inflation. In the short term it is possible that the main consequence of slowing of the rate of monetary expansion will be to raise unemployment, while the slowing of the rate of inflation is delayed for a year or more — until inflationary expectations are revised downwards. It has been argued that wage-price controls, *by forcing* a slower rate of inflation on the economy while the rate of monetary contraction is being slowed, can force people to revise their inflationary expectations downwards. If so, the upset that occurs if inflationary expectations remain high while the rate of monetary expansion is lowered could be avoided.

What is involved here is a technical debate among economists about some quite subtle economic theories that have not yet been fully tested. For this reason I will say little about the debate, and will confine myself to a few relevant points.

1. What is involved is trying to avoid some transitory costs in terms of a temporary rise in *the unemployment rate* that may accompany a slowing of the rate of inflation when expectations about the future inflation rate do not adjust quickly.

2. These costs are likely to be *lower* the more *gradually* the actual inflation rate is lowered.

3. The economic theory that gave most credence to the claim that controls could avoid these transitory costs (the theory of adaptive expectations) is now under rather heavy attack. Furthermore, there is no body of evidence showing that, in the past, wage-price controls have led to a downward revision of expectations of inflation. Since it is quite possible that they could lead to an upward revision — people expect the lid to blow off once the controls are removed — no strong conclusion can be ventured at this time.

4. Thus there is neither accepted theory nor well-documented empirical evidence to suggest that controls will succeed in forcing inflationary *expectations* downward. Anyone who does accept this view at present does so mainly as an act of faith.

Controls might be used to give the government a pause in which to introduce structural changes in the economy

This argument was used in the government's 1975 White Paper on Inflation. There is, however, no evidence that the passage of legislation to increase the degree of competitiveness in Canada has been accelerated during the 'breathing period' provided by incomes policies. Indeed, there are good reasons to believe that if you give government, or anyone else, 'breathing time' they will spend the time breathing rather than acting under accelerated crises conditions. If you wish to get crisis behaviour and suitable solutions out of governments, it would seem reasonable to expect that a clearly apprehended and existing crisis is more conducive to this behaviour than is a crisis whose effects are temporarily suppressed by direct controls. Certainly I know of no evidence of past government behaviour to suggest otherwise.

Short-term costs

The above discussion exhausts the list of alleged short-term benefits. The obvious costs are the administrative costs, and they are borne both by the public and the private sectors. The less obvious costs concern the distortions that are introduced into the economy by any centrally administered set of prices and wages. These costs, of course, get larger the longer the controls are in place because the controlled prices at least start by bearing some close relation to market conditions. There is also a further set of hidden costs that concern the quality changes that occur when prices are effectively controlled. These short-term costs clearly exist and are not negligible. I will not, however, pay them any further attention in this paper since they are insignificant when measured against the long-term costs discussed in Section IV.

III. WILL WAGE-PRICE CONTROLS BECOME A COMMONLY USED POLICY TOOL IN THE FUTURE ?

A great deal is made of the argument that the Canadian government is now engaged in a once-for-all policy experiment, probably never to be repeated. If this turns out to be the case, many of the longer-term costs of controls with which I concern myself in Section IV may not be a matter of serious concern. I feel, however, that this belief that the experiment with controls is a 'once-only' attempt should not be taken at its face value. Indeed, there are forces at work that make it highly likely that the experiment will be repeated.

First, there will be positive future pressure to repeat the experiment even if it actually fails. When the wage-price controls are removed, economists will no doubt set to work studying their effects. It is in the nature of all economic estimation, however, that results cannot be exact. The government is committed to its wage-price controls in the face of severe opposition, particularly from labour unions, and it would be unreasonable to expect it not to claim such positive achievements for these controls as cannot definitively be ruled out by careful study of past experience. This will lay the basis of another resort to controls when inflation threatens in the future.

Inflationary pressures were clearly subsiding throughout the world by late 1975 and, as was predictable then, the Canadian inflation rate began to decelerate even before the controls, and a more restrictive monetary policy, made their effects felt. The general public knows little about monetary theory and monetary policy. Ordinary voters will thus, quite understandably, give to controls much of the credit for the reduction in inflation rates that will occur in the next year or so. When the next sustained inflation occurs in Canada there will be heavy pressures placed on the government in power not to eschew the use of a tool that was claimed by the government, and perceived by the public, to have had some effect in the past. Even if the existing government is hostile to such a course of action, the opposition may become committed to such a policy; and the opposition may win a subsequent election.

Second, there is the argument that controls are needed to reduce inflationary *expectations* when a sustained inflation is being attacked by fiscal and monetary policy. It would be a rash economist who would predict that a sustained inflation will never occur in Canada again. A government which then wished to reduce this rate of inflation would be faced with the argument that reducing the inflation rate, when expectations of the existing rate are established, would require controls to break these expectations. This is because the transitional harm caused by lowering the rate of inflation unexpectedly depends on the *discrepancy* between the rate of inflation that people expect and the rate that the monetary authorities plan to validate. Thus, insofar as the argument about inflationary expectations is valid, it applies to *any* sustained rate of inflation. Bringing the rate of inflation down to five per cent when expectations are for a ten per cent inflation has approximately the same real effects as bringing the rate down to zero when expectations are for a five per cent inflation. It seems inconceivable, therefore, that we will not, in the foreseeable future, be faced with the same argument that the government has used today for the necessity of controls in order to reduce inflationary expectations as part of a policy package designed to reduce inflation further.

Third, as I have already observed, the general public understands little about monetary theory and monetary policy and is not aware of the mass of evidence establishing that inflations cannot long persist unless the government expands the money supply, no matter how militant are the country's unions. By giving credence to a policy of wage-price controls, the government will strengthen the erroneous theories of inflation already held by many members of the public. This will make more difficult the task of any future government that tries to control an inflation by sensible fiscal and monetary policies while ignoring the siren calls of wage-price controls.

For all of the above reasons, it seems to me that we would be unduly sanguine to assume that the present Canadian controls will be a 'once-only' experiment. Thus it is important to consider the evidence of what wage-price controls do *when they are applied several times in succession in order to resist bouts of inflation that developed from time to time.*

IV. LONG-TERM COSTS AND BENEFITS OF WAGE-PRICE CONTROLS

Wage-price controls have many potentially serious long-term effects. The more frequently the controls are resorted to, the more serious do the long-term effects become. Further, and much more upsetting, these effects persist long after the controls are removed. Let us look at some of the most important of these effects.[2]

Some controls outlive general wage-price controls

One of the most disturbing aspects of wage-price controls is that they often leave behind them certain specific controls which are not dismantled when the general controls disappear. As a single illustration let me mention rent controls. The trend towards provincial rent controls has been strengthened by the urging of the federal government who sees them as part of its package of anti-inflationary policies. Rent control measures that will not seriously affect the supply of new housing can, no doubt, be designed to operate for some time. If, however, rent controls persist, and do succeed in keeping the price of rental accommodation below the free market price, they will inevitably reduce the supply of new

29

rental accommodation in the long run.

Two of the best documented predictions in economics are the following. First, rent controls that are effective do end up creating serious housing shortages; the longer the rent controls persist, the more serious do the housing shortages become. In the words of Assar Lindbeck, Professor of International Economics at the Institute of International Studies, Stockholm:[3]

> In many cases rent controls appear to be the most efficient technique presently known to destroy a city — except for bombing.

Second, when an effective rent control apparatus is dismantled, the short-term effects are genuine hardship brought about by large increases in rents with little short-term gains, since it takes some time for the supply of new housing to be increased. The greater the housing shortage, the greater the genuine short-term hardship caused by removing rent controls.

These two factors have a serious political consequence. The longer effective rent controls have been in operation and the greater is the current control-induced housing shortage, the harder it is politically to dismantle the rent control apparatus. The evidence of rent controls throughout the world is that it is only possible to get rid of them easily if they have been in place for a short period of time; as the duration of the rent controls increases, even say to as much as five years, the political difficulties in removing them increase very rapidly and for obvious reasons. Thus the longer the controls have been in operation, the more likely they are to persist indefinitely.

Income distribution

Controls that have transitory effects on wages and prices usually influence the distribution of income at least while they are in operation. This is partly because the controls inevitably vary in their effectiveness. Sectors that are easy to control tend to suffer relative to sectors that are hard to control. It is also partly because administrators can seldom refrain from using controls to affect directly the distribution of income.

Canadian controls policy has been no exception to this rule. The moves, although modest, are quite unmistakable. In particular the protection given against inflation falls steadily as incomes rise above $25,000. Each person is allowed to get the guideline proportional increase in his wage or salary, but only up to a maximum of $2,500. This ceiling is ten per cent of an income of $25,000, and only five per cent of an income of $50,000. Clearly, income differentials will be steadily narrowed at the upper end of the scale for as long as this policy persists. There is also a surtax on high incomes which was instituted as part of the anti-inflationary package. Once again, governments have shown that they cannot resist the temptation to hit hard at the higher income groups which include, of course, the successful innovators and businessmen, senior professionals, and the upper managerial groups.

Observing this behaviour throughout the world has led me to suggest Lipsey's *first law of the rationalization of jealousy.* The law runs as follows: *Any income up to the amount that an individual could expect to obtain over his lifetime is regarded as gained through hard work and fully justified. Incomes significantly in excess of one's own lifetime expectations are regarded as immoral and a suitable subject for confiscation without serious economic effects.* As an illustration, the level of income at which full protection against inflation ceases to be given is often closely related to the incomes of the legislators who set the controls. Very rarely does full protection cease to be granted at a level below the median income of the legislators — all of whom know that they earn their incomes by sheer hard work.

Competition and industrial concentration

Price controls tend to increase the concentration of industry and reduce its competitiveness. Many Canadian industries contain a few large, fairly profitable firms and a larger number of smaller less-profitable firms. Canadian controls are designed to reduce the profits of the most profitable firms by forcing them to charge lower prices than they would otherwise charge. If the policies work, they will have the effect of driving smaller, more marginal firms out of business. Periods of controls often foster communication and cooperation between firms who normally compete with each other. Often with the blessing of government, competing firms open communications with each other to try to design ways of meeting government objectives without, for example, too much loss of investment incentives. These lines of communication do not disappear with the wage controls.

Such effects are observable elsewhere. For example, in the bakery industry in the United States the wage-price freeze of 1971 had the effect of driving out a substantial number of the smaller independent producers. Such changes are difficult to reverse once the controls are removed.

Canadian controls were meant, according to the White Paper on Inflation, to give a breathing space for the adoption of policies intended to increase the degree of competitiveness within the economy. *If the policies work, however, they themselves will have the effect of reducing the degree of competitiveness and increasing the amount of concentration.*

Non-market power is given to organized labour

Consider next the effects of repeated applications of periods of wage controls on the relations between organized labour and government. Just as they often were in the U.K., the first experiment with controls in Canada was forced through against the opposition of labour unions. If, as I have argued above, these policy experiments are repeated in the future, it is inconceivable that the second and third attempts will be forced through in the same way. The history of wage-price controls elsewhere suggests that subsequent attempts must be instituted with the support of the labour movement. How will this come about?

Wage-price controls represent an attempt to ask labour to reduce its wage compensation below what the market would provide, at least in the short run. One price for labour's support will be that there must be no suspicion, let alone any actuality, that the distribution of income is to turn unfavourably against labour. This means a fiercer set of administrative controls over prices than the present set, with consequent harmful effects on investment and long-term growth. A second price will be that labour must be offered something other than direct wage compensation in return for its cooperation. If the labour movement does not have clearly formulated objectives of this type, it will have to develop them in a hurry since, if it is going to sacrifice its members' short-term claims to higher wages, it *must* deliver something else in return.

The British experience is particularly instructive in this context. The *quid pro quo* for union support for the current severe wage restraints has been the Universal Closed Shop Legislation. Under this legislation all workers must belong to a union before they can be employed. The unions to which they belong are officially designated and workers are unable to form their own small independent unions. Furthermore, the unions have the right to expel any member from the union without significant right of appeal. The unions desired this policy in order to kill the growth of 'bread-and-butter' unionism in Britain. An increasing number of workers had become disenchanted with the political activities of the major trade unions. There was evident an active movement, still small but growing, towards unions which were primarily concerned with wages and working conditions and not with political activities. This healthy decentralization of unionism has been killed utterly by the Closed Shop Legislation. This, however, was not its only effect. If newspaper editors, as well as typesetters, must belong to the union and if the union can evict editors, and thereby deny them the right to work, the rank and file can exert pressure on publication policy. The House of Lords perceived this as such a threat to the freedom of the press that they were prepared to engage in the first major revolt against the House of Commons in over twenty years. Unfortunately, the Lords failed in their efforts to persuade the House of Commons to introduce some rudimentary safeguards. I worry generally about the great power given to unions to determine who can work and, therefore, to influence people by holding their livelihoods in hostage.

The United Kingdom, at the end of a long series of successive bouts of wage-price controls, has gone far in the direction of narrowing income differentials. The relative earnings of managers, academics, doctors, lawyers, and other members of the middle class have been ground down slowly until they are now often no more than what can be earned by a senior man on the shop floor. The effects on emigration and the supply of effort and risk-taking are only too obvious and they can hardly be regarded as anything other than disastrous for the workings of the economy. Current Canadian efforts are more modest, but then we are in our first bout of peace-time controls. Future bouts will no doubt be accompanied by more serious efforts in this direction. If so, they will be instituted at heavy cost, since Canadian management and professionals are highly mobile with respect to the United States. Such policies provide, among other things, an incentive to emigrate, an incentive to switch income from brackets covered to brackets not covered, an incentive to just plain cheating, and eventually a force for social disillusionment.

The paradoxical result is that, whenever they persist for very long, wage-price controls that were first instituted to control the power of unions end up by giving unions a degree of power they could never otherwise have hoped to attain — and might never even have aspired to.

This of course would never happen in Canada, I hear many people mutter. Most people said the same thing a decade ago in Britain. If controls do recur in Canada, it will be necessary to offer labour unions some non-wage incentives to obtain their cooperation in restraining wage demands. This forced alliance between labour and government, whereby many labour goals which have serious long-run effects on the economy are accepted by government in return for labour's short-term cooperation with controls, is a very serious matter. Those of us who believe in a pluralistic society and do not wish to see any group gain dominance must be little short of alarmed.

I do not wish the above remarks to suggest that I believe the labour movement to be anti-social. Special interest groups who protect the interests of their members are needed in our society. I become frightened, however, when the government creates a political environment that greatly enhances the power of one particular special interest group. Indeed at this point in time every Canadian has cause to be grateful to the CLC for resisting the present wage-price controls by every legitimate means at its disposal rather than cooperating with them, and then demanding its political *quid pro quo.*

Destruction of social capital

The history of countries which have used controls has often been that the early policies curbed wages more than prices. This is partly because it is easier to control wages than prices, and partly because the general climate of opinion at the beginning of a series of wage-price controls is that wage behaviour is primarily responsible for inflation. The controls are then found to do more to redistribute income from wages to profits than they do to affect inflation rates. Thus, when successive rounds of controls are introduced, tougher and tougher administrative procedures are designed for the control of prices at each round. It was rather interesting to see Canadian businessmen accepting wage-price controls fairly calmly at the outset. Business will gain some short-term advantages if wages are controlled more rigidly than prices. But past history suggests that these advantages are at best only temporary. If the experiment is repeated in the future, it will be the business community rather than labour that will have cause for most serious complaint.

Problems arise when the pressure for ever tougher controls on prices encounters a fundamental fact of political economy: *the average life of a government is very much less than the average life of the economy's capital.* Five years is the maximum assured life for a government, four or even less, the usual; twenty years or more is a reasonable life for much of the economy's capital stock. The effects of this discrepancy are profound: short-run political gains can be obtained by adopting policies that cause the economy to live on its capital stock. If controls are effective enough, prices can be held down to a point where much new investment becomes unprofitable. Production of consumer goods in the short run is not greatly affected since the country can live for a considerable time on its existing capital stock. After ten or fifteen years, however, the effects become serious, and it is then too late to reverse the process easily. Firms such as Chrysler in the U.K. are finally pushed to the point where not only do they need some new capital investment, they need sufficient investment to change their entire stock of models. Such enormous investment is beyond the usual ability of private firms to raise capital. Government intervention becomes necessary. It is clear that U.K. price restraints have operated so long and so severely that many firms in that country are no longer replacing their capital stock and investment has shrunk to an alarmingly low level. Although this is now appreciated, the U.K. government already has the tiger of wage-price controls by the tail and finds it difficult, if not impossible, to change its policy to make it more favourable to investment. The British newspapers over the last several months have been full of reports of the inability of the government and the Confederation of British Industry to agree on a formula that would restore the incentive to invest while still retaining a stiff form of price control and not allowing profits to rise 'inordinately.' While both sides argue, investment and innovation languish at all time lows.

Another very important asset of any country is the social attitudes of the population. For example, the income tax works only as long as the people not subject to deductions at source feel a strong social or moral obligation to pay the tax. Professionals and other middle class people usually accept such social obligations. This feeling can be exploited for quite long periods of time without serious consequences in the same way as can the economy's stock of physical capital, but the obvious inequities that arise from a bureaucratically determined wage and salary structure erode this sense of obligation. The Kitimat workers, for example, settled for the guideline increase in wages early in the life of the AIB. Later they discovered that others had obtained much more. This kind of thing happens frequently, and it affects attitudes, as it is always the people who try to cooperate who get hurt most.

U.K. incomes policies that hit hardest on middle and high incomes groups exploited these attitudes and finally, after a decade or so, these attitudes have been seriously eroded. As an illustration, the Autumn of 1975 saw a doctors' strike in the U.K. All but emergency services were withdrawn and even emergency services were supplied spasmodically. Ambulances were turned away from one casualty department after another at various London hospitals and some patients died in the process. The cases of actual death were few, but the change in the social attitudes over the decade is dramatic. If anyone had told the British voter or doctor in 1960 that this would occur in 1975 he would have been dismissed as a madman.[4]

The sense of social obligation is very resilient to short-run influences, but it can change in the long term. It can be, and in many countries has been, exploited for the short-term gains of the controls policies. The long-term effects, once the attitudes change, are extremely serious and not easily or quickly reversible.

The politicization of economic relations

These observations lead on directly to my final point. Controls politicize everything. He who makes a big noise gets. A big noise is a political big noise. Economic contribution is less important. If a group is not so structured as to be able to make a political noise then the group must change its structure. It must unionize, it must set up a pressure group to make its wishes politically effective.

The Prime Minister in his 1975 end-of-year comments suggested that he has been greatly influenced by Galbraith's views on *The New Industrial State.* Aside from his nonsensical views that social attitudes are amenable to prime ministerial injunction, the Prime Minister himself has done more through his wage-price controls than any other single individual in Canada to bring about the conditions of the Corporate State that he ostensibly fears. Wage-price controls, by increasing the degree of politicization, by increasing the degree of industrial concentration, by increasing the importance of political power on the part of labour unions, work powerfully in this direction. Of course, we do not have perfect competition in Canada, but we do have many of the protections that are afforded by decentralized markets. Continued bouts of controls weaken the forces of the market and tend to concentrate power in the hands of politicians, union leaders and large industrialists. The next step is for them to sit down around a table, behind closed doors, and plot the economic course for Canada. When this happens — and there are signs that it would not be wholly unwelcomed by some of our political leaders — we will be well on the way to the complete realization of the Corporate State.

Long-term benefits

The only two *alleged* benefits that I have heard claimed for controls are that they strengthen the forces of centralization in the economy and that they are a way of disciplining the population. The first of these I have dealt with at length and it seems hardly to be counted as a benefit — except by those who would welcome the advent of the Corporate State in Canada. The disciplining of the population is something that appeals to some political leaders. It often also appeals to groups in society — as long as it applies only to other groups. Consumers and firms would like to see unions disciplined, and unions would like to see firms disciplined. The evidence of experience elsewhere is that if we yield to the temptation to have the government discipline others, we ourselves will end up being disciplined as well. Whenever I hear a politician say something like the following (Hugh Faulkner, Secretary of State, quoted in the *Globe and Mail*, 21 January, 1976, p. 8) ". . . we are living too high on the hog in Canada, getting too fat, getting too lazy and lacking in the discipline that has been enforced on people in other countries . . ." and discover that these remarks are in relation to the discipline of wage-price controls, I become worried. In a free society the government creates the structure within which free individuals play most of the economic game. Once governments decide to play the whole game for us, because they feel we have become 'fat,' 'lazy,' and 'undisciplined,' we have cause to worry about the preservation of individual liberty.

V. CONCLUSIONS

I have stated some extreme things in this paper. Because of this, two comments preliminary to the conclusion would seem to be in order. First, I do not intend to frighten the reader with horrors created solely from my own imagination. In each case there is both a reasoned argument as to why forces that I identify can be expected to operate and an actual example of the harm that these forces have done elsewhere. Second, I do not write as an advocate of extreme *laissez faire*. I believe that although the price system can do a great deal, it also has many failings and permits much suffering. I also believe that it is not beyond human wit to design methods that would improve the workings of the price system without interfering unduly with those things that it already does well. It seems to me that we must strive to help governments do things that will lead to a more efficient and a more just society than the unaided market will produce. This attempt, however, must be guided by a careful empirical appreciation of how governments do behave, and of how we must expect them to behave; rather than by our analysis of what they might usefully do.

It is important to note that the harmful effects of controls are *quite independent* of the monetary and fiscal policies that accompany them. The effects follow directly from the impact of particular types of government intervention on the economy, the economic changes that this impact creates, and the durability of these changes. There is, therefore, no more reason to be sanguine about the harmful long-term effects of repeated applications of controls when they are instituted along with sensible monetary and fiscal policies (as appears to be the case in Canada) than when they are accompanied by self-defeating monetary and fiscal policies (as was often the case in Britain). My main message then is as follows. Wage-price controls are shown by economic theory, and demonstrated by an enormous wealth of factual evidence, to have no permanent effect on the price level. If these controls are never repeated in Canada, the long-term effects of this one attempt are not likely to be too serious. There are forces, however, that will be at work to cause the experiment to be repeated. If this does happen, then the

39

time for alarm will already have passed. If these forces for repetition are to be resisted, and the long-term consequences are not to occur, then an appreciation of the long-term effects of repeated controls policies are needed in Canada now.

I say, therefore, that *now* is the time to stand up and be counted. Now is the time to say loudly and clearly that wage-price controls are ineffective in their main objective and extremely harmful in all of their other effects. Now is the time to do everything that we can do to influence public opinion. In doing this economists will be fighting for the integrity of their own subject, since economic analysis clearly shows that the price level cannot be permanently determined by legislation. It is my considered opinion that, not only will we be fighting for the integrity of economics, we will also be doing battle at the barricades in a not insubstantial fight in the defence of human freedom.

References

Walker, M., ed. *Rent Control: A Popular Paradox* (Vancouver: The Fraser Institute, 1975).

Walker, M., ed. *The Illusion of Wage and Price Control, Essays on Inflation, Its Causes and Its Cures* (Vancouver: The Fraser Institute, 1976).

Notes

[1] Much of the voluminous and overwhelming evidence that supports these conclusions is summarized in my Economic Appendix to the Legal Factum submitted by the Canadian Labour Congress to the Supreme Court of Canada in support of its contention that Canadian wage-price controls are *ultra vires.*

[2] Since writing this article, I have had a chance to read an important new book edited by Michael Walker (1976), which details much of the voluminous evidence in support of my own theses. I warmly recommend it as 'further reading' for anyone concerned about the issues that I discuss.

[3] Quoted in Michael Walker (1975); 'destroy' is not quite to be read literally; 'do great harm to' and 'greatly reduce the quantity and quality of rental accommodation available' might be more accurate, although less arresting phrases. The seriousness of the matter is illustrated by the fact that only a modest exaggeration is required to enable the writer to say 'destroy'.

[4] The immediate cause of the doctors' strike was the phasing out of the last vestiges of private hospital treatment in state hospitals. There can be no doubt, however, that the erosion of income differentials of doctors as part of a general attack on income differentials operated through a wage-price control policy was a major contributing cause for discontent among doctors.

Are Wage and Price Controls Working?

MICHAEL WALKER

Research and Editorial Director
The Fraser Institute

THE AUTHOR

Michael A. Walker is the Research and Editorial Director of the Fraser Institute. Born in Newfoundland in 1945, he received his B.A. (Summa) at St. Francis Xavier University and his Ph.D. in Economics at the University of Western Ontario, 1969. From 1969 to 1973, he worked in various research capacities at the Bank of Canada, Ottawa and when he left in 1973, was Research Officer in charge of the Special Studies and Monetary Policy group in the Department of Banking. Dr. Walker has also taught Economics and Statistics at the University of Western Ontario and Carleton University. Immediately prior to joining the Fraser Institute, Dr. Walker was Econometric Model Consultant to the Federal Department of Finance, Ottawa.

Dr. Walker was editor of, and a contributor to, three of the Fraser Institute's previous books: *Rent Control - A Popular Paradox* (1975), *The Illusion of Wage and Price Control* (1976) and *How Much Tax Do You Really Pay?* (1976).

Are Wage and Price Controls Working?

MICHAEL WALKER

Research and Editorial Director
The Fraser Institute

I. INTRODUCTION

Whether or not to abolish the controls depends in part on whether or not they are doing any good. There seems to be a feeling that the controls have done some good — if only because the AIB itself has gone to considerable lengths to claim victory. If the AIB has reduced inflationary pressures to an extent that more than compensates for its side-effects on everything from business confidence to labour relations, then perhaps controls should be retained. If, on the other hand, controls have not worked and are, in Professor Lipsey's words, merely an exercise in sympathetic magic, then they should be abolished. This determination alone would be reason enough for attempting to ascertain, in a preliminary way, the effects that controls have had.

An even more important reason is that we should be in a position to correctly assess events if, through happenstance, the eventual termination of controls was to coincide with an outbreak of inflation. In that event, it would be all too easy to infer that the renewed inflation was a consequence of the abolition of controls. If controls haven't worked, however, there would be no reason for such an inference.

The objective of this section is to document in as precise a fashion as possible what we now know about the effect of controls in the Canadian case. As is indicated by Professors Laidler and Parkin, in their essay in Part Two, a definitive analysis of the effect of controls is not possible at this time.

II. WHAT WOULD HAVE HAPPENED?

During September 1976, the Government of Canada ran a series of advertisements in Canadian newspapers claiming that the inflation rate was slowing down as a result of the AIB's efforts. There can be no doubt about the fact that the inflation rate has fallen since October 1975 when the Board was announced, (Table 1). The question is, *what would have happened without the AIB and its efforts?*

TABLE 1
CANADIAN INFLATION
Percentage Increase in Consumer Prices

		%	
1975	I*	11.7	
	II	10.5	
	III	10.9	
			Anti-Inflation Board Created
	IV	10.1	
	YEAR 1975	10.8	
1976	I	9.2	
	II	8.5	
	III	6.5	
	IV	5.7	
	YEAR 1976	7.5	

*Inflation rate is calculated as percentage change in quarterly average year over year.
Source: Bank of Canada Review, November 1976, Table 61.

As Professors Laidler and Parkin suggest, one way to determine this would be to build a mathematical model of the Canadian economy and experiment with it to determine what would have happened without controls. Another way is simply to examine what professional observers thought was going to happen before the control programme was announced. While no one would claim a high degree of scientific accuracy for this exercise, it does reflect what the "implicit models" of these forecasters were saying at the time. In addition, this exercise has the merit that it can be done now and at least provides the chance for a preliminary assessment.

In Table 2, I have assembled the forecasts for the change in the rate of inflation during 1976 made by Canadian and foreign economists. All of these forecasts were completed prior to the announcement of controls. In almost every case, the forecasts were for a decline in the rate of inflation. Ignoring those predictions calling for an increase in the inflation rate (only four out of fifteen predicted an increase) the average of Canadian forecasts of inflation (the increase in the Consumer Price Index) was -1.84 per cent. In other words, the expectation was that the rate of inflation would fall by about 1.84 per cent in 1976.

Foreign observers of the Canadian economy were even more optimistic calling for reductions in inflation ranging from .5 percentage points in the case of the OECD, to at least 4.0 percentage points in the case of the U.K. National Institute for Economic and Social Research. The average of foreign forecasts was 2.5 percentage points decrease in the rate of inflation.

There seems little doubt that the rate of inflation in Canada would have fallen during 1976 quite apart from the influence of the Anti-Inflation Board. The average of foreign and domestic forecasts indicates that there would have been a reduction in the inflation rate of at least two full percentage points. If our estimates for the overall inflation rate during 1976 (7.5%) are correct, the total reduction in the rate of inflation in 1976 over 1975 will have amounted to 3.3 percentage points. In other words, fully two-thirds of the reduction in inflation that has occurred was foreseen and cannot properly be attributed to the effect of the anti-inflation programme.

It is interesting and perhaps indicative that when the Federal Minister of Finance was confronted with the implications of these predictions his reply was (referring to the eve of controls) "I don't think that forecasters generally would have said that."† But that is precisely what forecasters generally were saying.

---

†Finance Minister Donald MacDonald, quoted in *MacLean's*, October 18, 1976.

TABLE 2
INFLATION FORECASTS FOR 1976
Forecasts Made Before Anti-Inflation Programme

Forecasts Predicting Decreased Inflation	Predicted Change in Inflation Rate (- signifies downturn)
Domestic Forecasters:	
Bank of Nova Scotia.	-2.0
Bank Canadienne Nationale.	-1.0
Canadian Imperial Bank of Commerce	-1.7
Dominion Securities Corp. Harris & Partners Ltd.	-1.5
Greenshields Incorporated.	-1.0
Informetrica Ltd.	-2.5
Nesbitt Thomson and Co. Ltd.	-3.0
MacMillan Bloedel Ltd. (July, 1975)*	-2.1
Royal Bank of Canada Economics Dept.	-1.1
Wood Gundy Ltd.	-1.3
Woods, Gordon and Company.	-3.0
Average of Domestic Forecasts Predicting Decrease	-1.84
Foreign Forecasters:	
Japan Economic Research Centre (July, 1975)	-3.5
Organization for Economic Cooperation and Development (Paris) (June, 1975)	-0.5
Chase Econometrics (September, 1975)	-2.0
National Institute for Economic and Social Research (U.K.) (August, 1975).	-4.0
Average of Foreign Forecasts Predicting Decrease	-2.5
Overall average of Forecasts Predicting Decrease	-2.17

Forecasts Predicting Increased Inflation

The Conference Board in Canada.	+0.4
Fry Mills Spence Ltd.	+0.8
Institute for the Quantitative Analysis of Social and Economic Policy, University of Toronto	+0.1
James Richardson and Sons Ltd.	+0.4
Average of Forecasts Predicting Increase.	+0.43

Source: Unless otherwise indicated, the domestic forecasts cited were published in the Autumn 1975 issue of the Canadian Business Review, Volume 2, Number 4. All forecasts were made prior to the announcement of controls.

Other Sources: Japan Economic Research Centre Quarterly Forecast #30, July 1975.
Organization for Economic Cooperation and Development Outlook, #17, June 1975.
National Institute Economic Review 3, 1975, #73, August 1975.
Chase Econometrics International Service, September 1975.
*MacMillan Bloedel's forecast was provided by Csaba Hajdu, Chief Economist.

Unforeseen events and the rate of inflation

At the time when the forecasts reported above were made, the Canadian dollar was worth from 97¢ to 98¢ U.S. — down from "par" at 1974 year end. In other words, the Canadian dollar was falling in value and becoming worth less than the U.S. dollar. As a consequence, all of the things that Canadians import (about 28% of total spending in Canada is on imported goods and services) were becoming more expensive. During the period between the time that the forecasts were made and November of 1976, the value of the Canadian dollar rose dramatically and the situation that had existed at the time of the forecasts was reversed.

Due to the large inflows of borrowed funds, the value of the Canadian dollar rose from a low of 96.5¢ U.S. in August 1975 to a high of $1.028 U.S. in November 1976. Consequently, the price of imports into Canada could have fallen by as much as 6.5 per cent — a fact that probably was not included in the forecasts mentioned above.

It is difficult to know whether or not all of the potential saving to consumers was passed on. It is also difficult to know to what extent the forecasts took this factor into account. (Although usually forecasters do not build exchange rate changes into their forecasts.) The potential saving was in the order of 1.8 percentage points on the Consumer Price Index. If we regarded 1 percentage point as a firm estimate then it would not be unreasonable to add .5 percentage points reduction to the 2.17 percentage points that forecasters expected. This yields a probable total reduction in inflation *due to factors other than the AIB* of about 2.7 percentage points.

Thus, of a total reduction in inflation from 1975 to 1976 of 3.3 percentage points, 2.7 percentage points or eight-tenths of the total reduction can be traced to factors other than the AIB. That is, factors that had been identified by forecasters before the AIB was formed and the unforeseeable escalation in the value of the Canadian dollar.

The foregoing estimates do not take into account the very pronounced alteration in the stance of monetary policy that has occurred since the end of 1975. Presumably some of the effects of this policy switch would be reflected in the inflation rate for 1976 - particularly during the later months of the year. The fact that these effects are ignored in the calculations makes the estimates that have been made even more credible.

What about wages?

In a cover story on October 18, 1976 *MacLean's* magazine ran a commentary-interview about the Anti-Inflation Programme one year on. In the course of the interviews that were conducted with various people, the business editor, Peter Brimelow, threw out for reaction the above evidence on forecast inflation rates versus the actual rates. One of the reactions that he got from officials in Ottawa was, "They just weren't looking at the 20 per cent and 30 per cent wage claims we were looking at."

Well, what about those wage settlements.?

According to statistics published in the Bank of Canada Review and reproduced here as Figure 1 and Table 3, wage settlements (in percentage increases awarded) reached their peak in May 1975. This was five months before the AIB was established and, in fact, wage settlements did not show an increase in their rate of increase until five months after the AIB had been established.

Similarly, average hourly earnings peaked in June of 1975, some four months before the AIB was announced. The trend from June on was very clearly falling and, in fact, the trend was not reversed until October 1975 — the month that the AIB was launched. Since October the growth in average hourly earnings has again increased and at latest reading was nearly back up to the rate of increase experienced in September 1975. The interesting fact is that the growth in hourly wages had already slowed to the smallest increase in 16 months before the AIB could have had any effect.

Figure 1 — Canadian Wages and Wage Settlements, 1974-1976

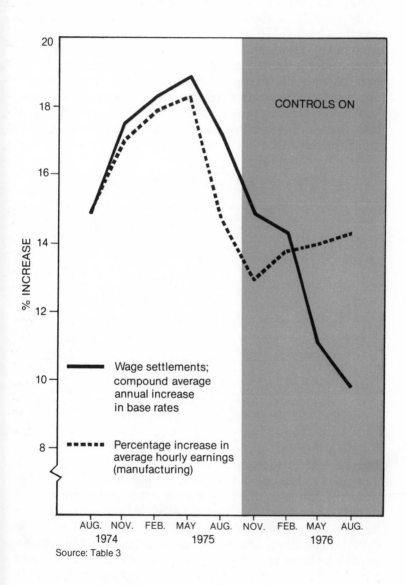

Source: Table 3

51

If one were to assess the effect of the AIB on wages by comparing the percentage increase in wages during the month that the Board was established with the most recently available information, one would conclude that the net effect of the AIB was to increase wage growth by about two percentage points. Of course, this is not quite legitimate since we don't know what would have happened in the absence of the AIB, (except to observe that the wage bargains reflected in settlements were showing a downtrend and settlements do portend the course of actual wages.) At the very least, these are interesting facts against which to weigh the impact of the AIB.

TABLE 3
WAGES AND WAGE SETTLEMENTS

		Wage Settlements Compound Average Annual Increase in Base Rates (per cent per annum)	Percentage Increase in Average Hourly Earnings (Manufacturing)
1974	III	14.8	14.9
	IV	17.5	17.0
1975	I	18.2	17.9
	II	18.8	18.2
	III	17.1	14.8
	IV	14.8*	12.9
1976	I	14.3	13.8
	II	11.1	14.0
	III	9.8	14.3

*AIB established in October but unlikely to have affected this number very much.
Source: Wage Settlements: Bank of Canada Review, November 1976, Table 62.
Average Hourly Earnings in Manufacturing: Bank of Canada Review, November 1976, Table 62. Quarterly average of year over year percentage changes.

A policy mistake?

There is one further aspect of these inflation and wage data that bears at least passing mention. First of all, it is obvious from the Minister of Finance's remarks (cited above) that somebody, at least, in Ottawa was expecting an *increase* in the inflation rate during 1976 and probably was advising the government during that tense period before the AIB was announced. If that was the case it was not a forecast that would have received very widespread support as we have demonstrated.

Secondly, the wage and wage settlement data available at the time the AIB was announced only covered the period up to June 1975. As Figure 1 shows, the trend in both wages earned and settlements changed rather dramatically at precisely that point in time.

On the basis of these two factors one cannot help but speculate that if the forecasts in Ottawa had been more 'conventional' — accurate — and wages earned and wage settlements reached as at the end of September had been known, the AIB might never have been created. If that is the case then the AIB should now be recognized for the mistake it is. On the other hand, as is clear from the analysis of Professor T.J. Courchene in this volume, public sector wage settlements were higher than private sector settlements during 1975 and were in fact rising. If this was the information that led to the adoption of controls — and it is the *only* information that indicated things were getting worse — surely a system of public sector controls as suggested by Professor Courchene, would have been the solution. Indeed, as Courchene, Reisman and others in this volume have indicated, public sector controls still are the solution.

about turn;
Canada after controls

The Economy Without Controls

GRANT L. REUBER

Professor of Economics and Academic Vice-President
University of Western Ontario
and
Chairman, Ontario Economic Council

THE AUTHOR

Grant L. Reuber is Professor of Economics, Academic Vice-President and Provost of the University of Western Ontario. He has been Chairman of the Ontario Economic Council since 1973, and is a past president of the Canadian Economics Association. Born in Ontario in 1927, he received his undergraduate degree from the University of Western Ontario and his Ph.D. from Harvard University in 1957. He has served with the Bank of Canada (Economics Research Department), the federal Department of Finance (Economic and International Relations Division), and has been a consultant to the Organisation for Economic Co-operation and Development and the Economic Council of Canada. He is a Fellow of the Royal Society of Canada.

Professor Reuber's publications include: *Price Stability and High Employment: The Options for Canadian Economic Policy* (with R.G. Bodkin, E.P. Bond and T.R. Robinson), published as Special Study No. 5 by the Economic Council of Canada in 1967; "Incomes Policy: Canada's Experiment with Organized Voluntarism to Curb Price Inflation" and "Canada's Economic Policies Towards the Less-Developed Countries" in *Canadian Perspectives in Economics*, edited by J.F. Chant and published by Collier-Macmillan Canada in 1972; "Stagflation: The Canadian Experience" in *Issues in Canadian Economics*, edited by L.H. Officer and L.B. Smith, published by McGraw-Hill Ryerson in 1974; and "Foreign Ownership and Competition Policy," *Canadian Competition Policy*, L.A. Skeoch, editor, published by Queen's University in 1972.

The Economy Without Controls

GRANT L. REUBER

Professor of Economics and Academic Vice-President
University of Western Ontario
and
Chairman, Ontario Economic Council

I. INTRODUCTION

The purpose of this essay is to address a variety of issues related to Canada's economic prospects in the period after the current wage and price control programme ends. The most obvious question that must be answered is *what will happen when controls are abolished.* The most important questions, however, are those relating to the policies that must be pursued in the post-control period. The bulk of the essay is devoted to sketching out what must be done in the general area of monetary and fiscal policy and pointing out specific structural difficulties that must be resolved.

II. THE DIRECT EFFECTS OF ABOLITION

Suppose the Government suddenly announced that, effective immediately, the AIB is abolished. Suppose also that other policies remained unchanged. What would happen?

The most predictable effect of decontrol is that there would be some short-run realignment of *relative* wages, prices and profits. This realignment, ensuing as market forces unravelled the distortions introduced by the AIB, would generally increase productivity as well as employment, output and prices. I do not believe, however, that these consequences would be very significant, since on both the wages and profits side the AIB has functioned with fairly high ceilings and these have frequently been exceeded.

To the extent that the AIB has succeeded in bottling up inflationary forces, another short-run impact might be general upward pressure on the *level* of prices and costs. Those who believe that the effect of the AIB has been marginal — say, no more than 1 per cent on the CPI over the last year — would not expect this effect of removing controls to be particularly significant either. The general result, in any event, will simply have been to reallocate price increases over time rather than to change the long-term level of prices.

Policy and power politics
Perhaps the most serious legacy to be inherited from the AIB will be its effect in further politicizing economic decision-making in this country, in increasing trade union militancy, and in enlarging the already-serious difficulties in labour/management relations. This is likely to be reflected not only in a lengthy series of bitter industrial disputes and strikes as the controls are lifted but also by increased demands for more government intervention in the economy. In addition, there will doubtless arise more demands for new institutional forms to permit more direct influence on the economy and economic policy by strong vested-interest groups.

In brief, if all we do now is abolish the AIB and nothing else, the economy, after a painful readjustment of perhaps six to nine months, may not be much different than if we had never had the AIB. However, labour relations may well be worse and the political constraints impinging upon private and public economic decisions could be more restrictive.

A believer's prospect

The costs of mandatory controls have of course been widely recognized as have the difficulties of rescinding such controls after they have been in effect for some time. The advocates of temporary controls have argued that these costs are worth paying for two reasons, namely:

i) imposing controls temporarily makes it feasible to engender more realistic short-run expectations and thereby avoid the more serious readjustment costs later when unchecked, allegedly unrealistic inflationary expectations turn out to be wrong, and

ii) imposing temporary controls provides "breathing space" for governments to undertake more basic policy reforms that will bring the situation under control from a longer-run standpoint.

Without denying that the advent of the AIB may have had some influence on expectations, one may question its importance even in the short run. Be that as it may, it is apparent that for those who believe that the impact on expectations was significant, the prospect of removing the controls may appear particularly serious. Their removal opens the possibility of again unleashing excessive inflationary expectations, particularly when little has so far been done to inspire much confidence in the belief that inflationary forces are now more firmly under control than a year ago.

The main chance missed?

Whatever "breathing space" the AIB may have provided to reshape policies, to date not much has happened. The two major structural reforms that have occurred recently — partial indexation of the personal income tax and the adoption of a more "monetarist"-style monetary policy — pre-date the AIB. By contrast, the curbs on public expenditure have been marginal and conventional. Furthermore, no significant policy modification seems in the offing. The recent government policy paper entitled *The Way Ahead* provides little in the way of guidance. Indeed, that document may easily be interpreted as providing further evidence of government uncertainty and confusion.

III. WHAT MUST BE DONE IN GENERAL?

What are some of the nettles that need to be grasped if the future is to be much different than the immediate past? First and foremost, consider general monetary and fiscal policies.

Monetary and fiscal policy

As part of the decontrol process, especially if one is concerned about not unleashing another round of inflationary expectations, monetary/fiscal policies will have to remain relatively tight. For monetary policy this implies letting interest and exchange rates float and continuing to focus on controlling the monetary aggregates. In the year since October, 1975, currency and privately-held deposits — M_2 — which I claim is more significant as a policy guide than M_1, has increased by about 15 per cent, (seasonally adjusted). During the last quarter ending in October, 1976, the increase has been 11.4 per cent (at annual rates). (Currency and demand deposits — M_1 — has increased 5 per cent over the year at a comparable rate during the last quarter.) Within this context it is not obvious that there is much scope for easing monetary policy for purposes of expanding output and employment, particularly when faced with the prospect of removing controls.

On the fiscal side, a strong case can be made for reducing both personal and business taxes. Personal tax reductions would not only stimulate consumption but also might take some of the steam out of wage demands. On the business side, tax concessions would increase investment incentives, reduce costs and increase cash flow. Particular attention might be given to introducing such tax concessions in the form of inflation accounting for business, which would be a desirable structural reform as well.

Tax and spending cuts?

So far so good. The difficult question is how to finance the revenue loss associated with a tax reduction. The scope to finance the loss by increasing the money supply is obviously limited by the current, appropriate concern for monetary discipline. Resort to the "printing press" might simply entrench us even deeper in the same old inflation-biased rut from which we find it so difficult to extricate ourselves. Borrowing the money from the public would have the effect of crowding out private borrowers, raising interest rates and putting upward pressure on the exchange rate — all of which will have a depressing effect on short-run investment and employment. After a year these short-run indirect contractionary effects might be outweighed by the direct expansionary effects of the tax reductions, but this prospect offers small consolation in a situation where the economy is already functioning well below capacity.

The other alternative is to reduce the rate of growth in public expenditures. Here too there is difficulty in reconciling the need to stimulate economic activity with the widely-acknowledged long-run objective of restricting the growth of the public sector. Matching tax cuts with expenditure cuts, in the short run at least, will depress economic activity. Yet, from a longer-run perspective, this is the only way in which the growth of the public sector can be reduced.

A Hobson's choice?

In summary, at the general level of monetary/fiscal policy we currently find ourselves faced with the temptation to trade off the possibility of some short-run gains in output and employment, combined admittedly with a risk of more rapidly rising prices, against the longer-term benefits — in terms of price stability, growth and employment — resulting from maintaining steady control over the money supply and the size of the public sector within a longer-term context. It will be particularly important to resist the seductive temptation to engage in the kind of short-run "fine-tuning" practised in the past. A major structural change to be accomplished is the re-establishment of the credibility and integrity of longer-term monetary and fiscal policies through demonstrated performance.

Public sector controls

The related structural problem is how to get rid of the AIB while at the same time re-establishing the credibility of long-term monetary/fiscal policy. Here I see no alternative but to declare victory, to remove the controls very soon on the private sector and to retain some form of controls over the public sector until better arrangements can be put in place. Consideration might be given as well to retaining some kind of agency to monitor wage and price developments and to call public attention to situations where special action, such as deregulation, might be appropriate.

IV. WHAT MUST BE DONE IN PARTICULAR?

Turning now to specific sectors, one finds another set of structural issues to be tackled. These emanate largely out of the structural changes in the economy which have arisen as a direct result of government policies since 1970. They pose the difficult political problem of unscrambling and redesigning established policies that now are strongly supported by strong vested-interests both inside and outside the government. The general focus of these reforms should be to improve productivity and employment, lessen price inflation and secure adequate minimum incomes for the poor. In a number of areas, current policies are counter-productive in terms of most, if not all, of these objectives. Yet changing the policies to inject greater flexibility, responsiveness and efficiency into the system is likely to be dislocating and to evoke strong political resistance.

What are some of the priority areas to be considered within this context? I shall note six, though the list is by no means exhaustive, nor do I place them in any order of priority.

Food policy

Changes in food policy during the past decade have, in my view, contributed significantly to price/wage inflation and have failed to provide as strong an agricultural sector as we might have had. Essentially what we have is an income support policy that restricts the supply of food, raises food prices and penalizes the most productive farmers — features that are almost exactly the opposite of what we need.† What is required is to free the market from government restrictions and allow it to work while at the same time looking after poor people in rural areas through either direct income support measures or a deficiency payments scheme.

Competition and trade policy

Both of these areas are now under review. What will eventually emerge remains to be seen. Any steps actually taken to improve competition and remove trade impediments can bring immediate gains through lower prices and higher productivity and incomes.

Here and in many other areas the notion of deregulation, from the standpoint of increasing competition and efficiency, is at least as important as the notion of adding further regulation. In numerous instances, current government regulations provide the primary basis for monopolistic or quasi-monopolistic positions in the private sector.

Labour relations

It seems apparent that the whole complex set of government regulations impinging directly and indirectly upon labour relations needs to be reviewed from the standpoint of improving labour relations and our sorry strike record. In addition, there is a particularly pressing need to devise more effective measures for handling labour disputes in the public sector — a sector which broadly defined now makes up about a quarter of the labour force, a significantly higher fraction than is engaged in secondary manufacturing.

The advent of the AIB, in my view, can most sensibly be seen as an attempt to exercise greater control over public sector wages and salaries. While controls might well be retained on the public sector after being lifted from the private

---

†Editor's Note: Two Fraser Institute publications examine marketing boards for milk and eggs with a view to establishing the effect that the boards have on the supply and prices of these products. The study of the egg marketing board is forthcoming; that on the milk board has been published; see H.G. Grubel and R.W. Schwindt, *The Real Cost of the B.C. Milk Board, A Case Study in Canadian Agricultural Policy*, Fraser Institute, February 1977.

sector, such an arrangement could probably not last more than a year or two if the controls were indeed to be effective. What is needed is longer-term solutions that alter the bargaining positions of the parties concerned and establish more satisfactory processes. The possibilities that might be explored include:

● Deregulating or removing the monopoly position of certain public enterprises such as the post office and transportation and communication facilities.

● Reducing or eliminating cost-sharing arrangements among governments so that negotiating authorities bear the full cost of settlements agreed upon.

● Setting public-sector wages and salaries upon an agreed and realistic formula basis.

● Removing from the authorities any funds that accumulate as a result of work stoppages, possibly by compensating the victims of strikes.

In this context I might add that, while I do not pretend to have the answer, I regard the "right to strike" as largely a red herring. Simply removing this right where it now exists in the public service would in my view achieve very little.

Reform of the income support system
After several years of discussion and widespread agreement about the inefficiencies and inequities of the present system, nothing has been done. In broad terms there is considerable agreement about the direction in which changes should be made. Reform has been held up because improving the design of the system has been mixed up with enriching the system. Instead of focusing on the rationalization of present levels of outlays, including UIC benefits, family allowances and all the other parts of the patch-work system that has grown up, there is concern that in the process attempts will be made to expand the system beyond present levels. Unless

the discussion can be redirected on reform at current or lower levels of total outlays, it may prove very difficult to make any progress in this area. Among the difficulties to be corrected in the present system are its ineffectiveness in relieving relative poverty, the lack of horizontal and vertical equity, the disincentives to work and efficiency, and the cost-sharing arrangements.

Policies bearing upon investment and regulated prices
The more active role of governments in recent years has had an important effect on both the level of private investment and its allocation and productivity. Among the policies in question have been tax and subsidy policies, regional development policies, land-use and conservation policies, various industrial policies, policies on foreign investment — and one could go on. On balance, the net effect of these policies has probably been to reduce the level and productivity of investment and the income and employment potential of the economy.

Associated with these issues have been the difficulties arising from setting uneconomic prices for publicly-provided goods and services as well as for regulated industries. The price of energy is perhaps the most dramatic example.

Inter-governmental cost-sharing programmes and inter-governmental transfers
There seems little doubt that perhaps the most important factor leading to increased public expenditure programmes in recent years has been the cost-sharing arrangements developed among various levels of government. In a world where a large fraction of every dollar spent is provided by someone else, the usual constraints on spending are greatly reduced. Moreover, many of these programmes have been a source of serious friction among the governments concerned. On both economic and political grounds the whole cost-sharing system needs to be re-examined.

Similarly the basis on which inter-governmental transfers are made needs to be re-examined to take account of the huge shifts that have recently occurred in the terms of trade among various regions of the country and the changes in their economic circumstances.

V. THE TASK AHEAD

All of this provides a very large agenda that obviously can be further expanded and elaborated. It is widely-accepted that governments in modern societies condition the decisions and practices by individuals and institutions in the private sector as well as those of other governments. It is also widely acknowledged that governments today have a role to play in ensuring that a basic level of goods and services is available to all citizens. Accepting these principles, one is left with the difficult task of how to apply them in practical terms in relation to specific policy areas. For this reason, I do not believe that further attempts to specify the role of government in the abstract will prove very helpful.

In my view the main structural changes in the domestic economy since 1970 have emanated from government policies. What we face is the formidable task of redesigning many of these policies in a way which gives higher priority to efficiency and economic growth, increased employment and stable prices. All too often in the past, policies have been developed on a piece-meal basis with other laudable objectives foremost in mind and without recognizing adequately that the accumulated secondary effects of the full range of these policies have serious adverse consequences for employment, growth and price stability. Redesigning these policies will require a high degree of political skill and courage, perhaps unprecedented since World War II.

Unwinding
Wage and Price Controls

DAVID E. W. LAIDLER

Professor of Economics
University of Western Ontario

and

MICHAEL PARKIN

Professor of Economics
University of Western Ontario

THE AUTHORS

David E. W. Laidler was born in 1938 and educated at the London School of Economics, the University of Syracuse and the University of Chicago where he received his Ph.D. in 1964. After teaching (in both Britain and the U.S.A.), Professor Laidler was appointed Professor of Economics at the University of Manchester in 1969.

In 1975, Professor Laidler joined the Department of Economics at the University of Western Ontario. Professor Laidler is a member of the Editorial Advisory Board of the Fraser Institute.

Professor Laidler's publications include: *The Demand for Money - Theories and Evidence*, (International Textbook Co., 1969), and *Introduction to Microeconomics*, (Philip Allan Publishers, 1974); he edited (with David Purdy) *Labour Markets and Inflation*, (Manchester University Press, 1974). With Michael Parkin, he published "Inflation: A Survey" in the December 1975 issue of the *Economic Journal.* His most recent publication is *Essays on Money and Inflation*, published by the University of Chicago Press in 1976. His essay "An Alternative to Wage and Price Controls," was published by the Fraser Institute in 1976 in *The Illusion of Wage and Price Control.*

Michael Parkin was born in Yorkshire, England in 1939 and in 1963 was graduated from the University of Leicester. Until fall 1975, when he moved to Canada, he was Professor of Economics at the University of Manchester. Currently, he is Professor of Economics at the University of Western Ontario.

Professor Parkin's scholarly publications are numerous and include on the subject of inflation alone: *Incomes Policy and Inflation*, edited by M. Parkin and M.T. Sumner, University of Toronto Press, 1973; *Inflation in the World Economy*, University of Toronto Press, 1976; "Inflation: A Survey" (with David Laidler), *Economic Journal*, December, 1975; *Inflation in Open Economies*, University of Toronto Press, 1976; and "The Post-War Record. Wage and Price Controls: The Lessons from Britain" in *The Illusion of Wage and Price Control*, published by the Fraser Institute, 1976.

Unwinding Wage and Price Controls

DAVID E. W. LAIDLER

Professor of Economics
University of Western Ontario

and

MICHAEL PARKIN

Professor of Economics
University of Western Ontario

I. INTRODUCTION

The Federal Government of Canada introduced its programme of wage and profits controls in October 1975. Since then the rate of inflation in Canada has undoubtedly fallen no matter how we measure it. The rates of increase of consumer prices, wholesale prices, and wages have all come down. In this paper we ask whether this reduction in the inflation rate may be attributed to the effects of controls, and whether the control programme should be maintained or abandoned. As the reader will see we have considerable doubts that the controls have helped to achieve this reduction in inflation and therefore conclude that they should be abandoned. This conclusion leads us to face up to the issues involved in how best to unwind the programme. We divide our paper into two main sections dealing with each issue in turn. Our overall conclusion is that not only should controls be taken off, but that they should be taken off in one single, simple operation. All controls on wages and profits should be abandoned simultaneously and the final task for the Anti-Inflation Board, prior to its dissolution, should be to carry out as objective as possible an evaluation of the consequences that the controls programme has had for the Canadian economy.

II. THE EFFECTS OF CONTROLS

The view that one takes about whether controls should be taken off clearly must depend in large measure on what effects the controls are thought to have had and are continuing to have on the economy. The primary aim of the programme is to influence the overall rate of wage and price inflation. However, in addition to their effects in controlling the rate of inflation, controls, like any other anti-inflation strategy, inevitably have side effects on factors other than those which they are designed primarily to influence.

Slim evidence

In the current state of knowledge and given the short space of time that has elapsed since their introduction, there is no way in which anyone could provide anything approaching a definitive evaluation of the effects of controls. This observation applies equally to such things as the overall rate of wage and price inflation, which it was designed to influence, and to other matters, such as investment resource allocation, upon which it might also be having side effects. The data needed to carry out such a full evaluation simply have not yet been collected and processed, and even if they had been, there has not yet been time to carry out the large amount of detailed research that would have to underlie such an evaluation. Our evaluation of the effects of controls is then, of necessity, tentative. In order to supplement the impressionistic evidence that is available concerning the current Canadian experiment we draw on evidence generated by careful studies of other countries that have, at earlier times, experimented with control programmes.

On inflation

First, let us consider the effects of the controls on the rate of inflation. As we noted in the opening sentences of this paper, the rate of inflation has, during the year-and-a-quarter of controls, fallen significantly — the exact extent is documented in the Preface to the book. The first question that we must address, therefore, concerns the extent to which that fall in the inflation rate may be attributed to the controls. Can we attribute the reduction in the rate of inflation to the operation of controls, or would the rate of inflation in Canada have come down anyway in their absence? A full answer to this question would require us to carry out the following kind of exercise. First, it would be necessary to construct an econometric model of the Canadian economy using evidence generated during the pre-controls period. Then, making what some might regard as the heroic assumption that there were no changes in the structure of the economy during late 1975 and 1976 except those brought about by the institution of controls, that econometric model would be used to predict what would have happened to wages and prices in the absence of controls. Any difference between such predictions, and what did actually happen, would then be attributed to the influence of controls. Moreover, given that economists are far from agreed about the right way to construct an econometric model of the Canadian or any other economy, it would be advisable to carry out this experiment with a number of alternative models; only if all led to the same conclusion about the influence of controls would it be safe to advance a firm view of what the programme had or had not accomplished in the way of reducing the inflation rate.

Neither we, nor anyone else, are in the position to be able to perform so detailed a series of experiments, though they will undoubtedly be performed in due course. Nevertheless, we are not in a state of total ignorance. We do have some limited qualitative understanding of the forces which make for movements in Canada's rate of inflation. There is widespread agreement among economists that whatever other factors impinge on the inflation rate, the overall state of demand in the economy, and the movement of world prices taken in combination with exchange rate fluctuations, play an important role in influencing the behaviour of wages and prices in Canada.

Versus the effect of domestic demand

Consider first of all the behaviour of domestic demand factors. It is clear that the Canadian economy has, in common with the rest of the Western industrialized world, been through and is still only slowly emerging from, the worst recession in post-war history. It is a standard prediction of economic theory that when an economy is in a depressed state, where there exists an excess supply of goods and services not to mention labour, that the rates of inflation of wages and prices begin to fall. The competition between firms to maintain their level of sales in a market that is apparently too small to take all the output they are capable of producing makes them less eager to raise prices and more reluctant to grant wage increases. Though it has lately become fashionable in some circles to deny that market mechanisms still work in this way, the current world-wide recession is generating an overwhelming body of evidence that they do in fact do so. We can find such evidence in all the major countries of the world as Table 1 shows. The fall in the inflation rate has been particularly dramatic in countries like Germany and Switzerland where the recession began somewhat earlier than elsewhere, but it is also clear, in the cases of the United States, Britain, and many other countries, that the current recession has been associated with a marked reduction in the overall rate of inflation. Moreover, though Britain has used wage and price controls during this period — indeed it has had some kind of programme continually in force since 1972 — Germany, Switzerland and the United States have seen their inflation rates fall without resort to controls.†

---

†Switzerland has had a mild form of controls since 1972. There are no official guidelines but the price office can roll back price increases. The system works on a "complaint" basis and only applies to prices. The apparent aim of the system is to increase the transparency of the pricing mechanism and not to control incomes.

Canada was particularly late in entering the current recession and compared with other countries, though not with past Canadian history, that recession has been relatively mild. Nevertheless since 1975 there clearly has been considerable slack in the Canadian economy and it seems fair to argue that the Canadian inflation rate in 1976 would have fallen simply as a result of the depressed state of the economy even in the absence of controls. Whether that fall in the inflation rate would in the absence of controls have been greater or smaller than it has in fact been is impossible to say. However, the depressed condition of the economy must have exerted some downward influence on Canada's rate of inflation over the last year, so that not all of the fall in the inflation rate can appropriately be attributed to the influence of controls.

TABLE 1
INTERNATIONAL INFLATION & ECONOMIC ACTIVITY

Country	Inflation Rate				Real Growth Rate			
	1973	1974	1975	1976*	1973	1974	1975	1976*
	%	%	%	%	%	%	%	%
Canada	7.6	10.9	10.8	7.6	7.2	3.2	0.6	4.8
U.S.	6.2	11.0	9.1	5.9	4.7	-1.1	1.5	5.5
Japan	11.7	24.4	11.8	9.0	9.7	-1.2	2.1	7.0
U.K.	9.1	16.0	24.3	16.5	5.4	0.5	-1.4	2.4
Switzerland**	8.7	9.8	6.7	1.5	5.8	0.9	-12.0	12.2
Germany	6.9	7.0	6.0	5.0	5.1	0.4	-3.4	5.4

*Values for 1976 are estimates based on partial 1976 data.
**Real growth figures for Switzerland are based on industrial production rather than National Income.
Source: Organisation for Economic Co-operation and Development.

It might be argued that, with the unemployment rate in Canada being so extraordinarily high (by post-war standards) during the current recession, the reduction in the inflation rate should have been greater than it was if the forces we have just been discussing were in fact strongly at work in the economy. It must be remembered, however, that, since the late 1960's, structural changes have taken place in the Canadian labour market. In particular, rates of unemployment compensation have increased substantially and eligibility to receive such benefits has been widened. This has probably led to an increase in what is often called the "natural rate of unemployment," that is, the rate of unemployment, as measured by official statistics, at which the economy is working at its full productive capacity. The implication of this is that current measures of the unemployment rate are not directly comparable with those generated in earlier times as indicators of the degree of slack in the economy. Thus an official unemployment rate of somewhere in the neighbourhood of six per cent may well be that at which the economy is working at full capacity under current conditions whereas, in the early 1960's, the relevant rate was closer to four-and-one-half per cent.[1] If this is, in fact, the case, then it should not be too surprising that the rate of inflation, particularly of wage inflation, has come down as slowly as it has over the past year.

Versus the effect of monetary policy

A further domestic factor tending to push down the overall rate of inflation over the last year is the initiative taken by the Bank of Canada, in conjunction with the Department of Finance, to place the Canadian money supply on an announced growth path and to adhere to that growth path. Since late 1975, the Bank of Canada has been announcing a target growth rate for the money supply and has, indeed, roughly achieved that target growth rate. Such a policy should in theory encourage domestic price and wage setters

[1]See H. Grubel and Dennis Maki and Shelley Sax, "Real and Insurance-Induced Unemployment in Canada," *Canadian Journal of Economics*, 8, No. 2, May 1975, pp. 174-91.

to expect a reduction in the overall rate of inflation, and as a result to build that expectation into contracts settled after the new monetary policy was put into force. It is of course too early to expect any large effects of this policy to be showing up in the overall inflation rate, but to the extent that such effects are beginning to come through, they would put extra downward pressure on the inflation rate independently of the behaviour of excess demand, and independently of the influence of wage and price controls.

Versus exchange and international price factors

For purely domestic reasons, then, it is clear that a reduction in the rate of inflation was to be expected since the autumn of 1975 whether or not a wage and price control programme was implemented. But when dealing with an economy as open as that of Canada, it is vital to look beyond the domestic scene to the outside world. The movement of world prices converted into Canadian dollars at the going exchange rate is an important influence on Canada's inflation rate. With an approximately constant exchange rate, the rates of inflation of world commodity prices, food prices, and the like, which Canada both imports and exports, feed directly into the Canadian rate of inflation. The inflation rate in the rest of the world has fallen markedly over the last year or so, and this in and of itself must have had a moderating influence on the Canadian inflation rate, enabling it to fall more rapidly, given the existing degree of slack in the economy, than it otherwise would have done. This effect has been compounded by the appreciation of the Canadian dollar that took place between the autumns of 1975 and 1976, largely as a result of borrowing abroad by provincial governments if anecdotal evidence is to be believed.[†] The depreciation of the dollar in early 1977 will likewise eventually produce a certain amount of inflationary pressure later in the year.

[†] Editor's Note: For further analysis of this point, see the essay by Professor John Floyd in this volume.

Overall, our evaluation of the factors other than controls which influence Canada's inflation rate leads us to the conclusion that inflation would have fallen substantially, as in fact it did during 1976, even in the absence of controls. Of course the kind of qualitative and impressionistic analysis that we have provided here is no substitute for a series of systematic econometric evaluations of the effects of controls. Such evaluations will, as we have said, no doubt be forthcoming in the next year or so and, if they produce results similar to those generated by already existing studies in the United Kingdom and the United States (see the Fraser Institute's *Illusion of Wage and Price Control*), then they will show that, at best, the controls had a "shock effect" during the first few months of their operation, but that their main influence was to alter the timing with which the inflation rate came down during the last year, rather than to have had any influence on the *amount* by which it did so.

It is our guess, an informed one we trust, that this is in fact what such studies will show in the case of Canada. Our guess is based both upon the fact that this is what controls have been seen to accomplish in other countries at other times, and upon the fact that the behaviour of world prices, the exchange rate, and domestic aggregate demand were all acting to reduce the Canadian inflation rate during the period since mid-1975. The behaviour of the exchange rate in early 1977 is, however, likely to put some pressure on the inflation rate later this year.

On things other than wages and prices

Up to now, we have discussed the effects of controls on the overall inflation rate. We have said nothing about side effects. In dealing with these issues we are treading on much thinner ice. We need detailed data on allocative and distributional matters to guide us, and such data are not readily at hand. Moreover, precious little work has been done on the allocative and distributional effects of controls in other countries, so we do not have a firm base of evidence from previous experiences from which to extrapolate. In principle it is clear that direct controls on wages and profits will influence the distribution of income and the allocation of resources by having a differential impact on different groups in society. Inevitably some groups are well equipped to evade the effects of controls while others have little alternative but to go along with them at least in the short run. Professionals, such as doctors, lawyers and accountants, whose incomes depend upon charging fees for specific services to specific individuals are hard to police, as are those groups whose incomes are set on a commission basis. On the other hand, it is relatively easier (though not inevitably straightforward) to oversee and control wage agreements. Profits are difficult to measure at the best of times, and hence controls on them are likely to be less effective than those on wages, while incomes generated in farming and small business are exempt from controls in any event.

These considerations suggest an *a priori* presumption that the incomes of industrial wage earners will be more affected by the programme than those of others and the British experience provides some empirical support for this proposition. However, the prediction of what would have happened to industrial wages in the absence of controls is even more hazardous than that of what would have happened to the overall price level and we do not even hazard a guess based on Canadian evidence as to what has happened here in general over the last twelve months. Although it is not clear from the aggregate data that controls have had any effect on the overall distribution of national income between wages and profits, it is quite clear that there are particular cases, the evidence for which is anecdotal, where there have been perceptible impacts of controls. The notorious, not to say ridiculous, case of automobile mechanics at St. Johns, Newfoundland drawing different wage rates depending upon the size of the company that employs them is unlikely to be the only anomaly produced by the controls programme. (This particular anomaly was recently removed by the Administrator of the AIB but it nevertheless illustrates the point.)

The potential effects of controls on profits and investment are particularly worrying. Canada is a free open economy, and Canadians are free to invest their wealth either in Canada or elsewhere in the world. When an attempt is made to control profits, that attempt does not have to be particularly effective in order to persuade those looking for a profitable outlet for their funds to seek investment opportunities in countries where there are no controls on profits. It is quite sufficient to make would-be investors nervous about the future in order to have such effects. Once again, there is anecdotal evidence that such tendencies are at work in the Canadian economy, but one cannot take all such evidence at face value. There is no way of knowing how often, when the controls programme is given as a reason for a decision to cancel an investment project, or transfer it to the United States or elsewhere, it is not in fact being used as a public excuse for a decision that would have been taken in any event. Though it would be surprising if it was always the case that the controls programme was merely an excuse, it would be equally surprising if that was never the case. It has been a feature common to most industrial countries in the latest business cycle that the rate of capital accumulation during the recovery phase has been low as compared to the same phase of earlier cycles. Just as Canada was late to enter the downswing of the current cycle, so is she late to recover. An important question to be faced by those who will eventually work on the effects of the controls programme is the extent to which the lateness and weakness of the Canadian recovery is to be attributed to the effects of profits controls on investment.

Summary

To sum up then, the rate of inflation has fallen over the past year, but it is our informed guess that little if any of that inflation reduction should be attributed to the operation of the controls. Rather, we attribute it to the degree of slack in the Canadian economy acting in combination with the movement of world prices, themselves the direct consequence of the slack state of demand in the world economy as a whole. Further, the operation of controls has had and is continuing to have a depressing effect of unknown magnitude on the rate of capital accumulation and hence on the long-run level real income in the economy. The programme may also be distorting the distribution of income to a degree. If such adverse effects on capital accumulation, allocation, and distribution continue, they will make inroads into real standards of living of all Canadians, whether workers or suppliers of capital. And none of this is to mention the obvious political and social strains that the programme of controls is generating. In short, our view of the effects of controls is that not only are they probably serving no useful purposes, but that they are also doing positive harm. Moreover, since it is reasonably well established from previous experience that, if they affect inflation at all they do so in the first few months of their operation, and that the economic distortions and social tensions they create become more acute with the passage of time, the case against controls becomes stronger as time passes. Hence our conclusion that it would be wise to wind up the programme as soon as possible.

III. HOW TO UNWIND CONTROLS

There are a variety of ways in which the programme of wage and price controls can be phased out. Let us first of all set out what options are available and then attempt to evaluate them. There are two broadly-defined alternative approaches to removing controls; either they can be phased out gradually, or removed suddenly. Within the first, "gradual phase-out," approach it should go without saying that there are many alternative detailed ways which the controls could be removed. One possibility would be to do nothing more than enforce the existing regulations with less and less vigour, thereby permitting them to wither away in a haphazard fashion. A second, but potentially more orderly procedure, would involve attempts to identify the areas where controls were no longer biting, because market forces were resulting in wage contracts and profit levels that fell below permitted maxima; controls could be formally removed from those sectors first, the hope being that more and more sectors would fall in that category with the passage of time. A third possibility would involve the decontrol of profits in order to avoid the potentially serious distorting effects on capital accumulation that many believe this aspect of the programme to be having, while maintaining controls of the wages for a more extended period. The alternative, of sudden removal of controls, is sufficiently well defined that we do not need to elaborate on it further at this stage.

Minimum requirement

If our guess is correct that controls are having little effect on the overall inflation rate or that if they have had any effect, that is now largely over, then it might not seem to matter much how controls are removed. The only dictum to be laid down might appear to be that the measures adopted to remove them should not lead economic agents to expect a renewed bout of inflation. Such expectations could well be self-fulfilling, at least in the short run. Thus it would be important for the government to avoid giving the impression that its main motive for removing controls derives from a belief that they were no longer capable of containing inflationary pressures that they had for a while successfully held in check. Our diagnosis of events of the past year is that the controls programme is by now redundant as an anti-inflation device; if the case for phasing out controls is put in such terms, and provided that the public believes that case, then there is no danger of the removal of controls in and of itself leading to a further burst of general inflation. From this point of view, because an immediate phase-out of all controls would be the easiest policy to justify in terms of an argument that the programme was redundant — why take time about removing regulations if they are having no beneficial effect? — and because it would be the simplest procedure to implement administratively, it appears to be by far the most attractive alternative.

However, the effect of controls on the overall rate of inflation is not the only matter that needs taking into consideration here. Their side effects on the allocation of resources and distribution of income make it necessary to take more seriously the case for adopting one of the more gradual options. If the distribution of income and the allocation of resources have been seriously affected by controls, might not a programme of gradual removal make it possible for the economy to get rid of those distortions with less friction and instability than might be encountered if controls were simply removed at one swoop? Let us look at the more gradual options in the light of this question.

The fadeout option

Consider first the option of phasing-out controls by the simple expedient of gradually reducing the degree of rigour with which they are enforced. It is clear that, while it was in force, such a policy would have the effect of accentuating some of the worst features of the controls themselves. To the extent that controls are affecting some sectors of the economy more than others at present, when they are being enforced rigorously, it is likely that they are in fact biting hardest on the most law-abiding and socially-responsible members of the population. These are the people least likely to be looking for loopholes. Such tendencies as this would become even more marked in a situation in which controls were not being heavily policed. It would be rather like the situation that exists when speed limits on the highway are enforced only laxly. In such a case those who have little regard for the law break the rules with impunity and those who attempt to obey it suffer. If law-breaking is tolerated, then a burden is placed upon the weaker and more conscientious members of the community, a burden which eventually leads them to view the law with contempt.

The method of winding up controls by lax enforcement has in fact been used on more than one occasion in the United Kingdom, for example, during 1968-1970, and at the beginning of 1974. In each case it was adopted for want of a better alternative by a government that was doubtful of its own position, nervous of being able to carry a political consensus in favour of the replacement of controls by more orthodox but viable anti-inflation policies, and which felt itself unable to continue with existing policies. We could speculate that the uncertainties generated by laxly-enforced controls, not to mention the cynicism also created, has made a major contribution to creating the impression that Britain is, at present, "ungovernable."

Sectoral decontrol

The second gradual phase-out option we should consider involves attempting to identify sectors of the economy where controls are no longer effective, indeed no longer needed because market forces themselves have begun to lead to rates of wage and price change below those laid down, and removing them from those sectors. It appears to be much more attractive on the face of things. If the controls programme was in fact operating according to plan, so that wages, profits and prices in various sectors of the economy were being made to behave in a way compatible with the reduction of inflation without the simultaneous introduction of any distortion in the economy; if their effect was simply to smooth out the process whereby the economy responded to the stance of fiscal and monetary policy; then this would indeed be the natural way to phase them out. Those sectors of the economy already behaving in an appropriate fashion of their own accord could be decontrolled, and those not yet likely to do so of their own accord could be kept on track until they had learnt better.

The difficulty with this case for a gradual unwinding of controls is that it is based on the assumption that they are in fact working smoothly and having no adverse consequences. It is, as we have already made clear, our informed guess that, rather than smooth out the economy's adjustment to a lower inflation rate, the controls are by now making that adjustment rougher than need be. If we are correct, then adverse consequences would persist wherever controls were left in place, and the longer was taken over the process of removing controls, the more damage would be done in the meanwhile. Suppose, for example, that controls on the profits of a particular sector of the economy were seen to be biting and kept on for the very reason that they were biting, but that the consequence of so doing was to divert some new investment from Canada to the United States. The longer were controls kept in force in that sector, the more would it ultimately suffer in terms of inadequate capital and reduced productivity.

The which hunt

The key objection, however, to a systematic gradual unwinding of controls by identifying in which sectors they are having the least effects is the very impossibility of conducting the search for such areas in any objective fashion. *Are the levels of profits in a particular industry within the guidelines because they are at the maximum level market conditions will permit, or because firms in that industry are complying with regulations? Are wage settlements in a particular industry in excess of the guidelines because of market forces, or because of a tacit agreement between employers and employees to make allowances for a roll-back in their initial bargain?* The kind of careful econometric work to which we referred earlier might eventually settle such questions as these, but it is inconceivable that it could be carried out rapidly enough to serve as a reliable guide to the unwinding of controls.

The Anti-Inflation Board simply cannot obtain enough information rapidly enough to know with any degree of confidence where controls are pinching most tightly and where hardly at all. In fact, therefore, the Board would have no ready-made operational criterion for deciding on sectors to be decontrolled first. In practise, we fear that an attempt at an orderly gradual decontrol would be likely to degenerate into something very like the first option we have discussed, in which controls come off in a haphazard fashion with perhaps the political influence of specific groups playing a bigger role than economic criteria in deciding who was first to be decontrolled.

Staged decontrol of wages and profits

The final option for gradually unwinding controls, that of decontrolling either profits or wages first, would at least be operationally viable.† If it is the case, for example, that con-

---

†Editor's Note: A strategy similar to this was employed in the second freeze phase of the 1971-1974 U.S. experiment with controls. Wages were permitted to rise 5.5 per cent per year while prices were frozen. "Shortages and outright cheating became more common. Food shortages in grocery stores forced the administration to begin Phase IV food regulations on July 18, 1973." See Michael R. Darby, "The U.S. Economic Stabilization Program of 1971-1974," in M. Walker, ed., *The Illusion of Wage and Price Control*, The Fraser Institute, 1976, p. 143.

trols on profits are having worse side effects than those on wages, then it may be felt that to decontrol profits but to keep controls on wages, at least for a period, would be sensible. There are, however, two overwhelming objections to such a strategy.

First, nothing would be more likely to cause major industrial conflicts than such an action. We have already seen how much hostility and suspicion was provoked by the recent easing of regulations on profits. One of the major adverse consequences of inflation is the social and political strife that it causes, and the least that we can ask of anti-inflation policy is that it mitigate rather than exacerbate that strife.

Second, perhaps less serious but nevertheless important is the possibility that controls on wages are themselves having adverse effects on the allocation of scarce labour resources. These effects stem from the fact that controls make it more difficult for firms to use the price mechanism to attract labour into new, high profit, high productivity areas of activity. To remove controls on profits alone, while it would give the corporate sector better opportunity to raise its rate of capital accumulation and exploit new investment opportunities, would not give it the best opportunity to do so. Only if high productivity sectors were able freely to bid up wages to attract labour from more sluggish sectors of the economy would we have such a state of affairs.

IV. ABRUPT REMOVAL

All in all then, there appears to be little case for any of the alternative gradual programmes for unwinding the controls. A quick removal of the entire apparatus thus comes to seem the most desirable way of proceeding. This is not to say such a procedure would involve a smooth transition from a controlled to a decontrolled situation. If controls have been having differential effects across sectors of the economy, then market forces would begin to act to correct the distortions created by those differential effects the moment controls are lifted. The bigger the distortions controls have created, the more frictions there are going to be when they are removed.

Arguments for

The case for a quick removal of controls does not rest on the proposition that there are no adjustment costs to be borne, nor is it denied that in principle there could exist a plan for a gradual phase-out that would reduce those adjustment costs. Rather that case rests on the practical proposition that our knowledge of the distortions that controls have created so far is so scanty that it would at best be a matter of pure chance if any such gradualist plan in fact made things better rather than worse. But that is at best: in fact, the pressures that would inevitably be brought to bear on those designing the phase-out plan would be likely to lead to a scheme which gave special advantages to those with political muscle, and those willing to use that political muscle. In such a case the "orderly phase-out" of controls would be only too likely to exacerbate the distortions that the controls themselves had introduced into the economy, rather than reduce them. Hence it would put off the day upon which market mechanisms could begin to deal with the problem of ridding the economy of them, while simultaneously making that problem more difficult.

Loss of policy power?

The question must arise as to whether the abandonment of controls would leave a vacuum in economic policymaking which would have to be filled by something. There are two aspects to this question — one dealing with policy toward inflation, and the other dealing with more general matters of policy towards the distribution of income. It is clear that the programme of wage and profit controls has never been regarded as more than one part of an anti-inflation package. We have already referred to the monetary and fiscal aspects of that policy above, and provided the stance of those aspects of policy is not changed, there is no sense in which the removal of controls would leave a vacuum as far as the control of inflation is concerned. One of us has already argued that monetary and fiscal policies, appropriately used and coordinated with policy towards the exchange rate, are necessary and sufficient for the control of inflation.† It is unfortunate that it seems to be so widely believed that wage and profit controls are a new tool needed to deal with newly-emerging problems concerning the distribution of income. Nothing could be further from the truth.

The entire apparatus of the income tax and social security system is already in place, and in large measure is designed to deal with distributional problems. We certainly would not wish to suggest that the structure of that system as it currently stands is ideal. No doubt it could be improved, and will be improved. The point is simply that, in advocating the removal of wage and profit controls, we are not advocating that the government give up a newly undertaken responsibility towards influencing the distribution of income, or indeed suggesting that the abandonment of controls would leave a vacuum in this area. Governments at all levels have in fact long accepted responsibilities in the sphere of income and wealth distribution, and are already well-endowed with the tools whereby policies can be formulated and implemented.

Unwinding the AIB

One final loose end needs to be tied up. It concerns what should be done with the elaborate machinery embodied in the Anti-Inflation Board. Much of the manpower employed

---

†D. Laidler, "An Alternative to Wage and Price Controls," in M. Walker, ed., *The Illusion of Wage and Price Control*, The Fraser Institute, 1976.

by the AIB could readily be re-absorbed in other areas of the Civil Service. However, it might be difficult for all of it to be re-absorbed quickly. It may, therefore, be desirable to unwind the Anti-Inflation Board itself in a somewhat slower fashion than the controls programme which it is administering. While this slow rundown of the Board was taking place, it would be very useful to have the remaining staff employed to perform a careful evaluation of the effects which controls have had on the Canadian economy. The question of their effects on the rate of inflation would be important here but so also would their effects on the allocation of resources and the distribution of income. The AIB is the natural body to carry out such a study since it presumably has already collected a good deal of the information necessary to carry it out. As we have stressed repeatedly in our foregoing discussion, we have had to rely upon informed guesses, and extrapolation from experience of other economies, in order to assess what effects the controls programme is currently having. It would be most valuable to have those guesses subjected to rigorous empirical analysis.

V. SUMMARY AND CONCLUSIONS

To summarize, then, it has been argued that controls are not an important factor in reducing Canada's inflation rate, but that they are potentially important in causing misallocation of resources and distortions in the income distribution and in generating social and political conflict. In view of these facts, the controls programme should be removed, and furthermore it should be removed as quickly as possible.

Control and Decontrol

RICHARD G. LIPSEY

Sir Edward Peacock Professor of Economics
Queen's University

THE AUTHOR

Richard G. Lipsey was born in British Columbia in 1928. He was educated at Victoria College and the University of British Columbia, and did graduate work at the University of Toronto and the London School of Economics. He received his Ph.D. from the University of London in 1957. Dr. Lipsey is presently Sir Edward Peacock Professor of Economics at Queen's University, Kingston. He has held many posts in the academic and public sectors, including a chair in economics at the London School of Economics, the chairmanship of the Department of Economics at the University of Essex, member of the council of Britain's National Institute of Economic and Social Research (London), and panel member for the Policy Analysis Group of the federal Department of Consumer and Corporate Affairs.

Professor Lipsey is author of several textbooks, including *Economics: An Introductory Analysis* (with P.O. Steiner) which has had four American and two Canadian editions and has also been translated into Spanish and French. His latest book is *Mathematical Economics: Methods and Applications* (with G.C. Archibald), published by Harper & Row. He has contributed many articles to learned journals, including *The Review of Economic Studies, Economica, The Banker, Lloyds Bank Review*, the *American Economic Review*, and the *Canadian Journal of Economics*.

Control and Decontrol

RICHARD G. LIPSEY

Sir Edward Peacock Professor of Economics
Queen's University

I. INTRODUCTION

It is my intention in this essay to comment briefly on four issues: government fiscal and monetary policy both before and after the period of decontrol, policies for the transition to the decontrol period, the danger the controls will be reimposed at some future date, and the consequences of a lapse into subsequent periods of control.

II. SOME BACKGROUND FACTS

To begin with it is worth getting on the record a few well-established facts:

1. There is a strong consensus among economists that the great upsurge of world inflationary pressure in the 1970's followed from very large increases in world demand that in turn followed on large increases in money supplies. Once inflations became rampant, unions became increasingly militant in their efforts to protect living standards in the face of rapidly rising price levels. But the union militancy was mainly the consequence not the primary cause

of the rising inflationary tide. The sequence was: increasing rates of monetary expansions which have everywhere and always caused sustained inflations throughout history, rising demands, rising prices, rising union militancy.

Once, however, the union militancy is entrenched, along with the idea that rapid increases in money wages are necessary just to hold one's own against a rising tide of inflation, it is hard for the government to induce an alteration in this behaviour merely by slowing the rate of monetary expansion even though excessive monetary expansion is the root cause of the inflation. It is at this point that wage-price controls enter the scene.

2. Governments cannot permanently determine the price level by wage and price controls. The price level is determined mainly by the forces of total or aggregate demand which is in turn determined by monetary factors at least to a great extent. Thus wage-price controls have no long-run influence on the price level and to talk of using them to defend the long-run integrity of the dollar is irresponsible.

3. Wage and price controls can temporarily slow down an inflation during the period when they are in effect. Even here the magnitude of their influence is surprisingly small. A host of studies of British and U.S. experience suggests that reducing the inflation rate by one to two percentage points (e.g. from 9% to 7 or 8%) is about all that can be expected of them while they last.

4. The only respectable argument for temporary wage and price controls is that they may reduce inflationary expectations in a situation in which the government is using fiscal and/or monetary policy to reduce the rate of inflation. This is the argument used by John Young in the Report of the now defunct Prices and Incomes Commission and it is the argument the

government uses when it is addressing audiences that it regards as informed on the subject of inflation.

The main argument here is that wage and price controls can be used to avoid an increase in unemployment that would accompany an *unanticipated* slowing of the rate of monetary expansion. (If prices are being set and wage contracts are being drawn up on the basis of e.g. 10 per cent expected inflation and the government only makes available enough purchasing power to buy current output at say a 5 per cent increase in prices, then sales must fall and unemployment rise.†) *The function of wage-price controls, according to the expectations argument, is not permanently to affect the rate of inflation, but to keep the unemployment rate lower than it otherwise would be while the economy adjusts to a lower rate of inflation brought about by a reduction in the rate of monetary expansion.*††

III. ANTI-INFLATION POLICY

Controls of course are only cosmetic. They attack the symptoms of rising prices and wages while doing nothing about the causes. If the government follows inflationary fiscal and monetary policies, then the best that can be hoped from controls is that they postpone the inevitable inflation. The government's long-term anti-inflation policy depends, therefore, on its anti-inflationary fiscal and monetary policy.

The government, however, has taken the line that major changes in the degree of competitiveness are needed if inflation is to be restrained in Canada. They have emphasized that the controls were meant to buy time by re-

†Editor's Note: For a more detailed discussion of this point, see David Laidler, "An Alternative to Wage and Price Controls" in *The Illusion of Wage and Price Control*, M. Walker, Ed., The Fraser Institute, 1976, p. 198.

††These four points were accepted by virtually all the economists and representatives from business and labour who gave papers to the Conference at which the first version of this paper was presented. Point (4) may also be found in the Government's White Paper *Attack on Inflation*.

straining inflation until major changes to increase the degree of competitiveness in Canada could be introduced, these changes being intended to make the economy less inflation-prone. Most economists support any changes that the government can make to increase competitiveness in Canada — while many, myself included, remain skeptical of the government's ability and willingness to make more than marginal changes. In supporting the government in its pro-competition policy, economists are in danger of appearing to give support to one of the mightiest and most unreasonable myths now current in Canada. The myth is that by increasing competitiveness, the government can make the economy significantly less inflation-prone. This is the Galbraith theory that inflation is caused by monopoly elements in our society.

Galbraith himself, and those who accept his theory of inflation, argue that the lack of competitiveness is deeply in-grained in the economy. They hold that it results, first, from the nature of technology that makes large firms inevitable and second from the powerlessness of individual workers against giant corporations that makes the existence of large unions a necessary counterweight to the existence of large firms. They feel that any changes the government can make through such things as its competition policy can do little or nothing to change the amount of market power exercised by large firms and unions. They see permanent wage-price controls as the only cure for inflation. Thus the minority of economists who accept the government's view that lack of competitiveness is a major cause of inflation hold that there is little the government can do about inflation short of per-manent wage-price controls.

The majority of economists do not accept the Galbraithian market power theory of inflation. Indeed no one has ever gathered any significant body of evidence to support this theory — by showing, for example, that for given rates of monetary expansion less competitive econom-ies have higher rates of inflation than do more competitive economies.

We now arrive at the interesting conclusion that both the majority of economists who reject the Galbraith view on inflation *and* the minority who accept it would agree that the main plank of the government's long-term anti-inflation policy — increasing the degree of competitiveness in the Canadian economy — bears no relation to inflation one way or the other. One group reaches this conclusion because it holds that lack of competitiveness has little to do with inflation while the other group reaches the same conclusion because it holds that there is little the government can do to alter significantly the amount of competitiveness in the economy. Whether one adopts the majority *or* the minority view on the relation between inflation and competitiveness the same conclusion follows: the government's long-term inflationary policy is founded on a dangerous myth. The myth is dangerous because it may stop the government from accepting what the majority of economists accept — that fiscal and monetary policy must bear the main brunt of the long-term control of inflation.

What then of these two policies?

Fiscal policy is not now being used as an anti-inflationary device in Canada. Government expenditure continues to rise at a significant rate and there are no signs of any restraining forces being deployed on the tax front. American governments have pointed the way to the use of temporary tax surcharges as a fiscal restraint on the economy, but this does not appear to be on the cards in Canada. It appears, therefore, that monetary policy is to carry the whole anti-inflationary burden.

The sole reliance on monetary policy has a number of consequences. First it implies high interest rates and thus a continuing differential between Canadian and U.S. rates. High interest rates imply a large capital inflow into Canada — both because short-term funds will move into Canada to take advantage of high Canadian short-term rates and because much long-term borrowing will be done in the U.S. where rates are lower. This implies strong upward pressure on the Canadian dollar in the foreign exchange market.

And this in turn implies a current account deficit as the appreciation of the dollar encourages imports and discourages exports.

It is important to realize that these things (high interest rates, capital inflows, high valued Canadian dollar, and current account deficit) are all part of a single parcel — deflation of the economy through monetary policy. This is not always perceived by the general public and there is some tendency to laud the government's monetary restraint for its anti-inflationary effects while complaining about high interest rates, large capital inflows, and high value of the Canadian dollar and the poor export performance that results. The praise for monetary restraint qualified by criticism of other parts of the package is misguided, since, as monetary policy is the sole tool relied upon, the government must accept the whole of this package — *at least until we no longer need a more contractionary policy than the U.S.*

The Conservative party has recently been calling for a reassessment of the belief that high interest rates are a necessary part of the anti-inflationary package. Economists, however, are in no doubt that the Bank of Canada can either influence the money supply or it can influence interest rates; *it cannot do both.* If the Bank of Canada is to gain control over, and slow down, the rate of monetary expansion in Canada it must give up any attempt to control interest rates. It must let these rates rise as high as the free market dictates. If interest rates are to be held below their free market levels, the Bank will lose control over the money supply and hence over the inflation rate. An accepted body of well-tested economic theory makes this one of the least questionable propositions in the whole of economics.

IV. REMOVING THE CONTROLS

A great deal is made of the problems of transition from controls to no controls and of the need to phase the controls out gradually. Such discussion rarely makes explicit its implied theory of inflation and the precise nature of the harmful consequences that are to be avoided by gradual decontrol.

Two cases

There are basically two situations in which controls may be removed. First, there is substantial excess liquidity and an excess in a variety of instances of demand over supply at current prices. (In other words the controls have actually worked in holding prices below the level that would be justified by current demands.) In this case there is nothing that can be done: take them off slowly or quickly and a period of inflation will ensue taking prices to the levels justified by current demands.

Second, there is no excess liquidity in the system and no significant excess demand at current prices. (This does not mean the controls have not worked, for their real purpose is to allow the inflation rate to be lowered by monetary policy without there being an accompanying rise in the unemployment rate.) In this case it is critical that the controls be removed in such a way as not to create expectations that an inflationary explosion is to follow. (Since in the long run the price level is determined mainly by the money supply, an upward burst of wages and prices in the *mistaken* expectation of another burst of sustained inflation would cause a once for all rise in prices and in unemployment. This would be most undesirable since the government would have to allow unemployment to remain high long enough to break the expectations of a sustained inflation and then provide the monetary expansion that would permit a return to "full employment" at the new higher price level.)

The witch doctor effect

Controls that are designed primarily to affect expectations are really an exercise in "sympathetic magic" and hence getting out of them successfully requires more of the arts of the witch doctor than of the economist. Sympathetic magic consists of magical rites designed to bring on what is in any case inevitable, such as the Spring Thaw or the re-emergence of the sun from an eclipse. If the event is as regular as the Spring or the end of an eclipse it does not matter whether or not the witch doctor believes his own mumbo jumbo. But if the event is less regular and not necessarily inevitable, the success of the witch doctor depends on his not believing his own nonsense, for he must cunningly and with Machiavellian purpose, apply his measures just when he calculates the events they are supposed to bring on are about to occur in any case.

The government will go on telling the public that the controls are responsible for slowing the inflation rate. In fact we all know that the CPI is governed by many factors that the government cannot or does not directly control; food prices, energy prices and the exchange rate, to mention but three. If the government believes its own recent propaganda that the controls are actually determining the inflation rate they may be tempted to leave the controls on for the full three years. They may then be unlucky and find themselves having to remove the controls in a period when prices are rising. The observation of these rising prices plus acceptance of the government's own propaganda that controls were reducing the rate of inflation would combine to create expectations that decontrol would be followed by a burst of inflation. The controls would then have served to create the very situation they were designed to prevent — the expectation of rising inflation.

To avoid this possibility the government must understand that it is largely engaged in an exercise of sympathetic magic. The government must carefully choose the moment — the *first* possible time during the next two years — when the inflation rate is nearly as low as might reasonably be expected given world conditions, and when, preferably, the rate is currently falling. The government must then remove the controls and it might be best to do this in a sudden surprise operation with no transitional period.

As a precaution, a sharp *temporary* and well-publicized tightening of the monetary brakes would signal to everyone the government's serious intention not to validate by monetary expansion any wage explosion that did occur. In this way the government should be able to get out from under the controls without creating new inflationary expectations. But if it waits to the end of its three year period and is unlucky enough to hit a period of rising world inflationary pressure the removal of the controls may itself create unfortunate inflationary expectations.

I have advocated a sudden decontrol — done at just the right time. There is a lot of talk about a transitionary period of slow and selective decontrol. Politics being what it is this seems a likely path for the government to follow. It is very important to realize that if the government takes what it regards as the politically safe way out and decontrols slowly, it risks losing any economic gains it may have gotten from the controls. Selective decontrol will lead to a further set of maladjustments between wages and prices in the controlled and decontrolled sectors and an increase in the already alarming sense of hostility and frustration felt by the unions. Both of these could lead to an outburst of wage inflation in response to an expected price inflation that could once again bring in the very thing that the controls were designed to avoid: rising wages and prices in response to the expectations of rising inflation.

V. THE POST-CONTROLS WORLD

The government in many pronouncements, and the Prime Minister in his 1976 New Year's musings, have tried to create a second myth: that a new society or new social order would be prepared during the controls period and instituted when the controls were terminated. I do not believe that this myth is so widely-accepted as is the one that an increase in competitiveness is a necessary condition to controlling inflation. To the extent that it is believed, however, people are in for disillusionment. When the controls are removed we will go right back to the economic system that we have had over the last decade or two. Small, sometimes cosmetic and sometimes real, changes in competition policy may be made but their effects on the overall behaviour of the Canadian economy will be minimal. I see no evidence that the present government has any intention of suggesting changes that could be reasonably described as "a significant altering in the socio-economic order" let alone as instituting a "new order."[1]

The main problem in the post-controls world, it seems to me, will be to avoid a lapse back into a further bout of controls. This could occur because of disillusionment when the promised new socio-economic order does not materialize, because of government-created expectations that controls are the best way of fighting another inflation when it occurs, or because the monetarists may be seriously discredited when an inflation occurs that is *not* initiated by an inordinate rate of monetary expansion induced by the Bank of Canada. The first danger is self-evident. Let me briefly address the second and third.

The sympathetic magic has worked

Controls were put on at almost the exact peak in the inflationary period. The inflation rate began to subside about the time the controls were instituted and well before they could have had any conceivable effect on the CPI themselves. The controls will get the credit just as the witch doctors of old got the credit for the coming of Spring. It would of course be asking too much of any government not to claim the credit for their controls; the controls were unpopular and it is only natural for the government to say "see, they worked." The general public knows little about monetary theory and monetary policy. Ordinary voters will thus, quite understandably, give to controls much of the credit for the reduction in inflation rates that is occurring and that would have

---

[1]Nor do I see that such changes are necessary. An increased awareness of the dangers of inflation is a good thing and hopefully the chances of slipping into two digit inflation almost unnoticed have been greatly reduced. Governmental changes that make marginal increases in competitiveness are also to be welcomed. Beyond that each of us has his or her own pet schemes for social and economic reform. But by and large I see no evidence that we need to risk the living standards and growth rates that we now have by trying to build a whole new economic order. Who do we want to copy? — the British, the Swedes, the Japanese, the Indians or the Pakistanis? Of course there is always room for change and improvement, but looking around the world I am more impressed at how much worse off rather than by how much better off the average Canadian could easily become if there is too much additional government tinkering with the economy.

occurred without the controls. When the next sustained inflation occurs in Canada there will be heavy pressures placed on the government in power not to eschew the use of a tool that was claimed by the present government, and perceived by the public, to have had some effect in the past. Even if the existing government is hostile to such a course of action, the opposition may become committed to such a policy; and the opposition may win a subsequent election.

See, money doesn't matter

By far the most serious danger in the post-controls period is that the monetarist approach to inflation will be discredited. Over the past ten years economists have rediscovered what was well established by two centuries of work and only de-emphasized — forgotten by some — in the 1930's: that money plays a crucial role in inflation. The rapid world inflation of the 1970's was brought about by extraordinary increases in world liquidity made possible in part by abandoning the Bretton Woods international monetary system. In Canada, the rapid rate of increase in the money supply rising from 10 to 15 per cent to 20 per cent had its inevitable effect in rapid and accelerating inflation. The Bank of Canada has now accepted the monetarist lesson;† it has stated target rates of growth for M_1 and it accepts that reducing this rate is a major condition for the control of inflation.††

But we have not yet had enough experience to be confident of how tightly the inflation rate can be controlled by controlling M_1 (and possibly M_2 as well). As Milton Friedman himself agrees, the links between the quantity of money and total demand and the price level are complex and variable.

---

†Editor's Note: For a discussion of the "monetarist lesson", see M. Walker, Ed., *The Illusion of Wage and Price Control*, published by the Fraser Institute, 1976.

††Editor's Note: There are three commonly used measures of the money supply: M_1 which is cash and demand deposits; M_2 which is M_1 plus non-demand deposits at commercial banks, and M_3 which is M_2 plus deposits with non bank financial institutions.

Also we don't know how much a flexible exchange rate will succeed in sheltering one economy from inflations abroad (inflations that are possibly on a world-wide scale). This is particularly so when there are heavy capital flows that can cause the exchange rate to vary from the path that would be dictated by the needs for current account balance (where changes in the exchange rate should roughly reflect changes in relative price levels). We don't know how much inflation will be caused by further increases in Arab oil and other energy prices, to say nothing of rising prices of certain raw materials that become increasingly scarce. World climatic changes may create persistent and rising shortages of foodstuffs. For these and other reasons we must expect price rises in some very important sectors of the economy.

If the price level is to be held constant when some money prices rise, then other prices must fall (to keep prices unchanged on average). But can we be sure that large and rapid increases in energy or food or raw material prices will be accompanied by falling money prices elsewhere in the economy? It would, it seems to me, be a rash economist who would say "of course." If some money prices don't fall, then the adjustment of relative prices due to large increases in energy, food and raw material prices will all come through differential increases in money prices. This means an inflation. The high degree of substitutability between M_1, M_2, and M_3 may lead to an increase in M_1 that the Bank of Canada can do very little about in the short run. This would provide the finance necessary to permit the inflation to proceed.

The problem then lies in the Bank of Canada getting the rate of increase of M_1 down to say 5 per cent and then having the inflation rate jump unexpectedly. Monetarists who have currently said "without control of the money supply you can do nothing" are likely to be interpreted as having said — indeed some of them may have said — "with control of the money supply you can do everything." Such an event — a serious inflation *not* initiated by a major government induced monetary expansion — is quite possible, but there is a danger that the advocates of monetary restraint will have made such extreme claims that they will be discredited by the event.

The correct lessons would be that monetary constraint cannot do everything to control inflation — particularly in the face of short-term real disturbances — and that the failure of monetary policy to provide a perfect control does nothing to establish the viability of any alternative policy. The advocates of controls would, however, say "see, we were right all the time and controls are the only way to hold the inflation rate in check." The danger is present, and only advance warning and extreme caution on the part of advocates of monetary restraint in stating their case can guard against the possible discrediting of a sensible middle-of-the-road position that changes in the quantity of money are one very important determinant of the rate of inflation.

These are two of the many considerations that lead me to believe that the most important task during the post-control period will be to prevent the reinstitution of controls the next time a sustained inflation occurs — as most surely it must sooner or later.

VI. WHAT IF CONTROLS ARE REINSTITUTED?

I have dealt elsewhere[2] with the potentially disastrous effects on the Canadian economy of the repeated application of bouts of wage-price controls. The British experience charts our course to disaster if we wish to sail this way. The disastrous effects on industry of a plethora of bureaucratic controls that have seriously curtailed the incentive to invest or to reduce costs is the direct result of repeated and futile attempts to control inflation by price controls.

I can think of no easier way to seriously curtail the free enterprise system in Canada and bring about the onset of the Corporate State that Professor Galbraith thinks we already have than to engage in a series of bouts of wage-price controls similar to those that have wreaked havoc in the U.K. The very survival of our free enterprise economy requires that we educate public opinion to be hostile to any attempt to try controls again and again, and again . . .

---

[2] "Wage Price Controls: How to do a Lot of Harm by Trying to do a Little Good". Remarks delivered at Symposium on Wage-Price Controls at the Canadian Economics Association Annual Meeting, Quebec City, June 1976. Forthcoming *Canadian Public Policy*, Winter 1977. Reprinted in this volume in Part One.

Decontrol:
The Special Case of Rents

MICHAEL WALKER

Research and Editorial Director
The Fraser Institute

THE AUTHOR

Michael A. Walker is the Research and Editorial Director of the Fraser Institute. Born in Newfoundland in 1945, he received his B.A. (Summa) at St. Francis Xavier University and his Ph.D. in Economics at the University of Western Ontario, 1969. From 1969 to 1973, he worked in various research capacities at the Bank of Canada, Ottawa and when he left in 1973, was Research Officer in charge of the Special Studies and Monetary Policy group in the Department of Banking. Dr. Walker has also taught Economics and Statistics at the University of Western Ontario and Carleton University. Immediately prior to joining the Fraser Institute, Dr. Walker was Econometric Model Consultant to the Federal Department of Finance, Ottawa.

Dr. Walker was editor of, and a contributor to, three of the Fraser Institute's previous books: *Rent Control - A Popular Paradox* (1975), *The Illusion of Wage and Price Control* (1976) and *How Much Tax Do You Really Pay?* (1976).

Decontrol:
The Special Case of Rents

MICHAEL WALKER

Research and Editorial Director
The Fraser Institute

I. INTRODUCTION

Rent control existed or had been promised in several provinces before the act establishing the AIB was promulgated. This, together with the characteristic longevity of rent control in other countries and in other eras, suggests that rent control probably deserves special attention in a discussion about decontrol.

There is some evidence (discussed in my essay in Part One) that the anti-inflation programme was adopted under the false pressure of erroneous forecasts about the rate of inflation. Whether or not this was the case, the situation illustrates an important feature about economic policy and that is the fact that what matters is what is believed to exist and not what actually exists. Further, our understanding about the economy is highly imperfect and our measurement of its functioning, imprecise. Accordingly, there is considerable room for the exercise of judgment in the assessment of current economic events. So, to some extent, economic events are partially in the mind of the beholder and the unfolding of economic events is, as much as anything, the development of a consensus amongst observers about what is happening. (After the fact, sometimes long after, our measurements are usually more precise and there is often a final judgment about matters on the basis of more reliable evidence.)

In the case of economic policy, the economic consensus is only one of the many opinions that bears on the decisions that are made. Political considerations weigh heavily on policy-makers as do the "high profile" and behind-the-scenes pleadings of special interest groups. The consequence is that economic policy is seldom, if ever, designed with the single-minded objective of dealing with an economic problem. More importantly, perception of the economic problem is often badly distorted because of the effect that other considerations have on the exercise of judgment in the interpretation of economic evidence.

Housing policy seems to have been particularly prone to this weakness[1] and rent control has been one of the consequences. An essay about rent decontrol which ignored the intentions of the enacters of control could not help but miss the mark. Accordingly, having in mind the importance of judgment in the interpretation of economic events, we have in the first part of this essay examined the origins of rent control policies.

In the second section we examine some of the possible consequences of decontrol. The final section presents my view as to the necessary shape of decontrol policies.

II. THE ORIGINS OF RENT CONTROL

Rent control, in practise, is always adopted as a temporary measure to alleviate the hardship (real or imagined) that tenants are presumed to endure as a consequence of a rental housing shortage. For example, the British rent control scheme (now sixty-one years old), the Swedish rent control provisions of 1945 (finally abolished under pressure from tenants in 1975), the existing 1974 rent control provisions in British Columbia and 1976 legislation in Alberta and Ontario all have this in common. The critical and determining factor in most of these cases was the widely-held belief that the jurisdiction in question was experiencing a housing 'shortage' of crisis proportions. A housing crisis demands an immediate dose of strong policy medicine — particularly if an election is in the offing or if the steps of parliament are daily occupied by vociferous media-attracting tenants. If, as will usually be the case, the short-term benefactors of rent control (*sitting tenants*) are more numerous than those who lose (*landlords*) the strong medicine for a housing crisis almost invariably takes the form of rent control.

From the point of view of the politically-orientated policy-maker, rent control has everything to offer. It silences (at least for a time) the noisy activists, it shows that the government is doing something about the housing crisis and often as not it wins the political support of a large fraction of the voting public (over half of the households in most urban areas are tenants). Moreover, rent control does not involve the use of government resources and hence doesn't 'cost' the government anything.

In addition, the bad side effects of control take a long time to emerge and are slow to affect tenants on average and hence slow adversely to affect the political fortunes of those who enact controls. In this respect, housing is unlike most other commodities. The supply of housing services is provided, for the most part, from fixed stock. Hence, controls on the price of these services cannot result, in the short term, in a withdrawal of the service. It is this built-in inertia effect in the supply of housing that makes it particularly vulnerable to controls. The prices of other necessities of life such as food and clothing are seldom controlled because the shortages produced by control are immediately evident. (The attempt to freeze food prices — Freeze II, June 13, 1973 to August 11, 1973 — during the U.S. anti-inflation programme promptly produced food shortages and necessitated the introduction of food regulations. Similarly, price controls in the U.S. following World War II were abandoned in the face of widespread shortages.)

In short, given the nature of housing, rent control is excellent policy snake oil for squeaky wheels.

The process that leads to rent control usually begins during a time when the housing market is in the process of adjusting to the pressure of excess demand. The natural consequence of excess demand for housing services is an increase in rents. The rise in rents will, after a time, encourage landlords to increase the supply of housing that they bring to the market. In the very short term, however, the excess demand can only be accommodated by a more intensive use of the existing stock of housing.

From the point of view of the government department attempting to monitor the housing situation the market adjustment may or may not be evident. For example, in Canada, information on housing market conditions is very poor. Vacancy rate information for the whole rental housing stock is not available. (The extent to which this may be a problem varies considerably but, for example, in Calgary only about half of the rental housing stock is surveyed.) Measurements of rental rates are not collected province-wide, or nationally, on a consistent basis and the information that is collected by Statistics Canada is known to be biased. Furthermore, critical information on the real burden of rising rents is not available at all on a current basis. (The real burden of rents is measured as the percentage of income that must be spent to acquire accommodation. In terms of a given market situation, the real burden of rents would be deemed to have risen if tenants were having to pay an increasing fraction of their incomes to maintain their standard of accommodation.)

So, the government finds itself facing a market wherein rents are rising and measured vacancy rates are falling. Exactly what the level of rents is and exactly how many vacant units there are is not known. Furthermore, the effects that rising rents are having on people's ability to buy other things is not known. In the midst of this ongoing circumstance, enter the tenant activists whose objective it is to have rent control enacted.

Tenant activists generally do not start out from the premise that "we must first ascertain the facts." Quite on the contrary. The objective of the tenant activist is is to create a sense of crisis - to make policy-makers and other tenants believe that the situation is truly desperate. A book entitled "Less Rent More Control," which is "about rent control . . . and how tenants can organize to win and enforce it," advises:

> "Even if you can't get good statistics, it's often helpful to publicize specific cases of families paying a large portion of their incomes for rent."

> "Stories about specific families who are suffering from the housing crisis can be very useful in bringing statistics to life and in getting publicity for the rent control campaign."[2]

Since the process of market adjustment produces rising rents and there are people in most communities whose incomes are low or slow to rise, the rent control campaign will not have to look very hard to find the evidence of a crisis. The media for its part, always happy to advance the cause of the underdog - an admirable objective taken by itself - willingly cooperates in making notorious the plight of the under-privileged. Coincidently, the rent control campaign attracts to it the support of a larger number of tenants who, owing to their own situations, would not have pressed for controls but who identify with the disadvantaged. (And besides, they do have something to gain because rent control does reduce the rate of increase in rents.)

At this juncture, whether or not there is a housing shortage of crisis proportions is irrelevant to the government involved because the general public believes that a crisis exists. Hard facts to dispell this belief are not available and when available are discounted by the emotional content of the evidence of hardship cases. In the event, as so often happens, the government 'can't do nothing.' In the midst of this ongoing circumstance, careful demonstrations by economists of the disastrous long-term effects of rent control are unlikely to get a careful hearing. Besides, rent controls are only a temporary measure!

It would be foolish to pretend that rent controls are always adopted in circumstances like the foregoing. In the case of British Columbia, pressure for rent control actually came from within the government itself. During a programme of general wage and price controls rent controls are

simply imposed as an adjunct to the general programme —
whether or not there is tenant pressure for controls.
Nevertheless, our characterization of the process is important because it highlights the essential elements that must be
coped with during the decontrol process - namely, the lack
of information and the plight of the disadvantaged.

III. THE EFFECTS OF RENT CONTROL

The primary purpose of this essay is to talk about decontrol
of rents. The reason for decontrolling is the overwhelming
burden of evidence that rent control is not effective in its
main objective and has many long-term costs. Accordingly,
the essay would not be complete without some statement of
the effects of rent control. In view of the fact that the Fraser
Institute has recently published several books on the subject,[3] I will not engage in a complete discussion here but
merely summarize the main points and refer the interested
reader to the books.

Before getting on with the summary of the effects of
controls, it is important to note that we are here talking
about both long-term and short-term effects of controls. In
some cases, the effects will already be evident in Canadian
housing markets subject to control. In other cases, the effects will only be marginally present and hence not yet evident.

In addition, this discussion presupposes that rent control has been an effective ceiling on rents. In some instances
the permissible increase under controls is larger than would
have occurred in a free market. In these cases rent control is
redundant except to the extent that it imposes a sort of col-
lusion on rent setting decisions. This may, in the short run,
produce larger rent increases than would otherwise have occurred.[4]

Rent control worsens housing "shortage"

Rent control makes rental housing relatively cheaper than it
would otherwise have been. Accordingly, it increases the de-

mand for housing. At the same time it reduces the profitability of investment in rental housing and hence reduces the supply. If we use the vacancy rate (the percentage of suites unoccupied) as a measurement of the shortage, observable evidence of the effect of controls is available in the New York housing market. The New York area has both a controlled market and an uncontrolled market. The vacancy rate in the rent controlled market is consistently half that in the uncontrolled market.[5]

Currently the Canadian experience with rent control is producing evidence that seems to conflict with this view that rent control increases housing shortages. The evidence is that in spite of rent control, vacancy rates are starting to rise — especially in Toronto and Vancouver. This evidence must be carefully interpreted.

The principal reasons for the incipient increase in vacancy rates relate to government policy to make production of rental accommodation more attractive and to make homeownership an attractive option for many current renters. Construction of rental accommodation has been made more attractive by the reinstatement of the provision, abandoned in 1971, that allowed landlords to "write off" the capital cost of buildings against their other income. The abandonment of that provision in 1971 and its associated effects on supply was a principal factor in the rise in rents that occurred during 1973-1975.

Rental accommodation is also being directly subsidized by the government. There has been widespread adoption of assisted rental programmes which subsidize the capital cost of projects in return for controls on the rents that will be charged. In effect, these programmes are an acknowledgement of the fact that rents are too low and should be viewed as the first step in what could be a disastrous journey. The provision of these subsidized units will 'take the pressure off' the rental market in the short term but will succeed in maintaining rents that are increasingly unrelated to the market in the long term. Thus, while seeming to improve the situation, these programmes will ultimately create a situation where no construction is undertaken unless it is subsidized.

Various programmes have been adopted to increase the attractiveness of homeownership. These subsidized home-ownership programmes have the effect of artificially shifting demand from the rental sector to the homeownership sector at a faster rate than is justified by the underlying economics of these two sub-markets. As a consequence, the short-term condition of the rental housing market will improve — but the improvement is illusory and must not be permitted to deflect attention from the fact that rents are below the long-term or equilibrium level.

Rent control causes deterioration of the housing stock

Faced with a rate of return on investment that is too small, many landlords recoup their losses on a current basis by allowing the physical stock of houses to depreciate at a faster rate. That is, regular maintenance and repair is neglected. While this improves the landlord's cash flow in the short term, it has an obviously disastrous effect on the housing stock over the long term.

From the landlord's point of view, rent control reduces the capital value of the buildings[6] supplying the housing service. The extraction of capital in the form of repair and maintenance foregone is a rational way of equalizing the rent-controlled rate of return with the expected rate of return before rent controls.

Rent control redistributes income in haphazard fashion

Rent control is a form of tax that is levied on landlords, the proceeds of which are given to tenants. The amount of tax and subsidy varies according to the difference between the market rent and the controlled rent. It is often supposed that the redistribution effected by rent control is from high income earners to low income earners. While there is not much firm evidence on the matter, what evidence there is does not support this view. For example, the most recent taxation statistics for Canada (1973) show that about half of all rents reported were earned by landlords with incomes of less than $13,000. A detailed study by D. Gale Johnson of the U.S. data did not support the hypothesis "that landlords have significantly higher incomes than tenants." Further, he concludes, "if one of the objectives of rent control is to aid low-income people . . . it does not achieve that objective."[7]

Rent control leads to discrimination

To the extent that they are unable to discriminate amongst
tenants on the basis of price, landlords find it expedient to
do so on the basis of race or other characteristics.[8] Groups
particularly vulnerable are those tenants that may cause
higher costs for the landlord, such as large families or
families with children (more "wear and tear" on housing
unit) and people whose jobs require higher than average
mobility (less stable tenancy).

Rent control shifts the incidence of property taxation

Rent control reduces the value of rental property. With a
given - indeed increasing - revenue requirement, governments that rely on the assessed value of property as a tax
base must increase the tax rate on all property. Since the
assessed value of owner-occupied housing will, in all probability, rise under a rent control regime, the burden of
property tax is gradually shifted to homeowners.

Recent evidence of this effect of rent control has been
compiled for the City of Cambridge, Massachusetts where
against an inflationary backdrop similar to Canada's the
total assessed value of real property actually fell during the
1972-1974 period. The city assessor, in commenting on the
situation, noted that as a consequence of the shrinking tax
base, the tax *rate* had been increased by 70 per cent over the
1970 to 1974 period.[9]

Rent control reduces labour mobility

Occupation of a rent controlled apartment is an asset. The
yield on this asset is the difference between the market rent
and the controlled rent. Moving from one unit with controls
to another without controls therefore entails a "capital loss."
The extent of this effect obviously increases with the length
of time that controls are in force. To the extent that controls
cause inefficient use of space and lack of housing production
reduced immobility may result from the very lack of housing units - whether controlled or not.

117

Rent control does not improve housing conditions of the poor

It is often supposed that since rent control makes housing cheaper it, therefore, improves the housing condition of the poor. The evidence suggests[10] that the effect of rent control is to cause tenants to increase their expenditures on goods and services other than housing. In other words, under rent control people tend to occupy about the same standard of housing that they would occupy in a free market. The extra disposable income that they have because of rent control is used to buy things other than housing.

Rent control does not eliminate price rationing

One of the functions of price in a market is to ration the supply of a good or a service amongst the people that want it. Proponents of rent control argue that this *ability to pay criterion* ought not to be applied in the housing market because of the essential nature of housing and because the existing income distribution is such that there is wide variability in ability to pay. This argument for rent control is advanced in the belief that eliminating the formal price rationing mechanism will eliminate rationing on the basis of ability to pay.

In practice, imposing rent control on the market price rationing scheme doesn't have this effect because rent control doesn't much affect the existing distribution of income. Key money, large security deposits, phoney offers to buy, bribes to officials and the like take the place of formal rent increases and ability to pay, as ever, determines who gets what. Indeed, since rent control reduces the total supply available, and accordingly the need for rationing is more acute, the ability to pay could potentially be a more significant determinant of housing conditions in a rent controlled market than in a free market.

The tendency for black and gray markets in housing (i.e., informal price rationing) to arise in the presence of rent control also has side effects on the structure of rental housing supply. Since black and gray market activities are generally illegal, many landlords are reluctant to become involved. However, since the return from such activities is

118

fairly high and becomes higher the farther controlled rents move from free market rents, people who do not have a distaste for marginal illegalities are attracted to the market. And, since property values based on market rents are artificially depressed, such potential landlords find the cost of *buying into the market* quite attractive. The potential effects of this sort of evolution and the situation that could arise do not tax the imagination. Certainly, the *property management* techniques of the sort of landlord that thrives on the intra-legal margin are well known.

IV. RENT DECONTROL

Unfortunately for all concerned, decontrol of rents involves precisely the same set of considerations that arose when rent control was first proposed. Furthermore, except in rare circumstance, the rent control legislation could only have made the basic housing situation worse since it encourages demand and discourages supply. Because the issues involved in the adoption of rent control are largely of a political nature, the way out of rent control is also dominated by essentially political considerations. From the point of view of a government that is entertaining a decontrol policy the potential consequence of precipitous decontrol is possible loss of support either from the electorate or, as in the case of the current government of Ontario, from a parliamentary coalition that may be ideologically opposed to decontrol.

Whereas the potential political costs of decontrol are more or less well-defined and the prospect of their incidence immediate, the benefits of decontrol are long term in nature and not clearly defined. This fact, more than any other, explains why rent control once adopted is extremely hard to get rid of.

A factor that looms large in the thinking of governments about to undertake decontrol is the uncertainty about exactly what will happen. (Or, about what will be said is happening.) While it is impossible to remove this uncertainty completely, it is possible nevertheless to provide some analysis of the situation and perhaps thereby eliminate from the range of the possible some of the more extreme views of what will happen.

Consequences for rents

What will happen to rents if rent control is removed?

This is, of course, the essential question to be answered. The extent of the rent rise occasioned by decontrol will determine the amount of hardship imposed by the return to a free market and the amount of ill feeling directed toward the government.

The answers to what will happen to rents are as numerous as there are separate housing market areas in the country. In each of these areas, the basic housing supply and demand conditions are different and accordingly, the reaction to a lifting of controls will be different in each case. Fortunately, for our analysis, the circumstance can only be of three basic kinds. 1. Excess supply of housing. 2. Excess demand for housing. 3. Supply-demand balance.

Supply-demand balance involves an increase in rents that is mutually satisfactory to both tenant and landlord. In this case, decontrol of rents would have no impact since the market is in a state of balance in any event. Accordingly, in what follows we will not address ourselves to this case.

1. Excess supply of housing

Excess supply of housing exists if the actual number of vacant apartments exceeds the number that landlords would like to have vacant. (Or expected to have vacant on average when they built or bought the apartments.) If there is an excess supply of apartments, landlords would find it difficult to raise rents since tenants have the option to move to other comparable apartments - the owners of which are glad to accept lower rents rather than have too many of their suites vacant. If there is an excess supply of apartments, it is unlikely that a rent control programme of the sort currently in existence across Canada would be effectively constraining rents. The market-determined rate of increase in rents would be lower than the permissible increase - regardless of the cost structure faced by landlords - because of the competition among landlords to rent their vacant suites. Accordingly, rent control in these areas is redundant and its abolition would have no effect.

2. Excess demand for housing

There is excess demand for housing if, at the existing level of rents, people want to occupy more housing space (either space per unit or number of units) than is currently available. A condition of excess demand would normally cause rents to rise until people had adjusted their expenditures on housing (their demand for space) to coincide with the available supply. Of course, the rise in rents would also cause landlords to make more space available both in the short term (remodelling and speedy completion of projects underway) and in the long term (new construction). To the extent that supply expanded, the amount of adjustment required on the part of demanders of space would be correspondingly reduced. Rent control that effectively constrains rents produces an excess demand for, or shortage of, housing. Accordingly, the remainder of the discussion will assume that most areas concerned about decontrol are characterized by a condition of excess demand.

Supply response and decontrol

It is often said that the housing market is unlike other markets in that the supply of housing is "inelastic" or slow to respond to changing circumstances. In large measure this opinion arises from the fact that it takes time for new housing to be built. However, a significant degree of "elasticity" or responsiveness to changes in rents is provided by "doubling and undoubling." Doubling can take the form either of two households occupying the same housing unit or of an existing housing unit being remodelled to provide for separate, double or multiple occupancy. The phenomenon of "doubling" represents a simultaneous decrease in the quantity of housing services demanded and an increase in the quantity of housing services supplied (more intensive utilization of the existing stock).

Analysis of the housing market that relies on published information about changes in the supply of housing is likely to fall very short of determining the actual condition of the market because of the existence of this "unofficial" segment of the market. Statistics collected by the Central Mortgage and Housing Corporation do not even attempt to cover housing units containing less than six suites. However, most of the short-term "action" in the market is likely to occur in precisely these units. The extent to which analyses of published figures is likely to be erroneous can be inferred from survey evidence in Vancouver which indicates that between 10 and 15 per cent of the residential housing stock probably contains "illegal" suites.[11]

It seems reasonable to suppose that these conversions to multiple occupancy did not occur during periods of excess supply of housing. Rather it is highly likely that they occurred during times of excess demand when rents were rising and the official market appeared quite tight. To the extent that this is a correct assessment, analysis of official statistics would be quite misleading. In particular such analysis would underestimate the responsiveness of the supply of and demand for housing services to increases in rents.

Demand response and decontrol

The foregoing discussion notwithstanding, the principal adjustment to the rising rents necessary to eliminate excess demand would have to occur, at least in the short run, on the side of the demand for housing. A "shortage" of rental housing is symptomatic of - indeed is synonymous with - rents that are, relatively speaking, too low. At some level of rents there would be a glut of housing on the market as consumers, in an attempt to reduce their total outlays on housing, moved to increasingly smaller and less well-appointed quarters, doubled up, postponed leaving home, etc.

Since Canadians are the best housed people in the world, there is obviously a considerable margin within which housing demand could contract without appreciably altering housing standards. Furthermore, most of the necessary adjustment could come about as a result of doubling-up of non-family households. Nearly a third of total household formations are currently undertaken by single, unattached individuals and, reflecting their less pressing need for separate households, it is this group that probably would be most responsive to a rise in rents. Similarly, single individuals who have not yet left the homes of their parents may be encouraged by a rise in rents to delay their leaving. This, too, would reduce the quantity of housing demanded.

The question that we must address in this section is *by how much would rents rise if, upon decontrol, all of the burden of adjustment had to be borne by the demand side of the market?*

The first question that arises is *what would determine the extent to which rents would rise? When would they stop rising?*

Rents would stop increasing relative to other prices when supply and demand were in balance. In terms of conventional measures of housing market conditions, supply and demand can be said to be in balance once the vacancy rate reaches its "natural equilibrium" level. The trick, of course, is to know what this "natural" vacancy rate is.

Estimates, based on published housing market information, made by Professor L.B. Smith, suggest that the natural vacancy rate for Canada as a whole was in the 5 per cent range during the 1950's and 1960's![12] Bearing in mind the deficiencies in the published information (as outlined above), I am inclined to suggest a figure of about 4 per cent as a working estimate in the current circumstances.

Having fixed on 4 per cent as the natural vacancy rate, we must now determine what increase in rents would be necessary to reduce the quantity of housing demanded so that this vacancy rate will be achieved. To do this we have to know to what extent consumer demand for housing is responsive to changes in the relative price of housing (i.e., rents relative to the price of other things).

Various estimates of consumer responsiveness have been made and they range from insignificant to substantial. For example, some estimates indicate that a 10 per cent relative change in rents (rents rising 10 per cent faster than the overall consumer price index) would cause a 10 per cent reduction in the quantity of housing services demanded by consumers. Other estimates place the reduction in demand caused by a 10 per cent rise in rents at about only 1 per cent.

The demand for housing that is relevant for any calculation related to the vacancy rate situation is the demand for physical housing units. The estimates of consumer responsiveness that we have cited relate to the demand for the services of these housing units. Fortunately, estimates have also been made for the responsiveness of the demand for housing units. On the basis of estimates calculated by L.B. Smith, an estimate of 0.4 seems appropriate as a working assumption of the responsiveness of housing unit demand to relative changes in rents.[13] The implication of this estimate is that if average rents rise 10 per cent and nothing else changes, the demand for housing units will fall by about 4 per cent.

The required rise in rents

In order to illustrate the application of this formula, we will apply it to the current situation in the Vancouver area. The vacancy rate in the Vancouver area is currently hovering in the 1 per cent range. If the natural vacancy rate is assumed to be about 4 per cent, vacancies would have to rise by about 3 per cent before rents would stabilize. The relative rise in rents required to achieve this, assuming that nothing else changes, would be about 7.5 per cent. Since general inflation (the increase in the consumer price index) is proceeding at about 6 per cent at annual rates, a rise in rents of 7.5 per cent relative to other prices would require an increase in rents of about 13.5 per cent.

Of course, this calculation ignores the fact that population growth and growth in family disposable income will both increase the demand for housing. The exact extent of these effects is not known but on the basis of estimates that have been made for Canada and elsewhere,[14] it seems reasonable to assume that growth in real income (growth in incomes minus growth in prices) is reflected to the extent of about thirty per cent in increased housing demand. New family formation, on the other hand, can reasonably be assumed to have a "one for one" effect on the demand for new housing units.[15] In other words, a two per cent increase in the number of families would increase the demand for housing units by about two per cent. Similarly, an increase in real family income of two per cent would increase the demand for housing units by about 0.6 of one per cent.

The above calculation of the required rent increase also ignores the fact that at any given point in time there are rental units in the process of construction that will eventually come on the market regardless of changes in rents. For example, in the Vancouver area some 3,400 rental units are currently (March 1977) in process. This represents about a 3.8 per cent eventual increase in the total "official" stock of rental accommodation in the city.[16]

If we revise the simple calculation made above to include the effects of population growth (2 per cent increase in demand), income growth (1.5 per cent increase in demand) and construction in progress (3.8 per cent increase in supply), we arrive at an estimate of 6.8 per cent as the relative rent increase. This yields 12.8 per cent as the actual rent increase required to arrive at a vacancy rate of 4 per cent. (Table 1 summarizes these calculations.)

TABLE 1
CALCULATION OF RENT INCREASES
THAT WOULD OCCUR AFTER DECONTROL
(Using Vancouver Illustration)

Total rise in rents assuming no supply response . . . . A
    Equals

Growth in population . . . . B
    Plus

One-third the growth in real disposable family income. C
    Minus

Growth in rental housing stock already in progress . . . . D
    Plus

The difference between the natural vacancy rate and the
actual vacancy rate. . . . . E

All $((B + C) - D + E)$ divided by the rate of demand response   .4
    Plus

The actual rate of general inflation (percentage increase in the CPI) . . . . F
$A = ((B + C) - D + E)/.4 + F$
$12.8\% = ((2\% + 1.5\%) - 3.8\% + 3\%)/.4 + 6\%$

Total rise in rents assuming that supply response accounts for 10 per cent of
the adjustment. . . . . R
    Equals

Ninety per cent of the total rise in rents assuming no supply response
$R = A \times .9$
$11.5\% = 12.8\% \times .9$

1. Rents will rise until the "natural" vacancy rate is attained. The "natural" rate is assumed to be 4 per cent.
2. A 10 per cent rise in rents is assumed to reduce the demand for housing units by about 4 per cent.
3. Population and real disposable income growth are assumed to affect the demand for housing units. A one per cent increase in real income is assumed to generate a .3 per cent increase in the demand for housing units. Growth in population is assumed to affect housing demand on a "one for one" basis.
4. Housing units in process are deducted from the net increase in demand.
5. Increases in supply are assumed to account for 10 per cent of the total adjustment.

125

This calculation and those preceding it have assumed that all of the adjustment would have to be borne by the demand for housing. However, as was pointed out in an earlier section, at least some of the adjustment to higher rents would come from the supply side of the market - even in the short run. If we assume that, say, one-tenth of the total adjustment would be made up by supply response in the short run, our final estimate for Vancouver is that an 11.7 per cent rise in rents would increase the vacancy rate to about 4 per cent by early in 1978. At that vacancy rate there would be no tendency for rents to rise further - other things being the same. In view of the fact that this estimate is based on a variety of assumptions, Table 2 presents a range of estimates based on different assumptions.

TABLE 2
RENT INCREASES
UNDER DIFFERENT ASSUMPTIONS

	Text Assumptions %	Alternate 1 %	Alternate 2 %	Alternate 3 %	Alternate 4 %
Population growth	2.0	2.0	2.0	2.0	4.0
Real income growth	4.5	7.0	4.5	3.0	4.5
Housing growth	3.8	2.8	3.8	3.8	3.8
Vacancy gap	3.0	3.0	3.0	3.0	3.0
Demand response	0.4	0.4	0.2	0.4	0.4
Relative rent increase	6.8	10.8	13.5	5.5	11.8
Total actual rent increase (assuming 6% general inflation)	12.8	16.8	19.5	11.5	17.8
Total actual rent increase allowing for short-run supply response	11.5	15.1	17.6	10.4	16.0

A note of caution is appropriate in the use of this formula. The starting point for the estimation is the actual vacancy rate at the point in time when the estimate is made. If rent controls have been in force for an extended period of time, the measured vacancy rate may underestimate the true extent of consumer demand that has been stimulated by the "bargain" rents under the rent control regime. The vacancy rate cannot be zero — however, the extent of demand may be such that it would more than fill all of the existing housing units, implying a "negative" vacancy rate. In some areas, the vacancy rate may well be "negative" and if that is the case, the relative rent increase would have to be larger to offset this "queueing" or pent-up demand.

The consequence of decontrol

As the foregoing discussion makes clear, the prospects for decontrol in each area of Canada will differ according to the situation. The principal variables that will determine the rate of rent increase in each area are: the vacancy rate gap, the rate of population growth, the rate of growth in real family income and the rate of growth in the housing stock implied by projects currently underway. All of these variables can be roughly estimated for each area and the degree of uncertainty attaching to the consequences of decontrol thereby substantially reduced.

In the case of Vancouver the most pessimistic estimate suggests that decontrol would produce a rise in rents of about 18 per cent. A more likely outcome is that rents would have to rise by about 13.0 per cent to increase the vacancy rate to the 4 per cent range. These estimates relate to the situation that would obtain during the first year or so after controls were abandoned and may underestimate the short-term consequences. In all probability, rents would tend to rise sharply at the outset and overshoot their eventual rate of increase. Accordingly, the immediate effects of decontrol - assuming that the eventual increase was about 13 per cent - might be an increase in rent in the 16 per cent range.

Unfortunately, there is very little historical evidence against which we can compare our judgment about the current situation in Canada. This is because rent control, once installed, tends to become a permanent feature of the economic landscape and hence experience with decontrol is limited. Also, even in those cases where rents have been decontrolled, the documentation of the process has seldom been thorough. In the following paragraphs we will discuss the limited information available from decontrol experiences in the U.S.[17]

The only experience with decontrol that has been accurately recorded in detail, of which we are aware, was that undertaken in the United States in the last months of 1949. The U.S. Department of Labor conducted surveys in selected cities that were decontrolled to determine rents before and after decontrol. The results of this survey are contained in Table 2.

At the time decontrol came, in the last months of 1949, rent control had been in effect for eight years. During that period a general wage and price freeze was in effect. The general wage and price controls — except for rent — were dropped in 1946 under the pressure of events. (There were strikes in key industries because companies subject to price control could not yield to even the reasonable demands of unions; shortages of various foods such as beef, butter and oranges developed and there was a general proliferation of supply crises and their bedfellows — black markets.) From 1946 to the end of 1949, the general price level in the U.S. rose by 32.4 per cent[18] — a very large increase by the then existing historical standards and by current standards.

Against this backdrop of general inflation, rents in aggregate rose by only 14.5 per cent over the 1946-1949 period[19] and in the year of widespread decontrol, rents rose by only 3.5 per cent. In fact, it was not until 1954 that rents rose sufficiently to regain their pre-war relationship with other prices.

The data in Table 3 indicate that only in three cases did the rent increase after decontrol exceed 15 per cent. (Dallas, Beverly Hills and Knoxville). The average percentage increase in rents amounted to only 11.6 per cent.

It is difficult to know what to infer for Canadian circumstances from this evidence. What the exact condition of the housing market was in each of the U.S. cities at the time of decontrol is not known. The attitudes of tenants and landlords in those circumstances may have been very different than the attitudes of Canadians in the current circumstances. In short, there are many reasons to believe that we cannot simply transfer those results from the U.S. in 1949 to Canada in 1977.

Nevertheless, this historical evidence leads us to be very optimistic about the situation in Canada. Certainly, our estimates of relative rent increases (the increase in rents relative to the increase in consumer prices) are much larger than any of those experienced in the U.S. cities.

TABLE 3
Increases in Rents Free to Rise after
Termination of Federal Rent Control in Cities

ALL RENT RANGES

(EXCLUDES UNITS HAVING CONTINUOUS LEASES AND UNITS INDIVIDUALLY DECONTROLLED BEFORE AREA-WIDE DECONTROL)

City	Percent of All Units Having Increases	Their Average Percentage Increase	Average Percentage Increase In General Rent Level*	Survey	Date of Decontrol 1949
Houston, Texas	31	41.3	10.7	8/15/49-11/15/49	10/19
Beverly Hills, Calif.	74	41.0	26.7	10/15/49- 3/ 1/50	12/ 7
Dallas, Texas	67	35.4	20.5	4/15/49-11/15/49	6/23
Topeka, Kansas	40	30.3	10.5	7/15/49-11/15/49	9/14
Eugene, Oregon	38	30.3	9.4	6/15/49- 2/15/50	8/18
Knoxville, Tennessee	61	26.8	15.8	5/15/49-11/15/49	6/14
Jacksonville, Fla.	56	26.2	12.3	6/15/49-11/15/49	8/ 5
Oklahoma City, Okla.[1]	17	26.2	2.9	9/15/49- 1/15/50	11/23
Omaha, Nebraska	62	21.9	14.2	9/15/49- 1/15/50	11/ 2
Milwaukee, Wisc.[2]	60	20.2	12.2	5/15/49- 2/15/50	8/ 5
Spokane, Washington	46	18.6	8.2	5/15/49-11/15/49	7/25
Witchita, Kansas	35	18.2	6.4	10/15/49- 3/ 1/50	12/29
Salt Lake City, Utah	46	16.2	7.1	6/15/49-11/15/49	8/ 5
Madison, Wisc.	51	12.3	5.9	6/15/49- 2/15/50	8/ 5

[1]General Rent Increase of 20 per cent granted prior to decontrol;
[2]Includes all units — data on rents free to rise not available;
*(Includes rents which did not increase).

Source: "Hearings before the Committee on Banking and Currency, United States Senate," 1950, *Extension of Rent Control,* p. 462. Reprinted in "The Post War Rent Control Controversy," by Willys R. Knight, Director, Bureau of Business and Economic Research, Georgia State College, Research Paper Number 23, September 1962.

Recently, two cities in the U.S. have decontrolled rents - Miami Beach, Florida and Lynd, Massachusetts. Unfortunately, the consequences of decontrol have not been closely-monitored in either case - largely because of the lack of data relating specifically to these housing markets. Owing also to this lack of information it is doubtful whether meaningful analysis about these cases can ever be conducted.

V. THE DECONTROL PROCESS

In the foregoing sections we have identified several critical elements in the rent control-decontrol process. Before launching into a discussion of the proposals for decontrol policies it would be useful to reiterate the main points:

1. In the absence of "hard" information what is believed to be happening in the economy is as important as what is actually happening.

2. Government policy-makers must exercise judgment in their interpretation of economic events and this judgment is influenced by the political objectives of economic policy.

3. There is very little "hard" information available about the state of the housing market and hence government policy towards housing tends to be directed at what is believed to be happening.

4. It is the expressed objective of at least some tenant activists to create a sense of crisis about housing - whether or not this is justified.

5. The critical element in a successful campaign for rent control is the existence of low income tenants - people for whom the provision of basic accommodation is a problem. In effect these people are the evidence offered by the activist.

6. The true costs of rent control are seldom understood or appreciated.

7. If rent control has restrained nominal rent increases, the result of its abandonment will be an increase in rents. The exact extent of the increase is difficult to predict but our estimates suggest that the maximum increase would be in the neighbourhood of 15 per cent.

8. Current official rental housing statistics do not attempt to measure a substantial segment of the market and analysis based on them could be erroneous. In particular, the ability of the supply of, and demand for, housing services to accommodate to changing circumstances is likely to be underestimated.

The suggestions for decontrol that are contained in this section reflect these points.

Is a decontrol 'strategy' necessary?

The immediate question that arises in considering decontrol of rents is *why not simply remove them?* A variety of answers are given to this question. However, most of them are not relevant to the Canadian case since they relate to situations where rent control has been in place for a long period of time.[20] If rent control has been in place for an extended period it will have had an effect on the basic structure of the housing market and in this case some sort of elaborate decontrol scheme that may be appropriate. (If there is an optimal decontrol strategy, it is one that is enacted quickly enough to avoid the distortions created by long-term control of rents!)

Most arguments against immediate decontrol are similar to those used to justify controls in the first place and have the low income tenant as their centerpiece. It is argued, for example, that overnight decontrol would impose tremendous hardships on those with low incomes. The rise in rents would force these people either to move to truly desperate living quarters or to drastically reduce their spending on other necessities.

In the first place, the number of people for whom this could potentially be true is usually exaggerated.[21] Secondly, the fact that market adjustment causes hardship for some is not an argument for intervention in a particular market. It may be an argument for an income supplement of some form or for an expansion of existing supplements. It is clear that if hardship for low income groups does occur, it is a result of an inadequate income supplementation scheme and should be treated as such. As is discussed later in this section, a sound income supplement scheme is essential to the decontrol process.

If, as is sometimes the case, the "hardship" referred to is the fact that all tenants will, upon decontrol, have to pay a market rent for accommodation, it is very difficult to be sympathetic to this view. The burden of adjustment back to a market rent will fall on roughly the same group of people who enjoyed the "benefits" that accrued from control. The only way tenants as a group can avoid the burden is by reducing the amount of housing that they occupy. This is precisely what is required in a situation of excess demand. Unless the market is allowed to adjust, new entrants to the housing market (of all incomes) are forced to have less housing than they would like (or where new construction is not controlled, pay more for it) because of the preferred position of sitting tenants.

Schemes for gradual decontrol may have the effect of spreading over time the incidence of the burden of adjustment back to the market. To this extent, they may be seen as desirable. However, to the extent that they ease the burden for consumers, they increase the burden for landlords (and prospective landlords). Accordingly, protracted decontrol schemes may have an effect on the supply of housing that more than offsets the seeming short-term advantages for consumers.

There is a potentially unlimited scope for devising gradual decontrol schemes and it would be impossible to discuss all varieties of them here. However, one scheme that is frequently suggested deserves special attention — *namely the vacancy rate decontrol scheme.*

Vacancy decontrol

Vacancy decontrol schemes have been suggested in North America for as long as there have been rent controls. In particular, vacancy decontrol was widely–applied in the U.S. after the Second World War. The key element in this sort of scheme is the provision that rent control be abandoned after the vacancy rate exceeds some arbitrary level. In the case of post-war decontrol in the U.S., 5 per cent was the magic figure. Any area that had attained a vacancy rate equal to, or greater than, this level was automatically exempted from the rent control provisions.

Even if the vacancy rate information available is accurate (and I have argued above that it could be totally inaccurate - especially in a tight market) a vacancy decontrol scheme is at best an incorrect policy and at worst a disastrous one. The reason for this is that if the vacancy rate selected is the "correct one" then it may never be reached and rent controls would become a permanent feature of the system.

Vacancy rates are a measure of the difference between the supply of, and demand for, apartments. When supply and demand are in balance the vacancy rate will not be zero but some positive figure, 4 per cent, say. Now, if the plan is to decontrol when the vacancy rate is 4 per cent and the "equilibrium" or market balancing vacancy rate happens to be 4 per cent then, even in principle, the policy can be successful only by chance.

If the rent control legislation is keeping rents from rising as quickly as they would rise in a free market then the vacancy rate will be lower than the free market level. (Demand is encouraged by the "bargain" rents to be higher than the free market level while supply is lower.) As long as rents are successfully restrained below the market level, the vacancy rate will never rise to 4 per cent. Accordingly, the vacancy decontrol policy will never produce decontrol if the legislation happens fortuitously to select the true (but unknown) free market vacancy rate as the criterion for decontrol.

If the vacancy rate selected is above the market rate then the only way that it can be reached is for rents to rise more quickly than they would in the market. Again, if the rent control is effective, this situation can never arise.

The only vacancy rate that can be achieved under a rent control regime is the one consistent with the rate of increase in rents selected as the control ceiling. Once the ceiling rate of increase in rents has been selected, given the supply-demand conditions, the vacancy rate is more or less determined. Of course, this assumes that all of the other factors influencing the market are maintaining their usual relationship with each other and with rents. If there happened to be a large change in some important factor, say a decrease in population or income in a particular region, then the vacancy rate consistent with any given rate of increase in rents would also change. (In the case of decreased incomes or population, the vacancy rate would rise as the demand for housing at every rent level fell.)

Put in another way, it is simply not possible by controlling the price of a service to control the amount that will be demanded and supplied. Once the price has been set, the quantity demanded and supplied will find their own level and this level may or may not be the desired level. (Unless, of course, people's right to decide how much to demand or supply is removed as in the case of rationing.) The attempt to achieve a certain minimum vacancy rate while at the same time imposing a rent ceiling can only be successful if other factors influencing the market happen fortuitously to move in the right direction. It would appear that this policy of housing market roulette is not a very promising route to follow.

A rent decontrol programme

The most important element in a decontrol programme is the adoption of an income supplementation system that ensures access to basic accommodation for all.[22] The detailed structure of such a housing allowance system has recently been studied by the Fraser Institute[23] for the particular case of British Columbia. (A modified version of the scheme has recently been adopted by the B.C. government. At this point, only the elderly are covered by the provisions of the scheme.) It was found that a housing allowance could be provided to all residents of the province (tenants and homeowners) in need at less than half the cost of the current array of housing programmes which could be abandoned. The basic features of this system are universal coverage, unrestricted cash grants, and benefit levels tied to the cost of basic accommodation, family size and family income.

As an element in the decontrol process, this programme would ensure that low income tenants are not unduly disadvantaged by the adjustment back to market rents. If the activist is to be deflected, not only must this coverage exist, it must be seen to exist. Accordingly, the adoption of the housing allowance system should be made widely known. The provisions of the programme should be widely advertised and the programme should be constantly monitored to ensure that eligible people are taking advantage of it.

In practise, the housing allowance system should probably be handled in the same way that property tax rebates are currently handled. Tenant property tax rebates are currently handled via the income tax system in some provinces. If the housing allowance system were operated in this way no additional bureaucratic costs would be involved.

Once the housing allowance system is in place, the rent control ceilings (and a variety of other housing programmes) should be abandoned. The decontrol process should be designed to instill confidence in prospective landlords that future controls are not planned. In order successfully to accomplish this objective decontrol should be abrupt and without qualification.

In order to rectify the information problem discussed in the first section, some of the civil servants currently employed in rent control enforcement should be re-employed in monitoring the rental housing stock. Accurate count should be made of all housing units — particularly in the large urban areas — and a quarterly assessment of the vacancy rate should be made. In addition, rents payable for a wide range of accommodation in each area should be determined and published on a regular basis.

As an interim measure, say for the first year, landlords should be required to file notice of a rent increase - the dollar and percentage amount - and public record of the increases should be maintained.

One of the most serious deficiencies in current information about the housing market relates to consumer expenditure patterns. The most recent information currently available from Statistics Canada on how much of their income tenants spend on shelter is for the year 1974. Accordingly, an assessment of the "hardship" associated with decontrol is simply not possible. Therefore, as part of the decontrol programme, each province should use part of the resources currently employed in control enforcement to conduct regular surveys of consumer spending patterns. The results of these surveys could serve to better inform the public and the policy-makers as to the actual state of affairs.

The public information aspects of these proposals might seem to be trite and irrelevant. However, as has been indicated at the outset, we are currently in a situation where claims about the existence of a housing crisis go essentially unchallenged while public policies are devised and revised to deal with what is said to be happening in the housing market.

The political consequences of decontrol

In the introductory section, I discussed some of the political aspects of rent control. In this section I want to provide some commentary on the political aspects of decontrol. My interest in doing so stems from the fact that rent control is one of the world's most celebrated "political footballs." Parties out of power promise it while incumbents adopt it in self-defence.

Because elected officials have little to gain in the short run from decontrol, decontrol has not often been pursued. (In the long term, the effects of controls become evident to all and it is then in the interest of public officials to decontrol. However, except in rare circumstance, like the case of Sweden, extended controls so distort the market that decontrol becomes extremely difficult to manage.) Accordingly, there is almost no evidence on the political consequences of decontrol and to a very considerable extent the political fear of decontrol is based on pure speculation as to the result. By way of assuaging these fears and better informing political judgment I want to consider a rather famous case of decontrol — that of Los Angeles in the aftermath of the Second World War.

In July, 1950 the City Council of Los Angeles adopted a motion that said, in effect, that there was no housing shortage and that rent control should be abandoned. Under normal circumstances, that would have been that. However, a Mr. Tighe Woods, the Federal Government's Housing Expediter who was charged with overseeing an orderly transition back to the free market, had the notion very firmly fixed in his mind that no city should be decontrolled unless a vacancy rate of at least 5 per cent prevailed. Accordingly, Mr. Woods obtained an injunction to halt decontrol.

In the months that followed there was much debate about decontrol and the actual condition of the housing market. The City Council steadfastly persisted in its position that decontrol would be desirable. Finally on December 20, 1950 controls were abandoned. In the months following decontrol, rents rose by 21 per cent, on average.

In spite of the notoriety that the Housing Expediter had given the attempt to decontrol and the subsequent "stiff" increase in rents, there was no political backlash. In aldermanic elections held several months after decontrol, nine of the ten aldermen who had voted for the decontrol motion were re-elected.[24]

It would appear, on the basis of this evidence, that the political ramifications of decontrol are highly over-rated and less deserving of concern than is often supposed.

Notes

[1]For an analysis of Canadian Housing Policy in the 1970's, see L.B. Smith, *Anatomy of a Crisis - Canadian Housing Policy in the Seventies*, The Fraser Institute, 1977.

[2]Emily Achtenburg, *Less Rent More Control*, Urban Planning Aid Inc., Cambridge, Mass. 1973, pages 2, 29, 27. Ms. Achtenburg is better known in Canada in her role as project leader on rent control in the 1975 study undertaken by the Government of British Columbia. One of the objectives of that study was to assess the impact of rent control and advise as to its place in government housing policy. This study is discussed by Raymond Heung in *The Do's and Don'ts of Housing Policy*, The Fraser Institute, December 1976.

[3]F.A. Hayek, et al., *Rent Control - A Popular Paradox*, The Fraser Institute, 1975, and R. Heung, *The Do's and Don'ts of Housing Policy*, The Fraser Institute, 1976.

[4]This seemingly counter-intuitive result is explained by the fact that the relationship between tenant and landlord is a critical part of the rental agreement. Stability of tenancy has value to a landlord and out-of-line increases jeopardize this stability - increases sanctioned by government and universally applied do not affect the landlord-tenant relationship. In addition, some landlords - life insurance companies, for example - produce a joint product and are reluctant to jeopardize their "image" in the rental market because of the potential spill-over into the other markets in which they sell (i.e., the life insurance market).

[5]See, E.O. Olsen, "Questions and Some Answers About Rent Control, An Empirical Analysis of New York's Experience," in *Rent Control - A Popular Paradox*, F.A. Hayek, et al., The Fraser Institute, 1975.

[6]The capital value is determined by the expected revenue from rents in the future.

[7]Reported in Raymond Heung, *The Do's and Don'ts of Housing Policy*, The Fraser Institute, 1976, page. 75.

[8]See, Roistacher, Elizabeth Anne, "The Distribution of Tenant Benefits Under Rent Control," unpublished doctoral dissertation, University of Pennsylvania, 1972. Possibly in recognition of this effect of rent control the National Association for the Advancement of Colored People (NAACP), as early as 1974, was opposing the institution of rent control in California.

[9]Source: Letter from Charles R. Laverty, Jr., Assessor, City of Cambridge, Massachusetts, to the Honorable Donald R. Gaudetter, House Chairman, Joint Legislative Committee on Local Affairs.

[10]Olsen, Edgar O., "An Econometric Analysis of Rent Control," *Journal of Political Economy*, Vol. 80, Nov./Dec. 1972, pp. 1081-1100. Summarized in E.O. Olsen, "Questions and Some Answers About Rent Control," in *Rent Control - A Popular Paradox*, F.A. Hayek, et al., The Fraser Institute, 1975.

[11]A sample survey of residential housing in Vancouver indicated that 8.3 per cent of the residences contained suites about which there existed no official record. In view of the fact that these suites are illegal and since the enumerators had no power to coerce respondents to provide information, it is likely that the 8.3 per cent estimate is conservative. (Divulging the information could have led to prosecution under the planning by-law.) In addition, there were 1,660 "illegal" suites officially

known to exist. That is, 1,660 or 2.6 per cent of those houses classed as single family dwellings were known to have more than one suite. In total, therefore, a minimum of 11 per cent of the total single family residential housing stock was, at the time of the survey, housing two or more households. *Housing Conversion*, P. Johnston and D. Hayes, City of Vancouver Planning Department, 1975, p. 8.

[12]L.B. Smith, "A Note on the Price Adjustment Mechanism for Rental Housing," *American Economic Review*, June 1974, Vol. LXIV, pp. 478-81.

[13]L.B. Smith, *Postwar Canadian Housing and Residential Mortgage Markets*, University of Toronto Press, 1974, p. 30.

[14]See L.B. Smith, *ibid.*, p. 30.

[15]To some extent this assumption represents a summary of a variety of influences. The total demand from demographic sources arises from net household formation where household formation includes family and non-family households. Accordingly, it is often the case that zero population growth yields significant housing demand because of undoubling and young people leaving home to establish a separate household. Rather than launch into a discussion of household formation, I have simply assumed that the population growth number includes an allowance for this. In the range of estimates calculated below and reported in Table 2 I have used a high and low estimate of population growth.

[16]The estimate of supply expansion ignores the potential effects that movements from the rental market encouraged by the Assisted Home Ownership Programme will have on the supply situation. Research currently being conducted by Central Mortgage and Housing Corporation in Vancouver indicates that many of the people moving into AHOP housing are, in fact, leaving the Vancouver rental housing market. This means that, other things being equal, the net supply of available rental units will be larger than is implied in our calculations and the rent increases necessary to eliminate the vacancy gap will be smaller.

[17]The following account of post-war decontrol in the U.S. is taken from M. Walker, "Decontrol" in *Rent Control - A Popular Paradox*, The Fraser Institute, 1975, p. 191.

[18]U.S. Department of Labor, Bureau of Labor Statistics, *Monthly Labor Review*, various years.

[19]Some increases had been allowed by the "Housing Expediter" who was responsible for the administration of rent control.

[20]For a discussion of some of the objections see *Rent Control - A Popular Paradox*, F.A. Hayek et al., The Fraser Institute, 1975.

[21]See M. Walker, "What are the Facts?", in *Rent Control - A Popular Paradox*, The Fraser Institute, 1975.

[22]See, for example, F.A. Hayek et al., *Rent Control - A Popular Paradox*, The Fraser Institute, 1975.

[23]Raymond Heung, *The Do's and Don'ts of Housing Policy: The Case of British Columbia*, The Fraser Institute, 1976, p. 119.

[24]Of course, to some extent the 21 per cent increase in rents was a relatively modest increase — given the fact that consumer prices had risen some 46 per cent. Accordingly, it could be claimed that the example of Los Angeles is not a particularly relevant one for the current Canadian situation where relative rent increases are likely to be larger.

Post-Controls
and
The Public Sector

THOMAS J. COURCHENE

Professor of Economics
University of Western Ontario

THE AUTHOR

Thomas J. Courchene is Professor of Economics at the Universtiy of Western Ontario. Born in Saskatchewan in 1940, he was educated at the University of Saskatchewan and received his Ph.D. from Princeton University in 1967. He has also been Professor in Residence at the Graduate Institute of International Studies in Geneva, and has done postgraduate study at the University of Chicago. Professor Courchene has been a member of the editorial boards of the *Journal of Money, Credit and Banking* and the *Canadian Journal of Economics*. He has been a member of the Executive Committee of the Canadian Economics Association, and is a member of the Editorial Advisory Board of the Fraser Institute.

Professor Courchene is author of many books, articles and reviews, including: "Stabilization Policy: A Monetarist Interpretation," in *Issues in Canadian Economics*, edited by L.H. Officer and L.B. Smith, and published by McGraw-Hill Ryerson in 1974; "The Monetary Approach to the Balance of Payments: An Empirical Investigation," in *Inflation in the World Economy*, edited by M. Parkin and G. Zis, published by the University of Toronto Press in 1976; "The Migration-Unemployment Nexus or Why B.C. has a High Unemployment Rate," and "The Canadian Balance of Payments under Fixed and Flexible Exchange Rates: A Monetarist Interpretation," both in *Policy Formation in an Open Economy*, edited by R.A. Mundell and B.E. van Snellenberg, and published by the University of Waterloo in 1975. He has also written several studies for the C.D. Howe Research Institute, including: *Money, Inflation and the Bank of Canada: An Analysis of Canadian Monetary Policy from 1970 to early 1975* (1976) and *Monetarism and Controls: The Inflation Fighters* (1976).

Post-Controls
and
The Public Sector

THOMAS J. COURCHENE *

Professor of Economics
University of Western Ontario

I. INTRODUCTION

The road to controls was paved with monetary excess.
About this there surely can be little doubt. Even the Bank of
Canada now readily admits that monetary policy was far too
expansionary for the three-year period following the floating
of the dollar (June, 1970). Elsewhere, I have argued that unduly expansionary monetary policy lasted well beyond
mid-1973[1]. Canada's double-digit inflation was the direct
legacy of this inappropriate monetary policy and the imposition of wage and price controls was Ottawa's response to the
inflation. This is not to say that Canada would necessarily
have had smooth sailing over this period had monetary
policy been more restrictive: these were and are turbulent
times for the world's economies. The large and rapid increases in primary product prices, particularly in energy and

*I wish to thank my colleagues David Laidler, Michael Parkin, Grant Reuber, Lars
Osberg and Ed Saraydar and also Professor Morley Gunderson of the University of
Toronto for valuable comments in earlier drafts of this paper. Responsibility for the
views expressed rests entirely with me.

143

food, would still have generated substantial relative price changes within Canada and attempts by economic agents to isolate themselves from falling real incomes deriving from these price changes would have put substantial pressures on wages and prices across the board. But with a tight rein on the monetary levers these relative price changes would not have been transformed into "general" price increases, i.e., into inflation.

Monetary policy

Just as rapid acceleration of rates of money growth led to the current inflation, the key to unwinding inflation lies with a corresponding deceleration of monetary growth rates. With its recent policy shift toward a more monetarist approach to the design and implementation of monetary policy, the Bank of Canada is in full agreement with this:

> "Whatever else may need to be done to bring inflation under control, it is absolutely essential to keep the rate of monetary expansion within reasonable limits. Any programme that did not include this policy would be doomed to failure."[2]

The Bank's method of implementing its new policy has been to set progressively lower target ranges for the rate of M_1 † growth.[3]

The public sector

Having thus acknowledged the critical role played by monetary policy in the recent inflation, it is now possible to address the central issue of this paper, namely the appropriate role for the public sector in the post-controls period. The rationale for focusing attention on, and outlining a series of recommendations relating to, the public sector after the AIB regulations are lifted, must be that a continuation of the status quo with respect to governments will result in a rekindling of the inflationary fires and the threat of a return to controls. In turn, this presumes that the public sector played

---

†Editor's Note: M_1 is the symbol used to denote the most liquid form of money held by the general public. It consists of currency and demand deposits.

a significant role in generating the current inflation and the system of controls. To establish this presumption empirically requires documentary evidence of a type which I do not believe has as yet been produced. Nonetheless, I think that it is possible to isolate several areas where it is likely that the public sector did play a role in heightening both inflationary expectations and the actual pace of wage and price increases.

Viewed from the monetarist perspective, this means either:

a. public sector behaviour was responsible directly or indirectly for some of the excess rate of monetary expansion; or

b. for any given rate of monetary expansion, the role of the public sector was such that more of the resulting nominal income increases were in the form of price increases and less in the form of output increases.

Included under the latter category would be activities that have led to a shortfall in real investment and productivity or have generated unrealistic expectations with respect to rewards for factors of production and in particular with respect to wage rates.

In what follows I identify four such areas: mushrooming government deficits; the rate of public sector growth; the "indexing" syndrome; and the collective bargaining process in the public sector. There is some admitted arbitrariness in the isolation of these areas: others may have opted for an alternative slate. Each of these aspects of public sector activity is dealt with in turn, with the analysis focusing first on the manner in which these areas may have influenced the inflationary process. Concluding the discussion of each area is one or more recommendations or alternatives for the post-controls period. This procedure is modified for the section on public sector wage behaviour where it seemed appropriate, prior to proposing alternatives, to compare and contrast the collective bargaining process in the public and private sectors.

II. GOVERNMENT DEFICITS

A. Deficits and inflation

The cash deficits of all levels of government have mushroomed over the last few years. Specifically, the total amount of "new money borrowed by governments through the issue of securities (other than to the Canada and Quebec Pension Plans) rose from a little below $2 billion in 1973, to $7 billion in 1974 and to over $10 billion in 1975 ".[4] Of this $10 billion for 1975, approximately one-half is attributable to the federal government. And over the 1970-75 period Ottawa's accumulated cash deficit amounted to nearly 12 billion dollars. Since the Bank of Canada acts as Ottawa's fiscal agent and, in principle at least, the federal government has access to Bank financing, i.e., to printing money, Ottawa's deficit carries with it the most inflation potential.

There need, of course, be no necessary relationship between Ottawa's financial requirements and the rate of monetary growth. But in the circumstances of the post-float years, it is not difficult to make the case that the presence of these large federal cash deficits did in fact put pressure on the Bank in the direction of printing money, or monetizing the debt. In large measure, this was the Bank's own doing, adhering as it was to an outmoded policy of attempting to monitor *independently* both the cost and availability of credit. As Canada's recent monetary history indicates, the net result was that the Bank settled on too low an interest rate over most of the post-float period,[5] so that not only could no new federal marketable debt be placed, but at the same time the public was ridding itself of substantial amounts of Ottawa's existing marketable debt. In the final analysis these federal deficits were financed by a combination of printing money and the floating CSB's, both highly liquid forms of debt financing. In other words, with unacceptably low interest rates and mounting deficits the Bank had little room to manoeuvre except to print money to finance the bill. It is in this sense that Ottawa's post-float deficits served to ratchet upward Canada's inflation rate.

Purists may well argue that this does not constitute evidence of the inflationary impact of deficit financing but rather it is more an indictment of Bank of Canada policy. On the other hand, it is legitimate to argue that the government is ultimately responsible for Bank policy. Not much mileage is likely to be had from joining this debate. My position is a rather pragmatic one: had Ottawa's cash deficits over this period been lower, so too would the rate of monetary expansion. Viewed in this light, federal deficits did contribute directly to the inflationary process.

B. Recommendations for the post-controls period

The Bank's conversion to a more monetarist approach to policy, especially the targeting of M_1 growth within rather narrow (and declining over time) bands, will go a long way to ensure that Ottawa's cash deficit will not impact directly on money supply growth to the extent that has been the case in the past. Indeed, it is reasonable to expect that the Bank will endeavour to pursue its monetary policy targets independent of the deficit levels. Nonetheless, these deficits are still proceeding at or near their record-1975 levels. Recent estimates suggest that Ottawa's cash deficit for 1976 will remain in the $5 billion neighbourhood. Provincial deficits are also likely to remain high, with Quebec's burgeoning deficit offsetting any reductions elsewhere.

Therefore the Canadian economy is still faced with the difficult problem of providing governments with levels of saving that are substantially above the levels required only a few years ago. To the extent that the Bank does prevent these deficits from being monetized, the burden is then passed on to either the foreign or domestic sectors. If governments, especially provincial governments, once again go off-shore for their funds, Canada is in the running for large capital inflows which will serve to keep the Canadian dollar above its competitive level. If these deficits are financed internally, then domestic interest rates are bound to rise substantially as Canadians attempt to digest these massive government debt issues.[6] In its *Annual Report* for 1975 the Bank of Canada faced this issue head on:

"Once private spending and credit demands begin to expand again as economic recovery proceeds, there is both less need and less room for government borrowing. If such borrowing nevertheless remains at a high level it may become increasingly difficult to accommodate credit demands in total, private as well as public, within a framework of reasonable monetary expansion without substantial upward pressure on interest rates. Depending on the level of external interest rates, there may be a substantial diversion of government and other borrowing to foreign markets resulting in upward pressure on the exchange rate as well, even with a very large balance of payments deficit on current account. Such a sequence of events could at some point prejudice a healthy expansion of the Canadian economy. The Bank of Canada can reasonably be expected to see to it that inappropriately high interest rates do not arise from an unduly low rate of monetary expansion. However, the Bank should not be expected to attempt to deal with these matters by allowing the money supply to expand at an excessive rate since that would only shift the problem back to domestic inflation of prices and costs. *Problems of this kind will be much easier to avoid if governments manage to reduce the size of their borrowing requirements as the private sector of the economy recovers.*"[7]

Those who defend the present fiscal stance are quick to point out that government deficit increases over the recent past represent the operations of "automatic stabilizers" and that in the absence of the deficits the recession would have been much more severe. There is, of course, some truth to the assertion. But one can legitimately question whether or not full indexation (to the CPI) of unemployment insurance benefits, for example, was appropriate when even without indexation the Canadian programme was the most generous in the Western world. More to the point, however, given the pace of wage settlements in the public sector over the past few years (and realizing that it is one of the most labour intensive sectors of the economy), it is difficult to lay the blame for record deficits entirely or even largely on the operation of built-in stabilizers. I wholly support the Bank's position that there is really no viable alternative to reducing the overall level of government deficits.

III. THE GROWTH OF THE PUBLIC SECTOR

A. Public sector growth and inflation

There is a growing consensus in many quarters that the rate of overall public sector growth, independent of the position of the deficit, has had a substantial impact on the rate of inflation. William Mackness has put the point rather concisely in a recent paper:

> "Governments in Canada have effected a massive appropriation of national income over the last decade. Government spending has risen from 30 per cent to fully 42 per cent of GNP over the 1965-1975 decade. Even the most naive observer should be reluctant to dismiss this unprecedented reallocation of resources (in peacetime) as a neutral economic event.
>
> Taxpayers, not surprisingly, have attempted to avoid the large and persistent increase in average tax take required to effect such a large transfer of resources from the private to the public sector — higher wages, higher prices and around again. Some individuals and some firms were successful in paying less than a full levy, but equally others paid that much more. In the final analysis, the government share of national income was up to 42 per cent and the private sector share correspondingly reduced. The process has been highly inflationary."[8]

The inflationary potential of this process is threefold. *First of all*, straightforward Keynesian balanced-budget multiplier analysis suggests that a rise in the government sector of this magnitude (provided that private expenditure is not displaced) represents a significant stimulus to aggregate demand and, therefore, to prices, other things being held constant. Actually, the principal influence is likely to be an increase in the price level and not a permanent effect on increasing the rate of change of prices. Nonetheless, this will have a significant impact on the inflation rate, as it is conventionally calculated — i.e., the change in the price level (of a given basket of goods and services) over some time period. *Secondly*, an increase in taxes from 30 per cent of GNP to approximately 40 per cent over the past decade† has the potential of bringing with it growing disincentives with respect to work and enterprise so that the net result may well be a decrease in capital equipment put in place and, therefore, a decrease from trend in both potential growth of output and productivity.[9] This effect might have been offset to a substantial degree had governments utilized the revenue increases for investment purposes. But much of the increased revenues were used to finance Canada's very extensive transfer system. The net impact of this is that the potential for capital investment that these large increases in savings represent has, to a substantial degree, been dissipated in the form of current consumption. Hence, for any given monetary policy setting, the implied nominal income increase will be reflected more in terms of price increases and less in terms of real output gains.

Finally, and this relates more to the point Mackness is making in the above quote, the scramble by individuals to regain their pre-tax levels of real income will likely be translated into demands for higher nominal wages. In turn this implies that individuals do not, for whatever reason, value the government-supplied service as equivalent to their loss of purchasing power resulting from the tax increase.[10] Once again, it is relevant to emphasize that while this process has inflation potential, it is not inflationary *per se*. But in the milieu of the early 1970's where the Bank of Canada was rubber-stamping virtually any and all wage increases by pursuing a most accommodating policy with respect to the money supply, it facilitated the acceptance of these wage demands and the passing of them on in the form of higher prices.†† In the process probably not too much income re-

†Editor's Note: For a documentation of the rising burden of taxation in Canada see *"How Much Tax Do YOU Really Pay?"* Fraser Institute, 1976.

†† Editor's Note: In terms of the market power theory of inflation discussed by Professors Lipsey, Grubel and Dean in this volume, monetary expansion at an excessive rate removed the constraint of market discipline. For a simplified discussion of the point see M. Walker, 'Inflation Dialogue," in M. Walker Ed., *The Illusion of Wage and Price Control*, Fraser Institute, 1976, p. 220.

distribution was effected, but the accompanying monetary ease did serve to accelerate the wage and price inflation.

B. Public sector growth and post-controls

With its rather complex system of controls, it is rather incredible that the AIB has no mandate to recommend upon, let alone regulate, public sector growth. Hence, I suspect that it is not very realistic to argue that in post-controls the public sector should be required to grow at rates not in excess of, say, the growth rate of real GNP. Ultimately, this is the sort of issue that, in part at least, is decided at the polls. Nonetheless, I believe that the presence of wage and price controls has had some, perhaps considerable, impact on the way in which Canadians view the role of the public sector. While government expenditure growth has exceeded, by a considerable margin, the wage guidelines it is undoubtedly the case that public opinion has been brought to bear on unbridled government expansion. The proposed reorganization of the welfare system, which carried with it the potential for a substantial enlargement of the government's role in the economy, appears to have been a victim, at least temporarily, of this increased public concern. Likewise, governments at all levels are likely to think twice before embarking on a major expenditure programme.

Indirectly, therefore, wage and price controls have served to focus attention on the growth of the government sector even to the point where there appears to be a growing realization of the continuing inflation potential of maintaining the recent growth rate of the public sector. Included in this realization also appears to be a challenge to the implicit assumption that, in my opinion, has held sway in recent years, namely, that governments are inherently superior in providing a large range of services than is the private sector. For the first time in a long while there is a serious discussion of the possibility of returning to the private sector various activities that are currently in the public domain.

Hence the time is probably ripe for considering some significant alternatives or reforms for the public sector — reforms which will contribute to a marked deceleration of public sector growth. At the specific programme level, proposals for restructuring government activity abound. However, the proposals that follow are not meant to be specific to particular areas of government activity but rather are fairly general and, furthermore, *take as given* the current allocation of activities between the public and private sectors. Some readers may prefer to view the proposals as being directed toward increasing efficiency in the government sector. To a substantial degree they are, but to the extent that they will also serve to put a damper on government sector growth, they have a part to play in Canada's attack on inflation in the post-controls period.

1. Synchronization of expenditure and revenue-raising responsibilities

High on the action list should be an intensification of effort to ensure that those governments which have the responsibility for spending decisions are also the ones responsible for generating the revenues required to finance these expenditures. Probably the worst offender in this general area is the existence of the open-ended federal-provincial cost-sharing programmes for health, welfare and higher education. In these three areas, the provinces are spending 50-cent dollars since Ottawa essentially matches provincial expenditures, dollar-for-dollar. This is hardly conducive to allocative efficiency at the provincial level and probably goes some way towards explaining why expenditures on health, for example, have been growing at such fantastic rates.[11] As a result of the recent federal-provincial negotiations much of this has now changed and, it would appear, for the better. The cost-sharing arrangements for health and education have been terminated and will be replaced by a combination of taxpoint transfers (primarily on personal income taxes) and per-capita grants to the provinces. Over the longer run this structural reform should prove important to the provinces' abilities to establish more effective control over the growth of these areas. There will clearly be more incentive to monitor expenditure growth since any over-expenditure will now have to be financed 100 per cent from provincial coffers.

Somewhat the same situation exists with respect to provincial-municipal fiscal relations, as the following excerpt from the Ontario Economic Council's study on education indicates:

> A large proportion of the funds with which they (the local school boards in Ontario) are bargaining are provincial and, as a result, local boards may not have appropriate incentives when reaching salary agreements with teachers: not all of the funds come from municipal property taxes and therefore school board spending is not fully a specific burden on those who have elected the school board. Perhaps school board bargaining behaviour would be rather different if more of the financial burden of the resulting agreement were laid on the municipal or, better still, the school board doorstep ...

> Limiting the rate of increase of public expenditure on education is difficult. Expenditure ceilings are a useful policy device if the ceilings represent real limitations. But if they are to have any effect they cannot be raised in response to school board pressures. If the provincial ceilings are maintained, and if unduly large demands for salary increases are met by school boards, an intensified squeeze is put on maintenance and supplies expenditures to keep spending under the ceilings. In the longer run this may seriously erode the quality of the system.

> A possible approach to salary negotiations would be for the province to negotiate minimum teacher salary increases with the Ontario Teachers' Federation and give the local boards the opportunity to pay more if they desired. These minimum increases, as well as other school expenditures, would continue to be funded on a

provincial-municipal shared basis as at present but any amount paid above the minimum which was negotiated between the local school board and its teachers would come from municipal tax funds and not from provincial sources. The result would be that the local school authorities would be bargaining in the harsh light of the local taxpayers' interest about the use of local funds. There would be no centrally-imposed limit on the satisfying of local demands but the local residents would have to pay any cost differences.[12]

While this quotation focuses principally on wage increases rather than on overall expenditure growth, the thrust of the message rings true to the theme developed here: in order to get a handle on government expenditure growth it is essential that those economic units responsible for generating expenditure growth are also responsible for finding the revenues required to finance the projects. To fail to adopt this simple and basic principle is essentially to invite severe resource misallocation and in the longer term to contribute to loss of control over the growth of the public sector.

2. Introducing incentives: the government bureaucracy

A second area where structural change is long overdue relates to the lack of incentives for cost minimization in the functioning of government bureaucracies. Bureaucratic inefficiency is undoubtedly not limited to the public sector. Nonetheless the public sector is apt to be more plagued by this sort of inefficiency since almost by definition the products of government bureaus are not sold in the market place and it is therefore all the more difficult to relate the role of any one department to the overall functioning of the system. The basic problem is that there do not exist adequate definitions of just what constitutes *output* in many areas of the public sector. This being the case it is not surprising that there are often no incentives for cost effectiveness — the typical reward for a government department that underspends its budgetary allocation and yet meets its objectives is simply a trimming of next year's allocation. Therefore, success in the bureaucracy is often linked to being able to obtain and spend the largest possible budgetary allotment.

Obviously the lack of appropriate definitions for output is not the only source of inefficiency in bureaucracy, private or public. For example, government departments are often run on the basis of being allotted *real* inputs, i.e., so much physical office space, so many employees at a particular classification level, etc. If between the time of any new budget allocation and the time of expenditures the dollar prices of these items rise, the budget is simply expanded to accommodate the acquisition of these real inputs. Obviously the problem is compounded if the existing as well as the new allocations are always defined in *real terms.*

Solutions to these problems run the gamut from the introduction of market-oriented incentives at various levels of the bureaucracy to more reliance on "cash budgets" (each department is allocated a given dollar amount to spend each year)[13] to "zero-base budgeting" (where each year *all* of a department's or agency's activities come up for review and not merely any new activities).[14] No doubt all of these proposals have obvious and considerable merit. And undoubtedly some variants of each of them, as well as other measures to increase efficiency, are to be found in many areas of government. Yet it is also the case, I would assert, that what has been accomplished to date is considerably less than one might expect. In part, this is due to the fact that not enough attention has heretofore been directed toward defining output in the public sector. The on-going efforts at the federal level aimed at addressing this output issue must surely be applauded.

However, part of the reason also has to do with the fact that policy analysts, or economists at any rate, do not as yet have a fully adequate theory to fall back on when it comes to analyzing governments and their decision-making processes. Introducing market-type incentives into a bureaucratic process only makes sense to the extent that the actors involved have preference orderings that will respond to these incentives. But this begs the important question of just what are the incentives and motivations of the various agents and agencies that comprise government bureaucracies. There has been some recent work on the theory of non-profit organizations and bureaucracies, and economists like Toronto's Albert Breton have made some significant inroads in the direction of devising a theory of government based on self-interest (e.g., politicians will maximize the probability of remaining in power).[15] But much more research is needed.

To my mind, the most insightful recent analytic work (and undoubtedly the most controversial as well) is that by Douglas Hartle.[16] He views the budgetary process as being composed of four teams of players: the politicians, the senior bureaucrats, the media, and the lobbyists or special interest groups. Hartle's analysis is not readily amenable to condensation for present purposes. Essentially, however, he details the sets of rules that appear to apply to each of these four "teams" and focuses on the complex set of interrelationships among and between the various teams and pairs of teams in the bureaucratic game. For example:

> "It is assumed that all players seek to maximize their self-interest as they perceive it, and that behavioural differences among the players in different games are largely attributable to the fact that they are subject to different incentives. This analysis implies, of course, that to change the outcome of the expenditure budgetary process it would be necessary to change one or more of the four sets of rules that, to a large extent, determine what the players seek to achieve and to avoid pursuing their self-interest. While changes in the different incentives that direct the play in each of the four games certainly seem a necessary condition for changing the outcome of expenditure budgeting, they may not be sufficient. Endless bargaining goes on between teams .... The result of this bargaining, and it takes many forms, is partly dependent upon the strategic skills of the players. It also depends in part on what they have to bargain with — what might loosely be called their relative bargaining power. This implies that still another way to modify the outcome of the expenditure budgetary process would be to change the

allocation of bargaining chips held by the players in each of the several games."[17].

Individual voters on the other hand often find it prudent to play a passive role in this process since obtaining information and exercising influence are very costly and the resulting benefits generally do not exceed the expected costs of obtaining them.[18] To this extent, the decision-making process is not responsive to the electorate. Hartle then proceeds to sort out some of the implications of his analysis for things like the rate of growth of expenditures, the implications for changing the relative share of expenditures devoted to existing programmes, the conditions under which the response to particular perceived problems is likely to take the form of a change in expenditures rather than a change in taxes, etc.

One implication of this analysis is that within this complicated game, simple decision rules may not work. For example, "politicians seldom find it expedient to reduce departmental budgets to the point where present employees must be laid off, because of the perceived retaliation of the bureaucracy as a whole."[19] This follows from the fact that many senior bureaucrats have about as much power to reward and punish ministers as ministers have to reward and punish senior officials. Successful senior officials have a complex and extensive network of alliances. They can conjure up or suppress information, they can delay or expedite activity, etc.[20] To some this is likely to appear to be a conspiratorial view of the budgetary process. Yet the purpose of Hartle's work, and the reason why it is important in the present context, is that it does attempt to focus on the process by which the bureaucracy operates and the manner in which expenditure decisions are formulated.

It is only when we have an appreciation of the factors involved in this expenditure process that progress can be made in terms of devising incentives that will be effective in terms of exerting influence over government expenditure. Hartle readily admits that his analysis is still at a preliminary stage. Yet it would appear that it is precisely the direction that future research should take. Unless we understand the complex set of rules driving the government expenditure process it is unlikely that proposals to change these rules in a manner that will alter behaviour of the players in an appropriate direction can be devised. It is in this context that some of the above-listed set of proposals, stemming as they do from an extension of the traditional economic paradigm to the theory of government, may prove to be second-best alternatives when it comes to efficient methods of increasing efficiency in the public sector.

3. Introducing incentives: specific programmes

There is another aspect of this incentive issue that is also contributing significantly to the mushrooming of the public sector, and that is the lack of incentives to economize on the services provided by governments. Health care is probably the best example. It is undoubtedly the case that Canadians overuse medical facilities since the marginal cost of visiting a physician is essentially zero. Indeed, it is rational for the *individual* consumer of health services to act in this manner. While this is frequently recognized as undesirable, the typical solution to this problem involves the imposition of a "deterrent fee" which apart from being regressive in its impact on the citizenry appears as well to be perceived as politically unpalatable. If this is indeed the case, more imaginative, but still effective, schemes must be found.

In its report on health, the Ontario Economic Council[21] advances several alternative approaches to this problem. One intriguing alternative, a variant of one of the OEC's proposals, would be to increase the medical exemption allowable for income tax purposes and allow the taxpayer to benefit from any excess of this exemption over the actual medical expenses he/she generates. The Ontario Economic Council also investigates alternative ways to provide some incentive for physicians and hospitals to curtail the existence of "medically unnecessary procedures, hospital visits, tests and referrals, encouragement of prolonged and more frequent hospitalization, the incentive to use better paid procedures more frequently and the lack of incentive to practise preventative medicine,"[22] all of which are encouraged by the present "fee-for-service" system. It is axiomatic that no progress will be made in reducing the size of the public sector as long as there exist no incentives (indeed, as long as there are *disincentives* may be more appropriate) for those who direct, administer and use the various government-provided services to economize on the production and consumption of these services.

4. The bankruptcy of tradition

Finally some attention deserves to be focused on governments' traditional methods of dealing with certain recurring economic problems. To the extent that a case can be made that government policies did play a role in heightening the current inflation, embarking on the traditional set of responses to recurring economic problems such as unemployment, regional disparities, and the balance of payments is likely to reproduce the same results a few years down the road. Therefore, it seems apparent that governments at all levels should evaluate these traditional responses. This is meant to be a general proposition, but it might be appropriate to relate it to a particular problem in order to make the point more strongly.

Consider, for example, the unemployment issue. With each passing month, Ottawa is under increasing pressure to take some action to cut Canada's currently high unemployment rate. The traditional response to rising unemployment has been to expand governments' role in the economy. Yet increasing the size of the government sector is as likely to be the cause of higher unemployment as the remedy to be used to control it. To a substantial degree, Canada's transfer system† has now built into it significant work-disincentive elements which have made unemployment at the same time a more desirable and less costly (in terms of foregone income) way of life.†† And not surprisingly, Canadians have

†Editor's Note: "Canada's transfer system" is the composite effect of the tax and "expenditure" functions of government where "expenditure" refers to direct cash payments to individuals for which the individual supplies no service. In effect, money is taxed away from — transferred from — some Canadians and given to others. Transfer payments include family allowance, unemployment insurance, social assistance, etc. In a different sense, inter-provincial income equalization payments are also part of the transfer mechanism.

††Editor's Note: This point is the subject of extensive discussion in Professor Grubel's paper in this volume.

tended to consume more of this now-lower-priced and high-er-yielding "good."

What this implies is that it is no longer appropriate to define full employment in terms of an unemployment rate in the 3 per cent to 4 per cent range. A figure near 6 per cent is probably more reasonable. The effect of the Unemployment Insurance Programme on the unemployment rate has been estimated to be somewhere in the neighbourhood of .5 per cent to .7 per cent on the low end[23] to 1.4 per cent on the high end.[24] Combined with the fact that Canada has one of the fastest-growing labour forces in the western world, this means that any attempt to restore rates of unemployment to the 4 per cent level are bound to be highly inflationary. If the 4 per cent range or thereabouts continues to be the ultimate target for government policy, it becomes increasingly important to introduce structural reform which would serve to reduce the degree to which Canadians find spells of unemployment to be a desirable alternative to employment. And most of these rationalizations of our social security system would entail *less*, not more, government spending. This is the major reason why an increasing number of policy analysts are calling for less government spending, coupled with appropriate structural reform, as a response to higher unemployment rates. If the past is any guide, all too frequently increased public sector expenditure on the employment front serves to drive up the natural rate of unemployment. In more general terms, the traditional policy responses are contributing more to the problems than to the solutions.

IV. INDEXATION

A third area where Ottawa may have contributed to the inflationary process relates to the issue of *indexing*. In periods of rising prices, there is a natural tendency for individuals to desire to protect themselves against increases in the cost of living. One seemingly attractive way to accomplish this protection is to build into contracts an automatic adjustment for inflation based on movements in an index of prices, such as the consumer price index (i.e., the CPI). Much of the Canadian economy is now *indexed*: UIC payments have been indexed, old age security and family allowance payments have been indexed; the personal income tax system has, in large measure, been indexed. The recent hikes in the rates of return on outstanding CSB's have effectively converted these issues into an indexed bond. However, the move toward generalized indexing is a mixed blessing when inflation is accompanied by large and permanent changes in relative prices. The large relative price changes that characterized the early post-float period dictated that the real incomes of the bulk of Canadians had to fall. Oil is the most obvious example, but the principle applies to other primary products as well. The four-fold increase in the price of oil simply cannot be effectively indexed. For consumers it represents a once-and-for-all fall in real incomes. Furthermore, Canadians have to accept the fact that rising oil prices must be accompanied by a shift in real income towards the energy sector and away from the rest of the economy so that the required factor reallocations can be effected.

How does all of this relate to the government sector? First of all, it is important to recognize that large real shocks (note that a permanent change in relative prices is a "real" not a "nominal" or "monetary" shock) require correspondingly large adjustments which a market economy may have difficulty in digesting quickly. Employees are going to have unrealistic wage expectations as they attempt to preserve their former standard of living. Some countries have let the shock be accommodated by high rates of monetary growth and in the process have generated high rates of price increase. Others have maintained tight money and have ended up with a much lower rate of inflation on both the price and wage side.† But all industrialized countries have had unusually high unemployment during the adjustment process, as one would expect with a shock of this magnitude. The important point as far as the Canadian situation was concerned was expressed very well by the following quotation from the 1975 *Annual Report* of the Bank of Canada:

> A contributing factor to the divergence between economic events in Canada and in the other main industrial countries was that from late 1972 until well into 1974 the international economic environment developed in a way that was very favourable to us and very unfavourable to them. During that period the demand for foodstuffs and other primary products was very strong and the prices of these commodities rose much more than the prices of manufactured goods. These circumstances added substantially to Canadian incomes and to the air of intense national prosperity that prevailed in Canada. The fact that the increase in income was initially very unevenly distributed served to strengthen greatly the scramble among groups in the country to share in it. The rising expectations of Canadians about the standard of living that they could attain were reinforced, and these expectations were not significantly dampened by the shock of the energy crisis that broke on the world at the end of 1973 because Canadians then regarded themselves as being largely insulated from that event [*quite wrongly, I would emphasize*]. For some time now developments in international markets have been much less favourable to Canada, but the change has been gradual and has not correspondingly altered expectations. The scramble for unreasonably large increases in money incomes has persisted long after the passing of the fortuitous circumstances that at first seemed to provide some justification for it.[25]

---

†Editor's Note: See the paper in this volume by Professors Laidler and Parkin for a discussion of this point.

One must readily grant that Canada could not isolate itself entirely from these effects: "Even in retrospect it is not easy to see how the large but temporary increment to incomes in Canada flowing from the world-wide boom of 1973 could have been prevented from causing economic disturbances of some magnitude."[26] Nonetheless, the Bank of Canada concludes this short discussion with what I consider to be a most appropriate comment, but one that embodies a substantial understatement: "No doubt a better appreciation of the inflationary risks inherent in the situation and more restraint on aggregate demand would have helped."[27]

While the Bank of Canada has to bear responsibility for the monetary ease which it generated in response to these international disturbances, governments were equally irresponsible in failing to appreciate these "inflationary risks." Ottawa's reaction was to index virtually all transfers to persons and to encourage the use of escalator clauses throughout the economy. Furthermore, it indexed transfers to provinces as well. This is perhaps less obvious since Ottawa did move to limit equalization payments resulting from oil increases by amending the formula to include only 1/3 of increased energy royalties above 1973-74 levels for equalization purposes. On the other hand, it also pegged the price of oil well below the world level and this required a substantial subsidy to oil consumers east of the Ottawa Valley — a subsidy that increasingly exceeded the revenues obtained from exporting Western crude to the U.S.A. The appropriate response should have been to move far more quickly to the world oil price. These actions, together with the poor timing of the M.P.'s salary boost, tended to create a situation where government appeared to be sanctioning the inappropriate wage expectations of Canadians. In short, individual Canadians came to believe that one and all had the right to ensure that his/her income kept abreast of the rise in the cost of living irrespective of the march of economic events.

The argument can be put somewhat differently. Indexation in the private sector maintains the real wage for the duration of the wage contract period, after which considerations of profits and productivity as well as inflation will influence the new wage bargain. Therefore, indexation in the private sector affects principally the *timing* rather than the ultimate level of wage rates. Indexation in the public sector could, of course, imply the same. Too often, however, indexation in the public sector is, in my opinion, really an attempt to *freeze* real values and sets up expectations that these real values will continue to be frozen.

Governments may well want to ensure that some sectors of the population are fully sheltered from cost-of-living changes. But even in this situation it is far from clear that "full" indexation to the Consumer Price Index is appropriate. This is so because changes in the CPI measure the increase in the price of a *given* bundle of goods over time. Hence, it overestimates the "true" cost-of-living increase over this time period if consumers *alter* their consumption patterns in response to these rising prices. And surely they do. One obvious implication of this is that considerably more effort should go into the analysis and presentation of the Consumer Price Index than is currently the case.

Consider another relevant example. In the wake of the Parti Quebecois victory, the Canadian dollar fell to 97¢ U.S. This depreciation was long overdue on economic grounds since the pace of wage increases in Canada has outstripped those in the U.S. One recent estimate suggests that average hourly earnings in Canada in 1963 were 73.5% of those in the U.S.A. By July 1975, this percentage had mushroomed to 114.8%.[22] If to this fact is added the further fact that the *average* productivity level in Canada is well below that of the U.S., one can grasp the extent of the "fundamental disequilibrium" that currently besets the Canadian economy. The depreciation of the dollar will lead to an increase in the CPI, since imported goods are now more expensive. Employees can be expected to ask for compensation in response to the CPI increase. Yet the fact remains that Canada's wage levels are currently too high relative to those of our trading partners. Full indexation will only lead to a further devaluation. Governments might do well to recognize this fundamental disequilibrium and not lend support to private sector expectations by indexing fully all government wages and transfers.

The concept of indexation can also be put in a much broader context: indexation can be interpreted as any discretionary effort to offset changes in internal terms of trade or comparative advantages among or across regions. Many of the activities of the Department of Regional Economic Expansion would fall under the umbrella of generalized indexation. Canadians appear to have accepted the fact that a considerable effort toward combatting regional economic disparities is essential to national unity. Yet the same principle applies. Complete indexation is not possible without totally jamming the allocative mechanism. No amount of federal transfers to the Maritime provinces, for example, is going to offset the fact that Alberta's relative economic position within Confederation has been enhanced substantially as a result of the quadrupling of the price of oil since the oil crisis. To attempt to do so with a monetary policy geared toward a reasonable rate of inflation is to invite severe unemployment. To attempt to do so holding unemployment constant is bound to be highly inflationary.

As far as the post-controls period is concerned, the message of this section is rather straightforward. Large and rapid changes in relative prices of many commodities have occurred in the recent past and this situation is likely to continue. These price shifts often usher in corresponding changes in the distribution of political and economic power both within and between nations. Where these disturbances are perceived as longer term in nature, governments should recognize that to attempt to index these changes fully is bound to be at the same time very inflationary and very disruptive of efficient allocation of resources. Social justice may require partial indexation or even full indexation for selected groups of persons, but attempts to do more than this will provide inappropriate expectations for the rest of the country to attempt to imitate.

V. COLLECTIVE BARGAINING IN THE PUBLIC SECTOR

A. Public sector wages and inflation

The final area I have chosen to focus on in terms of the inflationary potential of the public sector is the one that has attracted the most public attention, namely the role of public sector wage settlements in the inflationary process. It would, I think, be difficult to make the case that wage settlements in the public or non-commercial sector played a major role in influencing private sector wages in the early 1970's. However, the situation had altered dramatically by 1974 and especially by 1975. Wage increases in both the private and public sectors averaged approximately 10% in 1973 and 14% in 1974. But in 1975, public sector settlements increased to 18% (with lower-level government employees out-distancing their Ottawa counterparts)[29] while the private sector increases remained at 14%.

In addition, these figures do not take adequate account of the differences between public and private sector pension plans. Ottawa's recently negotiated pension scheme provides for indexing of pension benefits to the CPI *after* the retired employee begins to draw benefits. The present value of (or implicit lump sum necessary to sustain the benefits under) this pension scheme loomed very large in the year or so preceding controls because prevailing interest rates on financial assets were not sufficiently high to cover the rate of inflation let alone provide any *real* (i.e. after inflation) rate of return. One estimate suggested that an equivalent pension scheme for the private sector would, extrapolating conditions prevailing in 1975, require contributions in the neighbourhood of 16-20% on the part of both employers and employees.[30]

Finally, the wage percentages quoted above do not reveal the intensity of wage demands by high-profile public sector unions such as the postal workers and Ontario civil servants in the months immediately preceding the imposition of controls. Taken together, these events suggest that there was a distinct possibility that public sector wage settlements in 1975 would trigger an upward spiralling of wage expectations on the part of all Canadians. At any rate, in the year or so prior to controls there was little doubt that public sector wage settlements were proceeding at a much faster clip than those in the private sector.

What was not so clear was whether these public sector wage increases represented principally such things as wage "catch-up" with the private sector or the necessary transfer price to accommodate the movement of workers from the private to the more rapidly expanding public sector or whether they were evidence that public sector wages were, for all intents and purposes, out of control. While this is a testable hypothesis, my contention is that these wages were indeed becoming out of control and were threatening a re-kindling of private sector wage expectations. Elsewhere, I have taken an even stronger position.[31]

In the period prior to controls, the traditional factors in private sector wage negotiations, particularly profits and productivity, were increasingly forced to the sidelines in part because the private sector found justification for its wage demands in developments in the public sector. Even so, business may have been able to offer some effective degree of resistance were it not for the fact that all parties to any negotiation had come to take it for granted that Ottawa stood ready to provide the needed amount of monetary expansion to allow virtually any level of wage increase to be passed along to consumers in the form of higher commodity prices. The combination of these two factors meant that "whatever incentive the private sector may have had to resist wage demands was effectively eliminated. Bereft of any economic base, wage behaviour under these circumstances becomes principally a matter of expectations and political or social clout."[32]

To the extent that the above contention is correct, it suggests that the most serious challenge to the successful removal of controls may well come from public sector wage developments. This assertion is predicated on the two-fold assumption that *(A)* under de-control the Bank of Canada will continue with its policy of effecting a gradual deceleration of monetary growth and, *(B)* the private sector will respond, perhaps with a lag, to this policy of monetary restraint by moving towards reasonable and acceptable levels of price and wage increases.[33] It is far from clear that a programme of monetary restraint will impact much on public sector wage negotiations where consideration of profits and productivity are largely irrelevant. Therefore, some alternative to the present collective bargaining arrangements in the public sector may well be deserving of consideration. Prior to outlining some possible alternatives, it is convenient to devote some time to detailing some aspects of the process of wage determination in the public sector.

B. Wage determination in the public sector

1. The government as employer

Labour-management relations in the public sector take place in an environment that differs considerably from that characterizing most of the private sector. Governments are not constrained by profit levels or profit ratios when faced with wage demands. One could argue that to the extent increases in the wage bill imply increases in tax rates, these tax hikes would serve as a constraint similar to that of profits in the private sector. The analogy is not too useful, however. There exist several alternatives to increasing taxes, especially at the federal level. For the early part of the post-float period the quickening pace of inflation meant that Ottawa was garnering, thanks to the income tax system, an ever-increasing proportion of Canada's real purchasing power. In other words, governments were collecting an increasing proportion of *real* as well as nominal purchasing power in the form of increased tax inflows. In such a situation, large wage increases in the public sector simply meant that tax rates would be reduced less than otherwise would be the case — a situation that is considerably more politically acceptable than levying new taxes to pay for any increased wage bill.

With the indexing of the personal income tax system, the situation was altered considerably — Ottawa stood to gain considerably less from inflation in terms of tax revenue — even though the indexation is incomplete in the sense that it is applied with a one-year lag and it does not cover items such as capital gains. For present purposes, however, the relevant point is that by the time indexation was implemented, Ottawa was well on its way to resorting to printing money or floating CSB's to cover cash deficits. Granted that these features do not by any means assume that Ottawa would be likely to accede to large wage demands, the essential point is that Ottawa (and all levels of government generally) is not operating under the binding constraint that profits play in the private sector.

In the economist's jargon, Ottawa was not faced with the true "opportunity cost" for the funds it obtained. Some aspects of this lessened cost of borrowing funds have not been appreciated sufficiently. For example, the fact that chartered banks have to hold the bulk of their reserves in non-interest-bearing deposits at the Bank of Canada implies that Ottawa is in fact obtaining interest-free loans (the profits of the Bank of Canada go directly to the government). Moreover, the presence of the secondary reserve requirement ratio in the banking sector means that Ottawa can place part of its short-term debt at less-than-market rates of interest. Indeed, a few years back this constraint was so binding that chartered banks were willing to buy Ottawa's treasury bills at rates of interest which were a full 2% below market. The point of all this is simply that it is difficult for Ottawa to economize on its activities if it has access to several methods of financing that do not reflect the true cost of borrowing money. It is disappointing indeed that the recent White Paper on banking does not eliminate the two "captive markets" for federal debt.

The thrust of the above is that governments generally, and especially the federal government because of its interaction with the central bank, do not face the same constraints as private sector firms. There is one further point to be made in this context. If the constraint is less binding in the government sector, it is less binding still if it can be put off into the future rather than faced immediately. Hence it should not come as much of a surprise to find that Ottawa accepted a most generous pension scheme. This sort of remuneration scheme pushes the day of financial reckoning well into the future and, quite possibly, onto the shoulders of other governments.

2. Government employees

On the employee side the situation is likewise quite different. Public servants are essentially bargaining from a position of guaranteed job security. In turn, this job security implies that public sector employees will have less incentive to be moderate in their wage demands than their counterparts in the private sector because there is virtual certainty that the size of the wage settlement will have no impact on their work patterns. A 20% wage increase will lead to a 20% increase in annual income in the public sector, whereas the same rate of increase for, say, plumbers may not and probably will not translate into a comparable annual increase. Economic agents can, via capital substitution among other things, economize on the use of plumbers and other highly-priced trades when their wages increase. Furthermore, annual incomes in the private sector are subject to the overall economic outlook. The substantial layoffs and terminations of white-collar and blue-collar workers alike over the past two years are ample evidence that this is indeed the case for the private sector. Perhaps governments ought to contemplate the odd two-week employee furlough when economic conditions (record deficits or rampant government expenditure growth) dictate such a move.

3. Third party implications

There is a further significant difference relating to labour-management relations in the private and public sectors. Almost by definition the goods and services provided by the public sector do not have any close substitutes and certainly they are not in the class of internationally-traded goods and services. By definition, as well, services cannot be stockpiled in anticipation of a strike. Hence, a strike in the public sector implies that Canadians by and large simply have to do without the goods and services for the duration of the strike. Examples are not hard to come by: police protection, education, postal service, etc. The consuming Canadian public can easily weather a prolonged strike against even a giant corporation like General Motors. Domestic and international substitutes for Chevrolets abound. Moreover, with appropriate foresight, GM might be able to stockpile Chevs. In addition, strikes can affect both employers and employees adversely, apart from the loss of production and wages, respectively, during the actual strike itself. Employees and firms alike run the risk of substantial shifts in consumer preferences that will sharply curtail the need for their future services. And in the limit, the firm could go under.

As far as public sector strikes are concerned, the principal costs are borne by *third* parties, i.e., Canadians in their role as consumers of the services of education, postal services, etc. Two implications of this situation are worthy of highlight. First of all, Canadian citizens put tremendous pressure on the responsible government body to settle the strike and, normally, to settle it quickly in one way or another. Because governments often do not face appropriate "costs" for obtaining funds (as argued above) this suggests that the governments may be willing to make a more generous bargain with the workers than would otherwise be the case. Quite often, it is precisely these "third party" implications of a particular industry that were the original reason for the decision to shift the provision of its services from the private to the public sector. This being the case, Ron Bodkin has argued that it "could well be regarded as irresponsible, on the part of government decision-makers, to decree that a service is so important that it should be provided publicly without making certain that it would be provided continuously."[34] If strikes are allowed in such sectors, it seems to me that injured third parties should have some recourse in law to demand compensation from government and striking labour for the breaking of the implicit "social contract" of continuous provision of the public services. Such was clearly not the case last fall as numerous firms dependent on the mails suffered severe and in some cases irreparable losses.

An example may serve to focus this analysis further. What happens when, say, school teachers go on strike? Neither the school board nor the teachers necessarily suffer because of the "lost output." It is true that the teachers receive only strike benefits for the duration of the strike. But the unpaid salaries accumulate and probably go right back into the kitty to be used to determine the new salary levels.

Governments face adverse public opinion but no financial loss and perhaps even some gain if they can successfully siphon off some of the accumulated unpaid salaries from the eventual settlement. The real losers are third parties — the students themselves and perhaps the families of students if they were counting on the school to perform a babysitting role while they were engaged in work activity. If, however, the government or school boards utilized the accumulated salaries to issue education vouchers to students who could in turn use these vouchers to hire tutors during the strike the probable outcome might be substantially different. The teachers would lose access to unpaid salaries, governments would also stand to lose more financially from a large settlement, and the affected third parties would have access to a viable substitute for schooling services during the strike. In short, the collective bargaining process would resemble to a much greater extent that characterizing the bulk of such negotiations in the private sector. As a matter of fact, Milton Friedman, among others, has long advocated an education system that allows for more effective competition from private suppliers of education. Rather than resorting to education vouchers only when strikes arise, Friedman would issue permanent educational vouchers.

4. Arbitration in the civil service

As a result of legislation in the 1960's, either one of the parties to a labour dispute in the federal public sector can opt for arbitration which then becomes binding on both parties. More than the right to strike, this provision has led to the recent upward spiralling of wages in the public service. Arbitration in the public sector essentially means applying previous settlements in one area of the public service to another area. With little in the way of productivity or profit considerations to fall back upon, arbitration becomes incredibly susceptible to considerations relating to equity elsewhere in the public sector. The appropriate considerations should be the comparable wages for the particular, or a closely related, industry or occupation in the private sector. Alternatively, data relating to the supply of potential entrants into the industry in question should become a determining factor. Yet,

I am willing to assert (as a testable hypothesis) that arguments put before arbitration boards by public service unions relate principally to previous wage settlements elsewhere in the public sector and not to private sector developments.

The overall process might be best described in terms of the following scenario. The government steps in and takes over the service in question. In turn, this gives labour tremendous, but artificial, market power because it now has the power to interrupt this service. Note that this does not simply apply to government ownership or solely to the public sector. The presence of the government in the form of various regulations, be it for standards for plumbers or certification for doctors, bestows artificial but very significant market power on those being regulated. This is but another way of stating Stigler's Law: *regulation is in the interests of those being regulated*! Be that as it may, the basic scenario proceeds as follows. Public sector unions with substantial market power (and there are some, of course, who do have a strong market position) set the wage pattern. Compulsory arbitration then becomes the vehicle for unions with little or no inherent market power to share in the rewards of the wage leader. This process also applies to the provincial level as well. For example, it only takes one school board settlement in Ontario to set the target for the remaining boards.[35]

Given the proposition (and remembering that it is more in the nature of an assertion) that public sector wage behaviour is likely to pose the most serious problem to the successful unwinding of expectations in the post-controls period, are there any viable alternatives to the present collective bargaining process in the public service? This question takes on added importance since Ottawa, in its recent position paper on the future of government policy, also zeroed in on this same concern:

"Although one typically thinks of market power as characterizing the private sector, a serious administered pricing problem also exists in the public sector, where governments must often provide essential services that are widely considered to be 'vital at any cost', and where

173

labour does not feel there is any danger of 'driving the company bankrupt' by asking for substantial increases. The development of collective bargaining in the public sector has served to remove many of the inequities which existed between public and private sectors in the past. But the process has nonetheless directly contributed to higher spending by governments and can indirectly increase inflationary pressures by providing high-profile settlements which give other workers an inflationary target to aim at. It is important that public service collective bargaining not be allowed to overshoot and go beyond what is fair. Modifications in public sector employer/employee relations are an essential element in a broad anti-inflation strategy, along with improved labour-management relations in the private sector and policies to sustain and enhance competition."[36]

I turn now to a brief discussion of collective bargaining in the public sector in the post-controls period.

C. Alternatives to current labour-management relations in the public sector

The first recommendation is that controls be taken off the private sector before they are taken off the public sector. The reason for this is straightforward. The only major shift in overall government policy toward inflation since the imposition of controls has been the Bank of Canada's policy of gearing down the rate of monetary expansion. (Indeed, the Bank instituted this policy a few weeks prior to the advent of controls.) As was indicated earlier in this paper, monetary restraint is not likely to impact directly on public sector wage behaviour. Indirectly, of course, to the extent that the Bank remains steadfast in its pursuit of restraint irrespective of the size of the deficit, Ottawa may find that it faces a more realistic cost as far as obtaining funds are concerned and this in turn may lead it to be less willing to accommodate large wage demands. Nonetheless, it is probably fair to argue that monetary restraint will influence primarily private sector wage behaviour. Even here, the process may be a lengthy one. Hence, it would appear appropriate for the public sector to be subject to some sort of controls (patterned after average private sector wage responses) until the private sector has settled into a pattern of acceptable wage and price behaviour. To some extent this message has already reached Ottawa. At a recent Federal-Provincial Conference dealing with the process of decontrol and the post-control period, Finance Minister Donald Macdonald noted:

> " . . . A critical component of post-control arrangements will be the ability to offer reasonably convincing assurance that compensation in the public sector will not contribute to a new inflationary spiral, once the AIB controls are removed.
> For much of the private sector, it will be argued, market forces will exert a discipline on the setting of prices and incomes. Because this factor does not apply directly in the public sector, it has been widely suggested that a form of controls should remain in force for the public sector after they have been lifted from the private sector. This would undoubtedly raise major difficulties. Nevertheless, there is a need to consider carefully whether some form of continuing restraint should be established, particularly with regard to the public sector. Should the rate of some public sector compensation increases return to those found shortly before the AIB was established, governments might well be concerned about their ability to pay and about the demonstration effect that excessive increases can have."[37]

While recognition of the problem is most welcome, some action is also called for: an ounce of prevention . . .

This, however, is not a long-run solution to the problem of labour-management relations in the public sector. Something more is probably needed. This much is clear. The difficulty is deciding upon the nature of any changes. My own view is that it is appropriate to eliminate the right to strike in essential public services. I find Simon Reisman's suggestions on this issue embodied in his Address to the October 1976 Financial Post Conference on Inflation to be very attractive.† He recommends the establishment of a tripartite body composed of representatives of government, labour and the private sector which would be charged with the responsibility for identifying those areas of the government sector where prolonged work stoppage cannot be tolerated because of the resulting damages to the public interest. As far as remuneration for the employees in that sector, Mr. Reisman, the former Deputy Minister of Finance, recommends:

> "At the outset, annual increases in remuneration in such services should be geared to the rise in national industrial wages or some other appropriate yardstick. Maintenance of this approach over any extended time, however, would fail to take account of relative changes in pay scales required to reflect the changing needs of society. To provide for these necessary adjustments, I would propose that this same tripartite body periodically review relative pay scales, establishing as objective tests as possible to determine whether changes should be made on the basis of such factors as supply and demand inside and outside the public sector and compensation levels for comparable employment in private industry. As I see it, an approach of the nature I have outlined is necessary to ensure equitable treatment of the public employees involved, maintenance of essential public services, and elimination of this potentially dangerous source of renewed inflationary pressure."[38]

This is not meant to be a punitive measure. Every effort should be made to accommodate civil servants in these designated industries should they wish to transfer to other areas of the civil service prior to the imposition of the no-strike law.

Some changes are also needed in the "less essential" areas of the civil service. Arbitration of the variety now in force is not desirable. The process by which one strong

†Editor's Note: Mr. Reisman's remarks are included in this volume as the opening essay.

union "picks off" a large settlement which is then spread across the rest of the sector by allowing unions to opt unilaterally for arbitration binding on both parties tends, in my opinion, to result in pay hikes that are often quite unrelated to corresponding wages for like workers in the private sector. Outlawing strikes entirely in the public sector is probably not a viable solution. A preferred approach would be to allow strikes but require arbitration (if it remains in its present form whereby either party can opt for binding arbitration) to be of the "final offer" variety. The arbitrator, or team of arbitrators (again composed of government, labour and the public) would be required to select *in whole* one or other of the final offers — either that by management or by labour. This should serve to limit substantially the differentials in the wage offers or demands since an inordinately high demand or low offer will push the arbitration in the direction of selecting the other party's final offer.

Other procedures are deserving of consideration as well. Earlier in the paper an alternative approach to the present system of determining teachers' salaries in Ontario was presented — an approach that allowed for varying salary settlements across school boards but also required the local boards to obtain from local sources 100% of any wage increase beyond the provincially set floor wage. More extensive use of "cash budgets" for various government agencies would also be an improvement over the present system. Currently wage negotiations tend to be a major determinant of the total budget allocation of a given department — i.e., the total size of the financial allocation to any department is one of the variables determined by wage negotiations. It might be better were it the other way around. Finally, the time may be ripe for some degree of "privatization" of activities currently in the government sector or some methods of compensating "third parties" to any public sector strike so that collective bargaining in the public sector introduces some potential costs that impact on both sides in the case of a strike, i.e., to make public service collective bargaining subject to some of the same sort of risks that characterize private sector collective bargaining.

Much is at stake here. There is little chance for Canada to have a viable private sector if wage leadership falls into the domain of the public sector. For example, unless the present value of the civil service pension plan is taken into account when bargaining over future civil service remuneration packages, Ottawa will find itself in the position where the entire private sector will request to be covered by Ottawa when it comes to pension plans. This will mean a very substantial further expansion of the public sector but it would seem inevitable if the private sector finds itself simply unable to afford the generous pension scheme offered by the federal government. There is a bit of the "moral hazard" principle at work here, although I do not know to what extent it is relevant. Control over inflation currently rests in the hands of the policy makers. Yet it is precisely these people who stand to benefit, *relatively*, as a result of inflation. Personally, I would much rather see it the other way around, where the private sector had an indexed pension scheme and the civil servants an unindexed one so that civil servants would have a a substantial incentive to minimize the inflation rate in order to preserve the value of their pension scheme. As I stated this might not be an important point, but individual self-interest being what it is, it is worth pondering about.

In summary, in the enterprise system that characterizes our economy, considerations of productivity and profits should dominate wage determination. The role for the public sector is to ensure that its employees receive remuneration packages that match those in the private sector. The proposals in this section are designed to ensure that in the post-control period the public sector not be allowed once again to resume its position as the wage leader in the economy. The future of the private sector, let alone the concern over a re-spiralling of inflation, surely rests upon this proposition.

Notes

[1]Thomas J. Courchene, *Money, Inflation and the Bank of Canada* (Montreal: C.D. Howe Research Institute), 1976, Ch. 11.

[2]Governor Gerald K. Bouey, "Remarks to the 46th Annual Meeting of the Canadian Chamber of Commerce (Saskatoon, Sept. 22, 1975), reprinted in the *Bank of Canada Review*, Oct. 1975, p. 14.

[3]Essentially 10-15% for 1975 and 8-12% for 1976. While obviously siding with the Governor on the principle that is at stake, I believe that some aspects of the manner in which the Bank is implementing this policy of monetary deceleration leaves a great deal to be desired. The interested reader can consult Chapter 4 of Thomas J. Courchene, *Monetarism and Controls: The Inflation Fighters* (Montreal: C.D. Howe Research Institute), 1976.

[4]Bank of Canada, *Annual Report of the Governor to the Minister of Finance, 1975* (Ottawa: Bank of Canada), 1976, p. 12.

[5]The reason why the Bank was satisfied with such low interest rates was that it believed it could control the quantity or availability of credit, regardless of the level of prevailing interest rates, by focusing on chartered bank liquidity. But for this to be a viable approach to policy required the presence of a much greater degree of imperfection in the markets for money and credit than actually existed. In the event, the Bank lost control of the quantities of money and credit, principally because the interest rate setting was far too low — indeed for substantial periods of time the after-inflation rates of interest were negative. For a more detailed analysis of post-float policy the reader can consult Parts II and III of *Money, Inflation and the Bank of Canada, op. cit.*

[6]With substantial capital mobility between countries there would be little difference between the effects of domestic and foreign financing of these deficits.

[7]Bank of Canada, *Annual Report* (1975). Underlining added.

[8]William Mackness, Vice-President, Pitfield, Mackay, Ross and Company Limited, "Trade Payments and the Domestic Economy: Evidence of a Fundamental Deterioration in the Economic Climate," paper presented to Senior Executives Seminar, The Conference Board in Canada, Vancouver, Oct. 29, 1976, p. 11.

[9]There is some literature to fall back on when assessing the impact of, say, tax changes on work effort. But this is not of much help in the present context since the relevant issues are extremely broad, i.e., crowding out and its impact on the viability of the private sector, tax structure comparisons between nations, etc. The assertion or assumption underlying this paragraph is that this increase in the role of government has indeed led to a reduction in potential output and productivity.

[10]For example, this is likely to be the case for middle and upper class taxpayers if the proceeds of the tax are used to finance an increase in transfers, which are unlikely to be perceived as an adequate *quid pro quo* for the lost after-tax income.

[11]There are of course many other reasons; the high income elasticity of demand for medical care, the aging of the population, the low user cost of medical services (discussed below), etc.

[12]Ontario Economic Council, *Education: Issues and Alternatives, 1976*, p.p. 15-16.

[13]Essentially this is the opposite of "real term" budgeting referred to above, i.e., the agencies are not allotted physical units, but rather dollar allocations, so that if the cost of acquiring a given input unit increases, the agency simply has to economize on new purchases or make adjustments elsewhere.

[14]The process whereby only or principally new activities come up for review is referred to as "incremental budgeting."

[15]Albert Breton, *The Economic Theory of Representative Government* (Chicago: Aldine), 1974.

[16]D.G. Hartle, *A Theory of the Expenditure Budgetary Process* (Ontario Economic Council Research Study), Toronto: University of Toronto Press, 1976. Chapters 3 (A New Perspective on the Expenditure Budgetary Process) and 4 (Toward Some Testable Propositions) are particularly relevant.

[17]*Ibid*, p. 90.

[18]*Ibid*, p. viii.

[19]*Ibid*, p. 93.

[20]*Ibid*, p. 7l.

[21]Ontario Economic Council, *Health: Issues and Alternatives, 1976* (Toronto: University of Toronto Press), 1976, Part III.

[22]*Ibid*, p. 16.

[23]Christopher Green and J.-M. Cousineau, *Unemployment In Canada: The Impact of Unemployment Insurance*, Economic Council of Canada (Ottawa Queen's Printer), 1975, Ch. 5.

[24]H.G. Grubel, D. Maki and S. Sax, "Real and Insurance-Induced Unemployment in Canada", *Canadian Journal of Economics* (May, 1975), pp. 174-91.

[25]Bank of Canada, *Annual Report (1975)*, pp. 8-9.

[26]*Ibid*, p. 9.

[27]*Ibid*, p. 9.

[28]Mackness, *op. cit.*, p. 12.

[29]Department of Finance, *Economic Review, 1976* (Ottawa: Queen's Printer), 1976, Table 15.

[30]James Rusk, "Supplying Funds for Future Benefits Felt Impasse to Indexing of Private Pensions", *Globe and Mail*, Dec. 4, 1975.

[31]Courchene, *Monetarism and Controls . . ., op. cit.*, Ch. 7.

[32]*Ibid*, p. 83.

[33]For a discussion of the manner in which monetary restraint is likely to accomplish this unwinding of expectations the interested reader can consult the article by David Laidler, "An Alternative to Wage and Price Controls", *The Illusion of Wage and Price Control* M. Walker, ed., (Vancouver: The Fraser Institute), 1976, pp. 129-209, or Chapter 6 of Courchene, *Monetarism and Controls . . ., op. cit.*

[34]Ronald G. Bodkin, "A Proposal Concerning Collective Bargaining in the Public Sector," Research Paper 7517, Department of Economics, University of Ottawa, p.2.

[35]In a recent paper Douglas Hartle makes many of the same points that appear in this section. For example:

"Collective bargaining for public servants providing essential services has resulted in extremely large wage increases. This has produced a ripple effect as other workers have sought to maintain their old wage differentials. Allowing public servants to opt unilaterally for compulsory arbitration has resulted in large wage increases for groups with little or no bargaining power (e.g., economists and statisticians). Here too a ripple effect was created across the economy." (Douglas Hartle, "On Prophets and Power: A Comment on the Prime Minister's Revelation", *Canadian Public Policy/Analyse de Politiques*, Spring 1976, p. 253.

[36]*The Way Ahead: A Framework for Discussion*, a Working Paper published by the Government of Canada (Ottawa: Oct. 1976), p. 16.

[37]Donald S. Macdonald, "Decontrol and Post-Control". Notes for remarks to the Federal Provincial Conference of Ministers of Finance, Ottawa, February 1-2, 1977 (Department of Finance Press Release 77-14).

[38]Simon Reisman, "Controls: The Great Fallacy", Address to the *Financial Post* - AGF Companies Conference, Toronto, Oct. 7, 1976, pp. 17-18 (Reprinted in this volume).

which way ahead?

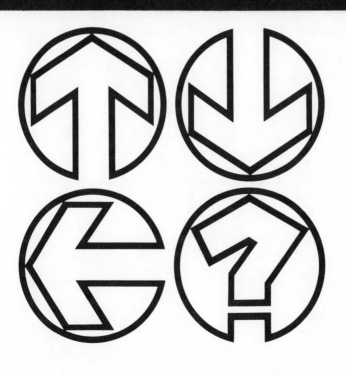

The Way Ahead:
A Promise Unfulfilled

DOUGLAS A. L. AULD

Professor of Economics
University of Guelph

THE AUTHOR

Douglas A.L. Auld was born in 1941 in London, Ontario, and educated at the University of Western Ontario and the University of Toronto. He received his Ph.D. from Australian National University in 1968. He has been at the University of Guelph since 1968, where he is now Professor of Economics. He has also been a member of the Intergovernment Fiscal Relations Committee of the National Tax Association, a member of the executive council of the Canadian Economics Association, and chairman of the Ontario Economic Council on Local and Regional Government. He has been an associate editor of *Canadian Public Policy* since 1974.

Professor Auld is the author or editor of many articles and books, including: *The Government Sector in the 1970's* (with T.R. Robinson), published by the Private Planning Association in 1971; *Economics: Contemporary Issues in Canada*, published by Holt, Rinehart and Winston in 1972; *Principles of Public Finance* (with F.C. Miller), published by Methuen Publishing Company in 1975; *Issues in Government Expenditure Growth*, published by the C.D. Howe Research Institute in 1976.

The Way Ahead:
A Promise Unfulfilled

DOUGLAS A. L. AULD

Professor of Economics
University of Guelph

I. INTRODUCTION

The Government of Canada's Working Paper, *The Way Ahead* (hereafter referred to as the *Paper*) is designed to provide a strong light at the end of the tunnel; not just to light the way in the tunnel but show the way ahead once the end of the tunnel has been reached. Unfortunately, only the promise is there; in fact, a more appropriate title for a large part of the *Paper* might have been *A Survey of the Principles of Freshman Economics*. A substantial portion of the *Paper* is devoted to informing the reader *(A).* how the free enterprise market system should work, *(B).* why it sometimes fails, and *(C).* options available to government to correct for the misdoings of the system. All of this is interspersed with a discussion of inflation. The level of the discussion is, I suspect, rather boring for most but this cost is not offset by its simplicity. What the *Paper* does accomplish is to reveal several fundamental points in connection with inflation and its control. These issues, however, are not exploited in a manner that would inform the reader about the federal government's policies. In addition, the questions surrounding controls and post-controls policy are muddied by extensive digressions into areas that are peripheral to the immediate concern. One of the worst examples is the emergence time and again, of platitudinous statements on the price system, attitudes of people and social goods. Finally, by the time the reader reaches the end of the *Paper* it has become annoyingly tiresome to read of "... ways and means to encourage...," "... mechanisms to encourage...," "... strategies for pursuing...," "... policies must help...," "... policies must provide..." and "... policies will have to be developed..." without once seeing a statement of specific alternative policies and the reasons why this government favours some courses of action over others. We have been told only that the government intends to follow a middle road.

This is a very broad-based reaction and not a terribly favourable one at that. There are a number of more specific areas that require analysis to validate my general reaction to the *Paper*.

II. GOVERNMENT POLICY AND INFLATION

On the question of government and its role in the inflationary process, the *Paper* contains some subtleties that are either almost impossible to decipher or subject to diverse interpretation. We find there is a statement that:

"... there may be instances where governments must bear a large share of the responsibility for inflation. To diagnose the inflationary spiral we have recently experienced as largely attributable to a profligate government, however, is simplistic to the point that it is misleading." (p. 15)

Later, the *Paper* states:

"The growth of government expenditure must bear some of the burden of responsibility for inflation." (p. 31)

What this amounts to is the admission that government is to blame (to some extent) for inflation but not for the inflationary spiral. What these statements do not reveal is in what instances government is to blame for inflation and who is responsible for the inflationary spiral.

Some hint of this comes in the section on *The Responsibility of Governments* when, in discussing *A Middle Road*, the *Paper* states that governments "... at any point in time ..." can initiate and exacerbate inflation through:

1. the levy of undesirable and unwarranted taxes,

2. financing deficits through the creation of money.

The tone of the discussion reminds one of the man who, having lost a considerable sum of money on the stock market, approaches an investment consultant at a party and says, "I have this friend who was wiped out in the stock market..." In short, the contents of the analysis in this section are really a catalogue of how the government has contributed to and/or sustained inflation in recent years. There is a very brave but nonetheless unconvincing and unsuccessful attempt to dismiss government spending and taxation in Canada as a contributing factor to inflation by stating that inflation has been a world-wide phenomenon for 30 years in all industrialized democracies.† There is no mention of the growth of public spending and taxation in most of these countries and their record of money financing the public debt except in an earlier statement where "international" liquidity is noted as a contributing cause of inflation. All of this is even more confusing when placed beside the *Paper's* assertion that,

> "The ultimate sources of inflation are to be found both in market 'failures' and the incapacity of the market system to serve social goals, with a consequent need for increasing government intervention." (p. 21)

†Editor's Note: As is shown in Professor Jack Carr's essay this claim of *The Way Ahead* is simply not true.

What this seems to say is that inflation is a permanent part of any market-orientated economic system with government at the centre of the price whirlwind. One is continually searching for a reconciliation of these diverse and almost conflicting statements but, alas, it is not to be found.

The final comment I wish to make is in connection with the statement,

> "Fiscal and monetary policies directed at the control of inflation, unless associated with other measures, will have increasingly costly and socially disruptive unemployment consequences before they have a significant effect on inflation rates." (p. 10)

This implies that fiscal and monetary policy is costless if used with other measures. What other measures? If the 'other measures' are an incomes policy, are there no disruptive consequences from that policy? Monetary and fiscal policy will, of course, be costly but what should be debated is whether or not the consequences are far less severe than controls over wages and profits.

III. RELATIVE PRICES, ABSOLUTE PRICES AND MONEY

Throughout the *Paper* there is frequent reference to long-run, internal and external forces that are likely to bring about increases in the prices of certain products. A recurring theme is that the economy must not allow these *relative* price changes to result in continuous upward movements in the *absolute* level of prices. In other instances, mainly those dealing with fiscal and monetary policy, there is recognition of the fact that continuous increases in the supply of money, beyond those required to finance real economic growth, can be inflationary. What is lacking is a clear statement combining all three issues. But it should be highlighted because it is the critical interdependence of absolute and relative prices, and the stock of money that is not (it would appear) widely recognized.† A rise in the price of certain resources and those products utilizing such resources is not, strictly speaking, inflationary. At best, the outcome would be a rise in the price of some products and a fall in the price of others as demand patterns and real incomes change in response to the initial price rise of certain products. At worst, there will be a once-and-for-all rise in price level, *not* a continuous rise in the price level. In a theoretical world of perfect competition where adjustments to price changes occur instantaneously and there are no costs to making adjustments, there is little prospect of inflation. It is, of course, implicitly assumed in such a world that the stock of nominal money remains unchanged.

The real world is not quite so tidy; markets do not adjust instantly at no cost; markets are not perfectly competitive (unions and producers' associations *do* exist) and unemployed resources in one sector do not flow quickly to other sectors. Because of all these imperfections in the real world, a rise in the price of certain products or inputs is likely to result in not just a rise in the overall price level but also in unemployment and changes in the distribution of income, not, perhaps, desired by government. These effects can be cushioned by ensuring that there is a sufficient once-and-for-all increase in the supply of money to accommodate the higher price level. How much is 'sufficient' is impossible to predict, and consequently it is little wonder that the monetary authorities can be wrong and therefore expand the money supply faster than is necessary to achieve a transition over to a new set of relative prices.

All of this is extremely important for the post-controls period and yet we find no recognition of it in the *Paper* (other than statements that monetary and fiscal policy will have to be constrained). In the event that there are 'bursts' of wage inflation following the removal of controls, there will be a great temptation to accommodate these wage increases through monetary expansion. This must be resisted.

---

†Editor's Note: For a discussion of these issues see M. Walker, Ed., *The Illusion of Wage and Price Control*, The Fraser Institute, 1976; the essay by J. Carr is particularly relevant on this point.

IV. PRIVATE PREFERENCES FOR PUBLIC GOODS

There is, in the *Paper*, a reference to the fact that growing tax revenues have been used to finance expanding government expenditure so that "... the fruits of growth were distributed to all Canadians in a just and equitable manner." There is also a reference to the fact that inflation could be initiated or exacerbated by taxation beyond the community's acceptance. The two statements are obviously related and have important repercussions for the post-control period. One of the worst features of our tax system (in terms of fiscal responsibility) is that as the economy grows there is an automatic rise in tax revenues that greatly exceeds the growth of the economy. This was particularly true before the income tax structure was indexed but is still true in spite of the indexing. The government has, therefore, been in a position to expand programmes and create new ones without having to impose higher tax rates (or only having to impose minor ones) on the community.

Did the vast majority of Canadians really want all these new programmes? How far were most Canadians really willing to go on income redistribution? Do Canadians really want the government to plan their life or would they prefer to do it themselves? We just don't know the answers to these questions and until we have some idea of the taxpayer's willingness to have widespread public intervention, further public sector involvement in the private sector should be resisted. This cannot be overemphasized. Although the *Paper* states time and time again that the government believes in the power of the market system to allocate factors of production, there are an equal number of statements about the need for government to 'correct' for the imperfections in the market system. In addition, the government has plans to initiate formal consultations with the private sector about what the government should do in the future. Informal discussions I favour, but formal discussions could well lead to formal, permanent institutions or agencies in which the federal government would always have the power of veto, the threat of retaliatory legislation and the maximum leverage. It is true that Ottawa has the supreme power, subject to the ruling of the Court, but this power is tempered by the openness of a parliamentary democracy, not the secrecy of a partisan-established agency or institution.

In fairness to *The Way Ahead*, I should explicitly recognize that its subtitle is: *A Framework for Discussion*. In that sense, it has fulfilled its purpose: people are discussing the government's views as expressed in this *Paper*. Much of the discussion will, unfortunately, take place in a vacuum until we have before us the specific options available for the future and the direction that the government favours.

Comments on
The Way Ahead:
A Framework for Discussion

JACK CARR

Associate Professor of Economics
University of Toronto

THE AUTHOR

Jack Carr was born in Toronto in 1944 and was graduated from the University of Toronto in 1965 before taking his Ph.D. at the University of Chicago in 1971. In 1968 he joined the Department of Political Economy in the University of Toronto and became Associate Professor in 1973. Professor Carr is also a Research Associate of the Institute for Policy Analysis at the University of Toronto. During the 1975-76 academic year he was a Visiting Scholar at the Department of Economics, University of California in Los Angeles.

Professor Carr's publications include: *The Money Supply and the Rate of Inflation*, a study prepared for the Prices and Incomes Commission in 1972; *Cents and Nonsense* (Holt, Rinehart and Winston), a book of popular essays on economic policy, and numerous contributions to scholarly journals. His essay "Wage and Price Controls: Panacea for Inflation or Prescription for Disaster!", was published by the Fraser Institute in 1976 in *The Illusion of Wage and Price Control*.

Comments on
The Way Ahead:
A Framework for Discussion

JACK CARR

Associate Professor of Economics
University of Toronto

I. INTRODUCTION

In October, 1976 the Government of Canada published a document entitled *The Way Ahead: A Framework for Discussion*. The stated purpose of this document was that "... in order to better focus future consultations and to aid national understanding, many groups and individuals have asked for a general paper outlining the economic and social directions the government intends to take after controls end. This Working Paper outlines these principles and strategies and provides a context for further consultation" (p. 5). The government provides a further rationalization for its Working Paper in arguing that "... it is a basic assumption of this paper that Canadians — when presented with the information necessary to assess our future options and opportunities to discuss the directions in which we should be moving — will make their choices in a manner that is both responsible and in accordance with their longer-term interests" (p. 32). Hence *The Way Ahead* makes two promises to its readers. It promises to outline what the government intends to do after wage and price controls are lifted and it promises to provide the reader with information to aid in assessing the direction

197

the government intends to take. Unfortunately, neither promise is fulfilled. *The Way Ahead* is an extremely vague document. It appears to have been drafted by a fairly large committee whose duty it was to make sure that every possible point of view was adequately represented in the document.

An outline of government policy?

A large part of *The Way Ahead* is devoted to providing so-called useful information to the general public on the subject of inflation. It is to this part of *The Way Ahead* that I will devote most of my comments. Before doing so, let me make a brief comment on the failure of *The Way Ahead* to live up to its promise of outlining government economic policy in the post-control period. I am sure that one of the major motives for writing a document such as *The Way Ahead* was to alleviate some of the fears and uncertainty businessmen, in general, felt as a result of the imposition of wage and price controls. As a result of a number of statements the Prime Minister and other Cabinet ministers made after controls were imposed, businessmen became increasingly alarmed at the prospect that post-control economic policy would be substantially different from pre-control economic policy. Exactly what form the new economic policy would take was not known but the feeling in the business community was that there was a good chance that post-control economic policy would be radically different from the pre-control policies.

This uncertainty that the rules of the game may be changed is not conducive to encouraging investment in Canada. Many businessmen indicated that they were postponing investment projects in Canada and in addition the flow of foreign direct investment in Canada almost dried up in the first half of 1976.[1] *The Way Ahead* is so vague and wishy-washy with respect to the government's future intentions that any uncertainty with respect to government economic policy in the post-control period that existed in the business community before the publication of *The Way Ahead* would certainly remain after its publication. *The Way Ahead* doesn't eliminate this uncertainty. In fact, it may increase it.

The Way Ahead tells the business community as well as all other Canadians that "the concept of a new sharing of social and economic responsibility is fundamental to the search for new directions that will ensure balanced growth without inflation" (p. 32). It does not say what this new concept of sharing will be. The document tells the business community that in the future the rules of the economic game as played in Canada will change; it does not say how the rules will change. *As far as outlining future government economic policy is concerned it would have been better if The Way Ahead had never been written.*

II. *THE WAY AHEAD'S* **THEORY OF INFLATION**

Let us now consider the basic ideas about inflation that are discussed in *The Way Ahead.* These ideas about inflation occupy a major part of the discussion. Unfortunately, *The Way Ahead* repeats most of the common fallacies that exist about inflation and in one case invents a new fallacy about inflation.[2]

1. There exists no single theory of inflation

The Way Ahead rejects any single theory about inflation. Inflation has at different times and different places a multiplicity of causes. "Simplistic explanations of inflation are bound to be incomplete and misleading. Inflation is a complex economic, social and political phenomenon, both in its origins and in its effects" (p. 8). No evidence is presented to support this statement. I would suspect that any single explanation of inflation is rejected in *The Way Ahead* because the most popular single theory of inflation, that inflation is at all times and all places a monetary phenomenon, squarely places the blame for inflation on the Federal government. From the point of view of the Federal government, such a theory is unpalatable, so theories of inflation which place the blame on anyone and everyone (i.e. greedy consumers, monopoly businesses, powerful trade unions, foreigners, etc.) are to be preferred.

But, what about the evidence?

The monetary theory of inflation argues that when the money supply is increased at a rate faster than the rate of growth of real output in the economy, then inflation will occur. There is substantial evidence both for Canada and for a large number of other countries of the relevance of the monetary theory of inflation. The authors of *The Way Ahead* chose to ignore this evidence. This empirical evidence was presented in an earlier piece of mine[3] and for convenience I reproduce it here. Table 1 presents the fifteen years of Canadian experience prior to the introduction of wage and price controls. This data provides a very good set of 'experiments' to test the monetary theory of inflation. With moderate monetary expansion there was no inflation in Canada. With

Table 1 — Inflation, Money Supply Growth and
Rate of Growth of Real Output, Canada 1960-1975

Year	Percentage Change in Consumer Price Index	Average for Period	Percentage Change in Money Supply*	Average for Period	Rate of Growth of Real Output	Average for Period
1960	1.3		4.6		2.9	
1961	.2		8.6		2.9	
1962	1.6		3.8	6.2	6.8	4.9
1963	1.8	1.7	6.4		5.2	
1964	1.9		7.4		6.7	
1965	2.9		12.0		6.7	
1966	3.6		6.5	11.9	6.9	5.7
1967	4.1	4.1	15.9		3.3	
1968	4.1		13.3		5.8	
1969	4.6		3.9		5.3	
1970	1.5		10.8		2.6	
1971	5.0		14.9	15.0	5.8	
1972	5.1	7.9	15.9		5.8	5.3
1973	9.1		18.3		6.9	
1974	12.4		16.8		2.8	
Sept., 1974	10.6		17.9		-1.3†	
Sept., 1975						

*Money supply is defined as the sum of currency in circulation outside banks plus all Canadian dollar deposits privately held.
†Output growth rate is for second quarter 1975 over second quarter 1974.

Source: Statistics Canada: *Canadian Statistical Review.*

expansionary monetary growth there was relatively mild inflation. When the monetary growth rate fell, the inflation rate fell. When monetary growth rates reached into the sky, Canada experienced double-digit inflation.

Although it is not as meaningful to look at year by year changes, Figure 1 plots for Canada, values for the rate of growth of the money supply minus the rate of growth of output against the inflation rate for the following year. It can be seen from this graph that, in general, as money supply increases, so inflation increases. Empirical support for the monetary theory of inflation not only exists for Canada over the last 15 years, but also over a much longer period of Canadian history and support also exists for this theory using the data from a large number of countries.

Figure 1 — Inflation and Money Supply Growth, Canada, 1960-1974

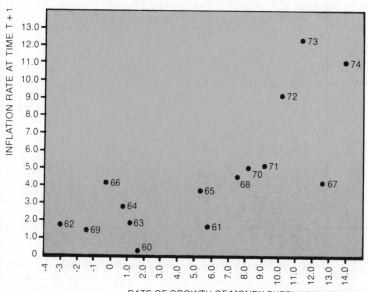

Source: Statistics Canada, *Canadian Statistical Review*

Figure 2 plots the rate of growth of money minus the rate of growth of output against the inflation rate for the period 1952-1969 for 40 industrialized countries.[4] Again this data supports the monetary theory of inflation. Inflation is at all times and at all places a monetary phenomenon.

Figure 2 — Rate of Change in Prices, and in M₁ per Unit of Output, Forty Countries, 1952-1969

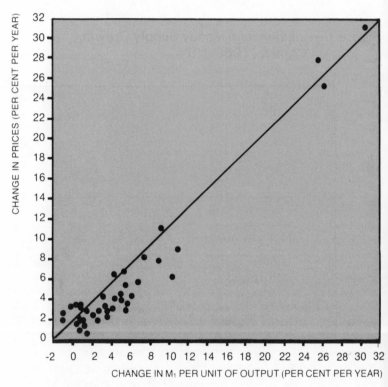

Source: Anna Schwartz. "Secular Price Change in Historical Perspective." *Journal of Money. Credit and Banking.* February 1973.

Monetarism is inconvenient

It should be noted that although the monetary theory of inflation provides a simple theory as to what is causing inflation, it only identifies the proximate cause of inflation, the excess printing of money. Why a government follows at any time any particular monetary policy is a much more complicated question. Government printing of money may be to finance government expenditures, it may be to help achieve certain economic goals or it may be necessitated because of the dictates of fixed exchange rates. Whatever the reason a government has for following a particular monetary policy, two points should be emphasized:

1. The government (including the Bank of Canada) controls the money supply.

2. Excess printing of money causes inflation.

From these two facts one cannot help but conclude that the blame for Canada's current bout of inflation rests squarely on the shoulders of the Federal government of Canada. As one might expect, this conclusion appears nowhere in *The Way Ahead.*

Factual errors in *The Way Ahead*

In fact, *The Way Ahead* cites what it feels is evidence against such a view. "The notion that inflation results from excessive government spending[5] is a popular one and, indeed, there may be instances where governments must bear a large share of the responsibility for inflation. To diagnose the inflationary spiral we have recently experienced as largely attributable to a profligate government, however, is simplistic to the point that it is misleading. Such a diagnosis ignores the fact that the recent acceleration of inflation was a worldwide phenomenon. It ignores the fact that all industrialized democracies have experienced gradually increasing inflation for at least the last three decades" (p. 15). The first thing about this evidence to note is that it is *not* a fact that all industrialized democracies have experienced gradually increasing inflation for at least the last three decades.

After World War II, Canada had inflation rates just under 15 per cent; at the outbreak of the Korean War period the inflation rate once again went into the double digit region; and from the end of the Korean War period until 1965 the inflation rate was under 2 per cent in most of these years. For Canada, it was only in the last 10 years that inflation rates have been increasing. And even in this period, there is at least one episode of a substantial fall in the inflation rate. The pattern in the U.S. during the last 30 years has been similar. The facts do *not* support the statement that inflation rates have been gradually increasing over the last 30 years.

Now what about the fact that inflation in the last 10 years appears to be a worldwide phenomenon? Does this absolve the government from blame? Does this negate the monetary theory of inflation?

The answer to both of these questions is a resounding *no.* In fact, the worldwide inflation that started in the late 1960's and early 1970's provides further evidence of the monetary theory of inflation. In the mid 1960's the U.S. started to increase its rate of monetary growth. One plausible reason for this is that the increase in the money supply in the U.S. was used to finance government expenditures on the Vietnam war. The increase in U.S. money supply caused inflation in the U.S. economy. This meant prices in the U.S. were rising faster than prices of the major trading partners of the U.S. and resulted in a decline in U.S. exports and an increase in U.S. imports. Under a system of floating exchange rates this U.S. trade imbalance would have resulted in a depreciation of the U.S. dollar. However, in the late 1960's most Western countries were on a system of fixed exchange rates. Canada, France, Germany, Japan all had agreed to peg their currency to the U.S. dollar. To prevent the fall in the price of the U.S. dollar, all these countries bought up the excess supplies of U.S. dollars.

These governments purchased the U.S. dollars with newly printed Canadian dollars or francs or marks or yens. Hence, the major trading partners of the U.S. were forced to increase monetary expansion. This increase in the rate of growth of the money supply, in each of these countries, was responsible for the resulting inflation in each of these countries. One of the lessons of fixed exchange rates is that under such a system a country cannot run an independent monetary policy. Canada cannot blame the inflation of the late 1960's on the U.S. — the blame should be placed on the nature of the exchange rate system.

The Canadian government freely adopted fixed exchange rates in 1962. Canada could have avoided increasing monetary expansion if it had chosen a system of flexible exchange rates. In fact, in 1970 Canada (and then subsequently most other Western countries) adopted a system of flexible exchange rates. Under such a system, the Canadian government is free to set monetary policy, independent of what is happening to the balance of payments. In fact, since most countries have adopted flexible exchanges, we see inflation rates in the world vary significantly from country to country. In the first half of 1976[6] the inflation rate was 2.2 per cent in Switzerland, 4.9 per cent in West Germany, 5.8 per cent in the United States, 7.9 per cent in Canada, 8.7 per cent in Japan and 15.3 per cent in Britain. It would be difficult to argue today that inflation is a worldwide problem.

In the late 1960's and early 1970's when inflation *was* a worldwide problem this was due to the nature of the fixed exchange rate regime. This system forced increases in world money supplies in response to the U.S. increase in its money supply. The increase in world money supplies led to a worldwide inflation. Thus the monetary theory of inflation is not only capable of explaining inflation in Canada, but it also explains the worldwide inflation of the late 1960's and early 1970's.

2. Confusion of relative prices with the absolute price level

One of the most common sources of confusion in discussions of the subject of inflation is the confusion of relative prices with the absolute price level. Economists refer to the price of all goods and services as the *absolute price level*. Inflation is defined as the percentage increase in the absolute price level. The price of any individual good or service in relation to the price of goods and services in general is known as the *relative price* of that good. When food prices or oil prices increase at a faster rate than other prices we do not have 'oil price inflation' or 'food price inflation' but rather an increase in the relative price of food or oil. This confusion between absolute and relative prices leads to a confusion about the causes of inflation.

The causes of *absolute price* change (i.e. inflation) are never to be found by looking at individual commodity markets. The causes of *relative price* changes always lie in changes in the demand for, or supply of, the particular good or service in question. Consider the case of an increase in the demand for cars by Canadians. This will, in general, increase the price of cars relative to the prices of other goods in Canada. With an increase in the demand for cars, Canadians will be spending more of their income on cars. As a consequence they must spend less of their income on something else and hence must reduce their demand for other commodities. This reduction in demand for other commodities will lead to a fall in the price of these other commodities relative to the price of goods in general. Hence, changes in the demand for, or supply of, one good cannot lead to a general price increase. Individual supply and demand factors are responsible for the fact that the price of one commodity has increased relative to the price of other commodities. They do not explain why the prices of all commodities have been rising. One will not find the cause of inflation by looking at the oil market or looking at the energy market or looking at any other individual commodity market.

The Way Ahead is filled with examples of the confusion between relative prices and the absolute price level. In talking about food and energy prices it is argued in *The Way Ahead* that "it is imperative, however, that price adjustments for particular commodities not be allowed to feed a general inflationary process, to the detriment of all" (p. 14). It is further argued that "excessive tightness in job markets, as in any market, can be an inflationary force" (p. 25).

3. Expectations of inflation are a major cause of inflation

In talking about the Canadian economy before October, 1975, *The Way Ahead* argues: "It was becoming apparent that rapidly rising expectations with respect to future levels of inflation posed grave threats to the stability of the Canadian economic and social system" (p. 7). In looking at theories of inflation one can find that for almost every phenomenon which occurs as a *result* of inflation, some investigator has taken that phenomenon and labelled it as a *cause* of inflation. This is true with the expectations theory also. There are those who believe that expectations of inflation are a cause of inflation. This is not the case. Expectations of inflation are not a *cause* of inflation but an *effect*. When inflation has been around for a while, people expect inflation. When inflation ends, expectations of inflation disappear.

The Way Ahead also presents the view that inflationary expectations were about to suddenly worsen in the summer and fall of 1975: "inflationary expectations had become deeply entrenched and there were indications that they were about to increase to extraordinary levels" (p. 13). Other than citing the example of a few large wage settlements, *The Way Ahead* presents no convincing evidence of this potential increase in inflationary expectations. In fact all the evidence points the other way. When inflationary expectations increase, market interest rates should also increase. Market interest rates as measured by the 30-day Finance Company paper rate were in the 11 per cent range in the fall of 1974 and in the 8 per cent range in the fall of 1975. The inflation rate in September 1975 was 10.6 per cent[7] and the inflation rate for 1974 was 12.4 per cent. In the fall of 1975 interest rates had fallen substantially over the previous year and the inflation rate also was falling. None of these facts point to a picture where inflationary expectations were about to increase to extraordinary levels.

4. Phillips Curve fallacy

During the 1960's some economists believed there was a stable trade-off between inflation and unemployment. This relationship between inflation and unemployment was known as the Phillips Curve. It was believed that to reduce unemployment an economy had to accept a higher degree of inflation. *The Way Ahead* adopts the position of a stable Phillips Curve. "For a large part of this period inflation was fairly moderate, though slowly increasing. It was widely, if reluctantly, accepted as a necessary and fairly tolerable cost of maintaining adequate levels of employment" (p. 9). The empirical evidence from Canada and other countries do not support the hypothesis of a stable trade-off between inflation and unemployment. From 1967 to 1972, and again from 1973 to mid-1975, unemployment rates exhibited a rising trend but so did inflation. Also, looking at a large number of countries there appears to be no correlation between inflation rates and rate of growth of real output or rates of unemployment. The Phillips Curve hypothesis does not appear to be a fruitful place to look for the cause of inflation.

5. The existence of market power is a contributing factor to inflation

"A balanced view must acknowledge that in some markets . . . organizations and institutions exist that have substantial economic power, including the power to set wages and prices in a way that may bear little relation to supply and demand. Although the ability to set prices in this way may not be a critical source of inflation, the use of market power to 'administer' prices can pass on and hence aggravate inflation originating from excess aggregate demand or from specific price increases" (p. 16). Hence, *The Way Ahead* views monopoly power as contributing to inflation. What this theory confuses is the concept of high prices versus the concept of rising prices. What is true about monopoly power is that monopolists restrict supply and cause a higher price to prevail in that market than would be the case if the market were competitively organized. Monopoly power can be responsible for a higher relative price in the monopolized sector; it is not responsible for high rates of increase in prices in the monopolized sector.

6. Economic growth or the lack of it may be responsible for inflation

At first glance, economists who believe in the monetary theory of inflation would find little to disagree with in the statement that the long-run rate of growth of real output will influence the long-run inflation rate. In fact, the monetary theory of inflation would argue that for any given rate of growth of the money supply, the greater is the rate of growth of real output, the lower will be the inflation rate. *The Way Ahead* introduces a new argument why economic growth may affect the inflation rate. This argument links economic growth to greed. In one part of *The Way Ahead*, it is argued that the higher the rate of growth of real output, the higher the inflation rate. In another part of *The Way Ahead* the exact opposite stance is taken. Lower economic growth, it is argued, leads to higher inflation rates. As we shall see, this is certainly a 'robust' argument.

(a) Higher economic growth leads to higher inflation rates

"Growth itself has been a contributing factor to inflation. While growth has brought about a substantial increase in average levels of economic well-being, the inequity of the distribution of its benefits both within and among nations has been a principal source of a restless quarrel over shares that has seriously escalated over the past few years" (p. 18). *The Way Ahead* seems to be arguing that although economic growth has improved everyone's lot in an absolute sense, it has not improved the lot of lower income groups in a relative sense.[8] It is hard to see the role that growth is playing in this process. If there were no growth it is certain lower income groups would be worse off in an absolute sense but in all probability there would be no change in their relative position. The major problem with this theory as with all theories that explain inflation in terms of greed is that the theory has no explanatory power. People have always been greedy. *Why didn't greed cause inflation during the Great Depression? Why didn't greed cause inflation in 1960 to 1965? Did greed break out in 1965, then subside in 1970 and then once again raise its ugly head in the 1971 to 1975 period?* It is hard to believe, as *The Way Ahead* states, that greed has seriously escalated over the past few years and this has contributed to inflation.

(b) Lower economic growth, caused by declining productivity, leads to higher inflation rates

"The confrontation that may occur between lower rates of future growth and increasing income expectations of Canadians could create new inflationary forces" (p. 17). Here, *The Way Ahead* seems to be arguing that lower economic growth will cause people's incomes in an absolute sense to be lower than they expected. Presumably, this causes an increase in greed and leads to inflation. As we have stated previously there is no theoretical or empirical support for the greed theory of inflation.

It is interesting to note though, that according to The Way Ahead, if we have economic growth this will lead to inflation. If we stagnate and do not grow, this will also lead to inflation. The Way Ahead thus appears to be fairly pessimistic about future inflation rates. In The Way Ahead it appears that inflation is inevitable. If the government seriously believed this, one cannot help but wonder what good temporary wage and price controls will do.

7. Even if the government plays a crucial role in the inflationary process, it is only doing so in response to social and economic needs

At various parts in *The Way Ahead*, the government comes close to admitting that there is a possibility that governments play a crucial role in the inflationary process. "To understand the inflationary process, and the issues surrounding the role that governments play in that process, it is necessary to examine those aspects of our social and economic structure that lead to inflation directly or indirectly through demands on government — to spend money and to intervene in the economic system" (p. 16). *The Way Ahead* seems to be making the case that if the government is doing anything to fuel the fires of inflation, the government should not be blamed. The government's action is only in response to social and economic pressure.

This view comes dangerously close to the proposition that the government can do no wrong. For whatever the government does, it is acting in the best interests of the nation. Of course the government is always acting in response to social and economic pressures. At various times these pressures are conflicting. A good government knows the long-run interests of the nation and knows which pressures should be acted upon and which should not. When the government errs in these choices it must be held accountable for its mistakes. Inflation in the last decade in Canada has been caused by excessive Federal government printing of money. The Federal government must bear the chief responsibility for the current bout of inflation in Canada.

Notes

[1] In the first half of 1976, 50 million dollars worth of direct investment entered the country while 220 million dollars of direct investment left the country.

[2] This fallacy is at least new to me.

[3] See J.L. Carr, "Wage and Price Controls: Panacea for Inflation or Prescription for Disaster?", in M. Walker, ed., *The Illusion of Wage and Price Control*, Fraser Institute, 1976.

[4] Figure 2 is reproduced from Anna Schwartz, "Secular Price Change in Historical Perspective," *Journal of Money, Credit and Banking*, February, 1973.

[5] According to the monetary theory excessive government expenditures which are financed by excessive printing of money will result in inflation.

[6] In comparison to a similar period in 1975.

[7] This measures the inflation rate from September 1974 to September 1975.

[8] The statistics for the Canadian economy show no appreciable change in the distribution of income during the post World War II period. This result is because no correction for such factors as age is taken into account in computing these income distributions. In fact, there is some preliminary evidence to indicate that when age is taken into account, income distributions in Canada show a significant trend towards a more equal distribution of income.

Thoughts on
The Way Ahead

LOUIS N. CHRISTOFIDES

Assistant Professor of Economics
University of Guelph

THE AUTHOR

Louis N. Christofides was born in Cyprus in 1946, and educated at the University of Essex in England and the University of British Columbia, where he received his Ph.D. in 1973. An Assistant Professor at the University of Guelph, he is also a member of the editorial board of the *Canadian Journal of Economics* and is a consultant to the Anti-Inflation Board. In 1974 he was a member of the Financial Markets Group of the Economic Council of Canada.

Professor Christofides' publications include: "Are Government Expenditures Likely to be Contractionary?" *Public Finance*, 1974; "Supply Variables in Term Structure Equations," the *Canadian Journal of Economics*, 1975; "The Conversion Loan of 1958: A Simulation Study of its Macroeconomic Consequences" (with J.F. Helliwell and J.M. Lester), the *Canadian Journal of Economics*, 1976; "Quadratic Costs and Multi-Asset Partial Adjustment Equations," *Applied Economics*, 1976.

Thoughts on
The Way Ahead

LOUIS N. CHRISTOFIDES

Assistant Professor of Economics
University of Guelph

I. INTRODUCTION

The Way Ahead is a "framework for discussion;" the introduction (pp. 7-8) sets the stage: the story begins in October 1975, when the government, faced with a high rate of inflation, instituted direct price and income controls, laying to rest all efforts to reach a voluntary agreement to that effect. *The Way Ahead* (henceforth also referred to as the document) makes it perfectly clear that no controls are preferable to voluntary controls which are, in turn, preferable to the current situation. Since the inexorable force of events led us into the worst possible alternative (the "breathing space" provided by our system of direct controls), it would be desirable to find our way out of it before 1978 when, in any case, controls will elapse. To that end, we must look for a set of conditions which, if attained, will signify that the AIB's objectives have been fulfilled. We are given a clue as to the possible nature of these conditions when we read that the programme of controls "is working," i.e. that the rate of inflation is decreasing. A related task is the achievement of a "shared appreciation of how the economy works" (p. 8).

What we might have expected

An introduction conditions the reader's expectations about the content of a paper. It seemed reasonable to look forward to a discussion along the following lines: *First*, an analysis of the forces that made the rate of inflation what it was in October 1975; this would also be consistent with the document's declared objective of educating the public. *Second*, a consideration of the possible costs and benefits associated with direct controls, voluntary controls and no controls and a clarification of the much brandished concept of the "breathing space." *Third*, an outline of how direct controls may impinge on the economy and hence how they might ultimately outlive their usefulness; at that point they can be abandoned. One expects to see here a discussion of how the economy might have behaved without controls and how it has with them, thereby also justifying the statement that the programme has been successful. *Finally*, the inevitable lessons from history: how can we prevent the rate of inflation from ever again attaining the heights of 1974-75.

II. WHAT WE GOT

About the causes of inflation

The first point is implicitly addressed in the first three sections of the document. Section one, "The Inflationary Process," mentions a number of plausible causes of inflation (p. 9), though at times (p. 10) it comes perilously close to confusing causes with characteristics of inflation. Section two, "Canadian Economic Performance: Retrospect and Prospect," outlines the sequence of events that led to the imposition of controls and documents their effectiveness in terms of the encouraging decline in the rate of inflation — we return to this point later. What is intriguing about this section is that it appears to downplay many of the accepted explanations of the inflation of 1973-76: the increase in the prices of food and oil only "compounded" inflationary pressures. Similarly fiscal and monetary policies merely "reinforced" such pressures.

The real villain of the piece appears in Section three, "Sources of Inflationary Pressure," which, on the basis of past experience, appears to be looking for pressures likely to arise in the 1980's. "To diagnose the inflationary spiral we have recently experienced as largely attributable to a profligate government ... is misleading. Such a diagnosis ignores the fact that the recent acceleration of inflation was a worldwide phenomenon" (p. 15). One is tempted here to retort that all governments may have been profligate! "To understand the inflationary process ... it is necessary to examine those aspects of our social and economic structure that lead to inflation directly or indirectly through demands on government — to spend money and to intervene in the economic system" (p. 16). This position constitutes the gist of the document and it is supported as follows.

It is first argued that economic actors with market power "pass on and hence aggravate inflation originating from excess aggregate demand or from specific price increases" (p. 16). This argument is not convincing since increases in demand and/or costs would raise prices even in perfectly competitive markets. The more familiar argument that monopolization results in lower output and higher prices requires increasing market concentration if it is to account for sustained price rises over a period of time. But even this argument holds only in a world of certainty. Galbraithians are now beginning to argue that firms with latent market power use it to reduce profit variance by *reducing prices* below certainty levels.

A second argument offered is that labour force and productivity growth may fall short of expectations of income growth, resulting in inflationary pressures. This is a plausible explanation of some inflation but it is not clear whether it is meant to apply to past or future experience in the 1980's.

The document then notes that Canada is, due to its substantial openness, likely to import inflations originating abroad. Even flexible exchange rates cannot protect us in periods of "worldwide and coincidental price increases" (p. 18). The reason is not at all clear unless the authors meant to introduce additional considerations such as an upper bound on the amount of exchange rate appreciation that will be politically tolerated.

Last, but not least, "growth itself has been a contributing factor to inflation" (p. 18), as individuals scramble to reap the fruits of growth. It is, however, all the more likely that this scramble will be more intense in a situation of no growth.

In addition to the above difficulties, what is sadly lacking from *The Way Ahead* is an attempt to assign explicit weights to all the factors mentioned; this omission plagues many a section of the document. However, one does get the impression that the problem lies mainly in the demands placed on governments *to re-redistribute incomes redistributed by inflation* (a good example of this was the Fall 1974 unilateral change in the terms of Canada Savings Bonds contracts, making it possible to pay holders a higher interest income), *to make good environmental degradation* caused by growth based on private, rather than social, cost-benefit calculations and *to act in the interests of power groups*. It is no wonder that the document pleads ". . . if we want governments to do less . . . we as individuals will have to do more" (p. 27). An optimistic interpretation of statements such as this one is that the government is hereby serving notice that it may refuse to be bulldozed into actions furthering the interest of politically-active groups.

About the costs and benefits of controls

Turning now to the costs and benefits of controls, one reads that inflation "posed grave threats to the stability of the Canadian economic and social system" and that direct controls were imposed "only after a sustained effort to arrive at a voluntary consensus had broken down" (p. 7). The failure to achieve a voluntary consensus posed a nasty philosophical dilemma for liberal ideology: controls had to be justified as a sort of War Measures Act, to guarantee "freedom from inflation" (p. 7). Thus the ultimate justification for controls offered in the document, and here one has to read between the lines, is a political one. A related, economic one, that of "freedom from inflation" as a public good, is not hinted at.

The concept of the "breathing space" is such a frequently used one that it is worthy of brief reflection. It is intended to evoke a picture of calm and tranquillity, a time during which physical processes are suspended, yet the mind continues to puzzle over problems of the land. Once solutions are found, undoubtedly by Oiko Nomos, blood rushes to hitherto immobile limbs and full life resumes. Unfortunately, this cannot be. Life, modified by an additional set of constraints, does continue during the breathing space. These constraints could have three effects. Controls could be redundant, an unlikely prospect. Second, controls could help us get further ahead than we would have without them. This is possible even if we would not voluntarily institute them, as controls may be a public good. Finally, controls may inhibit our progress, or even take us in a different direction than the desired one, with obvious costs. It is likely that even economists who support controls may grant the third possibility, but think that the second nevertheless dominates. In any case, the picture evoked by the term "breathing space" is hardly apt.

About the abolition of controls

The third point mentioned above that we might have expected to see covered is not addressed in *The Way Ahead*. There is, therefore, no basis on which to conclude that controls have outlived their usefulness and should be disbanded. Nor can we conclude that they have been successful (p. 7, 13). It is conceivable that the inflation rate would now be no different if controls had never been imposed. Indeed, some would argue that the AIB's *maxima* have been treated as *minima*, suggesting that wage claims would have been lower without controls. Given the approach taken in the document, it is no surprise that our fourth expectation is not addressed either.

III. OTHER COMMENTS

A number of other comments are now in order. Section three of the document concludes by identifying "three basic views as to the role of governments in the social and economic system" (p. 21). Supporters of a *minimal role for government* would argue that "the benefits to be gained by ... intervention ... are short-term and outweighed by the longer-run 'costs' of lost efficiency and output, and higher inflation" (p. 21). There is a confusion here between once-and-for-all and continuing price increases. Some government may lead to inefficiencies and, if aggregate demand is not correspondingly reduced, prices may conceivably rise. But inflation requires increasing government interference. A second group argues for a *continually expanding government role* and feel that "the ultimate sources of inflation are to be found both in market 'failures' and in the incapacity of the market system to serve social goals" (pp. 21-2). It is not at all obvious how market failures, as economists understand them, lead to inflation. As to the problem of attaining a particular income distribution the authorities should attempt to accomplish this through a system of transfers, rather than becoming involved in a host of productive activities best left to the private sector. The authors of the document opt for the third, *middle view*: "the inflationary consequences of government actions reside less in the ends that governments have sought to pursue than in a choice of means" (p. 23). This compromise basically accepts the view of the second group and reasserts that inflation is caused by market failures and various social pressures which lead to increasing government intervention. This position amounts to a virtual abdication of any responsibility with respect to control of inflation.

In the fourth and last section, "The Role of Government in the Post-Control Period," appropriate policies are discussed, apparently within the bounds set by the *middle view*. It is reassuring to find that the government is reluctant to assume sole responsibility for labour retraining and mobility programmes and to immerse itself further into price support programmes whose real purpose is to redistribute income. It is also reassuring to see some concern expressed about the inability of the current collective bargaining system to deliver binding contracts without a disturbingly high number of man-days lost. Unfortunately, the suggestion made by the Prime Minister to consider amalgamating bargaining units is not entertained by the document. The plans to encourage energy conservation and recycling, to discourage built-in obsolescence and some forms of advertising and to make polluters accountable for their actions are laudable, but one wonders why these are "post-control," rather than "right-now" policies. It is, finally, regretful that the plans to redesign and integrate social assistance programmes may, now, not materialize.

The Case for Continued Controls (and other Heresies)

JAMES W. DEAN

Associate Professor of Economics
Simon Fraser University

THE AUTHOR

James W. Dean is an Associate Professor in the Department of Economics and Commerce at Simon Fraser University. Born in 1941, he received a B.Sc. degree from Carleton University in 1962 and his Ph.D. degree from Harvard University in 1973. Besides having been Director of the Canadian Studies Programme at Simon Fraser University and a Research Officer for the Royal Commission on Taxation in 1963-1964, he has held academic posts at Seikei University, Tokyo, and the University of Reading in England.

Professor Dean's main research interests lie in the field of monetary policy and banking. Among his publications, he has contributed: "Monetary Policy in Canada: Instruments, Targets, and the Links Between Them," in *Canadian Perspectives in Economics*, which was edited by J.F. Chant and published by Collier-Macmillan Canada in 1972; "Problems in the Specification and Interpretation of Central Bank Reaction Functions" in *Economic and Social Review*, July, 1974; "The 1977 Bank Act: A Comment," in *Canadian Public Policy*, Summer 1976; "Bank Act Revision in Canada: Past and Potential Effects on Market Structure and Competition" (with R. Schwindt), in *Banca Nazionale del Lavoro — Quarterly Review*, March, 1976.

The Case for Continued Controls (and other Heresies)

JAMES W. DEAN

Associate Professor of Economics
Simon Fraser University

I. INTRODUCTION

Few will find the Government's *Framework for Discussion* [ref. no. 5] offensive. It reaffirms a fundamental belief in market mechanisms, but not without concessionary nods to a wide range of extra-market phenomena of which the modern Liberal must, to be fashionable, be apprised. One senses a faint tone of apology for growth in government and in particular its contribution to inflation. One senses further a note of promised retribution for the Prime Minister's Galbraithian outbursts last year and for the imposition of price and income controls. Nevertheless the authors, as Liberals, cannot ignore extra-market evils: beyond some empty exhortation to "all segments of society" to "work together" for "sharing, compassion, tolerance and responsibility towards others" (p. 28), they recognize their relegation to the tightrope path of "less expenditure-oriented [strategies] to serve the [growing] legitimate social concerns of government" (p. 23).

What the authors fail to consider are coherent radical alternatives to the eclectic "middle road" (p. 22) they advocate. Perhaps their reluctance to argue from the left reflects simply the political stance of a Government currently weakened and unpopular due to its adoption of controls and the Prime Minister's initial intimation of more to come. And to argue from the radical right would be most unliberal indeed.

A more generous reading would assign the Government at this stage the role of simple disgorgement and display of the issues. Judged by that criterion, the *Working Paper* is quite adequate. This interpretation, I would argue, assigns to us the citizenry a responsibility to state well-defined and contentious positions, so that meaningful debate may follow. This I will attempt to do.

I will argue in favour of continued price and income controls. I will argue further that such controls must and will be part of a more general framework of governmentally-planned resource allocation within the next few decades. To deny this is to deny the existence of inequitably distributed market and extra-market power.

II. THE INCONVENIENT ECONOMISTS

Just ten years ago, my fellow graduate students and I at Harvard were at best dimly aware of the shortcomings of neoclassical economic theory. J.K. Galbraith was considered an incompetent crank and W. Leontief, although more popular because of his relatively self-effacing personal charm, was judged a technocrat whose input/output tools could be sold at profit to the coal industry but whose politics were best ignored.

Seven years later, the challenge to neoclassicism was well enough established that the question of tenure for a left-radical junior professor united the graduate *corpus* behind him and split the senior faculty. These graduate students are now entering the profession; some have even infiltrated the University of Chicago. It would be naive to assume that they will not influence economic policy within their lifetimes.

The partial radicalization of Harvard is simply the most dramatic and potentially influential North American example of a revolution in thought that in time will profoundly affect government. Some of the early dissenters are now advisors to J. Carter. With the usual cultural lag, the revolution will also reach the Government of Canada. The academic revolution has also been aided greatly by recent events which neither neoclassicism nor conventional Keynesianism could digest; simultaneously rising unemployment and inflation rates is the most obvious example. Governments, with little support from reputable economists, have responded pragmatically with emergency programmes of control that have been doomed by their *adhoccery* and lack of coherence to limited success.

If conventional theory and policy is bankrupt, where should a responsible government turn? The new generation of theorists is too green. There exists, however, a small and motley collection of "inconvenient economists"[1] who have been with us all along but whom those of us in the profession have employed mainly as butts for our cocktail humour. To name a few: P.M. Sweezy, J. Robinson, J.K. Galbraith, W.A. Weisskopf, S. Weintraub, E.F. Schumacher, E.J. Mishan, K.E. Boulding and J.E. Meade.[2] These people cover a wide political spectrum running (very roughly) from left to right in the order I have listed them. But most of them would quite properly resist placement on a unidimensional political scale, and that constitutes part of their inconvenience. Their ideas are widely dissimilar, but their uniting virtue is that they all radically repudiate parts of current orthodoxy in economic theory and policy.

For this they have, understandably, been reviled by the profession and otherwise, as much as possible, ignored. Little wonder that no government which is closely in touch with established economic opinion will espouse them. Even P. Trudeau, normally known for his existential indifference, was so defensive when accused by *Fortune* magazine (August 1976) of Galbraithian leanings that he invoked his deep intellectual indebtedness to an economist whose belief in free markets was profound: Joseph Schumpeter.[3]

III. CONTROVERTING THE CONVENTIONAL WISDOM

The question of price and income controls is one on which the *Working Paper* predictably defers to current orthodoxy. It opposes their continuance. Yet one need not stretch plausibility too far to admit the existence of disparate degrees of market power in the Canadian economy. Our market structure is one of the most concentrated in the world. [ref. no. 1, p. 119]. Given this, one need not push logic too hard to argue that unions which possess significant monopoly power will obtain wage increases which exceed productivity increases and that firms with significant monopoly power will protect their profits by passing these wage increases forward in the form of price increases.[4]† Alternatively, the process may originate with firms which attempt to enhance their profits: the OPEC oil suppliers' recent price hikes illustrated this most dramatically (read "sheiks" for "firms"). It is important also to recognize that the rubric "firms" in this context applies equally to government-sanctioned monopolies such as marketing boards.

Moreover, and this is where orthodoxy would beg to differ, this process will prove inflationary even when fiscal

---

†Editor's note: The Canadian economy is also heavily dependent on international trade especially in the key resource extraction sectors. The reader might well ask how it is that Canadian industry can shift wage costs forward when the prices it receives in foreign markets are determined in world markets. The fact that the wage gains cannot effectively be reflected in higher prices explains why it is that monopoly power by unions leads to unemployment. This fact is acknowledged by the author in a subsequent paragraph. In any event, the question of the "power" of the firm and inflation has been thoroughly researched in Canada by the former Prices and Incomes Commission. In their final report they state, ". . . the Commission's studies make it seem unlikely that differences in price-setting behaviour associated with industrial concentration or the size of firms play any large or continuing role in the process of inflation." Prices and Incomes Commission, Final Report, *Inflation, Unemployment and Incomes Policy*, Information Canada, 1972, p. 63.

and monetary authorities attempt restraint.† The reason is that were the rate of increase of aggregate demand successfully held to the summed rates of increase of productivity and the labour force, the price and wage increases emanating from monopolistic sellers would necessarily result either in compensating price and wage declines elsewhere, or in factor unemployment, most importantly of labour. Given that price and wage decline in more competitive industries would be both inequitable and allocatively inefficient, and given in any case that prices and wages are notoriously inflexible downward, the realistic outcome of demand restraint accompanied by structurally-caused inflation is unemployment.

Therefore it is a rare government that will maintain demand restraint for long. Almost inevitably, sufficient money will be printed to fund the structurally-originating inflation without rising unemployment.[5] This, of course, eases the demand constraint to which monopolistic sellers were originally subject, and sets the stage for a second round of inflation which will build on the first.†† Eventually the inflation rate rises to such an intolerable level that government will

---

† Editor's Note: It is unclear which of the "inconvenient economists" the author is following here: it certainly is not Galbraith. ". . . As a practical matter, both under the competition model and with countervailing power, a continuing upward movement of prices requires continuing additions to demand beyond that made available by current production. *A government deficit*, consumer expenditures from past savings, *a boomtime increase in* business and consumer *bank borrowing* or some combination of all these is necessary to sustain the movement." (emphasis added). J.K. Galbraith, *American Capitalism*, Houghton Mifflin Co., Boston, 1952, p. 193. In other words, Galbraith is saying that one way or another there must be excess demand for inflation to occur. The examples that Galbraith has chosen all involve either increases in the money supply or its velocity of circulation.

†† Editor's Note: It is important to note that Professor Dean is herein acknowledging the fact that inflation cannot proceed without the tacit approval of government in the form of increased printing of money. In other words, structural changes, such as those associated with OPEC, are sometimes the *occasion* for money supply fueled inflations but are not *causes* in any sense of the word.

either sacrifice employment for monetary and fiscal restraint, or impose temporary wage/price controls (long enough to "break inflationary expectations").[†]

Current conundrums

But why is it only recently that this process has come to a head? Surely if we are to buy the notion of structurally-caused inflation we must, as one group analyzing the *Working Paper* has put it, isolate "the precise *shifts* in market power that account/for [its recent] inflationary impact" [ref. no. 3, p. 3]. Well, there have been some recent "shifts," most notably on the part of oil producers and other commodity suppliers that were encouraged by their example. Monetary and fiscal restraint would have proved much too draconian, or so most governments felt; thus demand-pull reinforced structural-push.[††] But I am not prepared to argue that the recent dramatic increase in inflation rates had its sole or even primary origin in structural pressures. It is undoubtedly true that governments have become less responsible about constraining aggregate demand. This is due to misguided Keynesian belief in a nonvertical long-run Phillips Curve, combined with the technical fact that output and employment respond more rapidly to monetary restraint than do prices, plus the political fact that governments have become increasingly sensitive to unemployment. Nevertheless to recognize that much recent pressure on aggregate demand originated independently of market power does not deny the partial originating, and more importantly exacerbating, role that such power played.

[†]Editor's Note: The possibility of the scenario that Professor Dean has outlined is well-known. For example, see my examination of the Canadian evidence of an indirect transmission of inflationary pressure from union power through the money supply. This evidence, while not strong, does not seem to support Dean's hypotheses. See M. Walker, "Inflation Dialogue," in M. Walker, Editor, *The Illusion of Wage and Price Control*, The Fraser Institute, 1976, pp. 223-225. The evidence from the U.S. doesn't support Dean's position either. See Milton Friedman, *Unemployment Versus Inflation?, An Evaluation of the Phillips Curve*, The Institute of Economic Affairs, London, 1975, p. 33.

[††]Editor's Note: It is unclear who "most" governments are. In the case of Germany, Japan and the U.S. the monetary brakes were firmly applied in the face of the OPEC oil price increases.

Moreover, if we are to accept the monetarists' policy prescription, we must live with a "natural" rate of unemployment in perpetuity.[6] Surely it is arguable that this "natural" rate is in part due to the fiscal and monetary restraint which is necessary if inflation is to be confined to that rate which market power makes inevitable.† Therefore it is also arguable that market power was an operative source of inflation and potential inflation, but more importantly an indirect cause of unemployment, throughout the fifties and sixties. One could also argue that in this country and elsewhere the market power of both labour and business has increased secularly over the last three decades due to the increasing scope of labour unions and concentration of industry.

The options

Therefore we are faced with a choice. On the one hand we can follow the monetarist prescription and confine ourselves to a policy of steady monetary and fiscal restraint. Restraint, I would contend, is unlikely in practice to prove lasting because of market pressure from sellers with monopoly power. To the extent it does last, it relegates us to a permanent "natural" rate of unemployment. On the other hand we can accept the reality of market power and attempt to control it directly.[7]

---

†Editor's Note: Perhaps a more significant cause of the increase in the "natural rate" has been recent changes in government policy toward employment insurance schemes. More generous programmes have, at the very least, increased the amount of time job seekers take to find a new job once they have become unemployed. This effect, in itself, increases the measured unemployment rate. For more analysis of this point for the Canadian Case see H. Grubel, D. Maki and S. Sax, "Real and Insurance Induced Unemployment in Canada," *Canadian Journal of Economics*, May 1975, pp. 174-191. In a forthcoming publication, the Fraser Institute will be publishing a series of studies that documents this effect in eight countries around the world. In this volume, Professor H.G. Grubel, a colleague of Professor Dean, presents an overview of the effects of government programmes on the unemployment rate.

It is no longer a novel notion that there would be a very high inflationary cost associated with attempting to reduce unemployment below, say, the "natural" level with aggregative tools alone. One must only concede the importance of "bottlenecks" due to labour immobility to support the use of disaggregative stimulatory measures such as government spending or tax reductions in low employment regions of the country. In cases of labour market disequilibrium across industries, it is generally wiser to retrain and otherwise subsidize labour mobility, but the principle remains: few would argue that secular unemployment can be reduced through ordinary monetary and fiscal policy.

It is surprising, therefore, that we are so reluctant to accept the notion of a disaggregative attack on inflation. Uneven sources of inflationary pressure can be viewed as an analogue of uneven sources of unemployment, requiring a similarly disaggregated response. To be sure, let us practice appropriate aggregate restraint, but let us also recognize that aggregate demand restraint does not homogeneously restrain prices across all markets.

The crux

We come now to the crux. Just how is it possible to administer wage/price controls without incurring unconscionable costs of resource misallocation due to the inhibition of relative price movements? *First*, it is important to remember that the costs of resource misallocation from unemployment and inflation are themselves immense; thus controls at *some* non-zero cost can be justified if they help at all. *Second*, no one advocates fixing a million prices: the markets that would be chosen are relatively few in number, although large in terms of volumes traded and important in terms of their impact on other markets.

Third, controls may take a myriad of forms. The more rigid the form, the more complementary control over resource allocation would be necessary. Controls during World War II were moderately successful because we ac-

cepted the presence of dollar-a-year men in Ottawa who controlled the production of everything from steel to wheat.†
Although planning to that extent would be unacceptable to most of us, the Government should and implicitly does recognize the inevitability of more planning in the future. The large corporations already prodigiously plan their own affairs and also spend large sums spying on the plans of others. Private agencies and governments at every level devote vast sums to forecasts and plans. But, in North America at least, coordinated planning at the national level is still in its infancy. There is little doubt that the private sector could gain from careful "indicative" planning.[8,9] National planning would also be an indispensible complement to strict wage/price control in order to effect relative price changes without excessive resource missallocation.

But we do not have indicative planning, or anything like it. Therefore the kind of wage/price control that I advocate would stop far short of actual price setting. I would suggest that some form of tax be levied on increases in those key wages and prices that are subject to administered pressures.††

---

†Editor's Note: It is doubtful that controls were even "moderately successful" during World War II. See R.L. Schuettinger, "The Historical Record," in M. Walker, Editor, *The Illusion of Wage and Price Controls*, The Fraser Institute, 1976, p. 87 ff.

††Editor's Note: This suggestion of Professor Dean was the subject of some debate in the Federal Civil Service during early 1970. In its final report, the Prices and Incomes Commission, in commenting on the implementation of such an excess income tax, said: "In the end, however, the conclusion was reached that it was extremely difficult to devise a system along these lines which was sufficiently equitable, administratively workable and reasonably certain to produce the desired effects on private behaviour." The Prices and Incomes Commission, Final Report, *Inflation, Unemployment and Incomes Policy*, pp. 54-55.

A tax on wage gains

For example in the British context, James Meade suggests the following [ref. no. 8, pp. 59-60].[10] The government would set, from time to time, an "x per cent norm" for the annual rate of increase of wage earnings. Should a wage agreement be reached in excess of that norm, regulations would come into effect which curbed the bargaining power of the relevant workers. Strikers would lose accumulated rights to unemployment payments, social benefits paid for their support would become their liability or that of their union, and the union would be taxed on strike benefits paid out to its members. I would suggest further that the sums saved and taxes raised in this way be diverted to the Unemployment Insurance Fund.

A proposal of the above kind would probably have the additional benefit of reducing strike time. Manhours lost in this country due to strikes have by now permeated the public consciousness sufficiently that strike-deterrent measures might even be popular. The connection between compulsory arbitration and a national wage policy hinges on the degree of decentralization involved in arbitration, but it is clear that the potential exists to attack two problems — lost strike time and inflationary wage claims — with one policy.

A tax on price hikes

But no incomes policy should confine its attentions to wages. To ignore prices would not only be politically infeasible, and for good reason, but would ignore a major source of administered inflation. The counterpart of the kind of wage strategy outlined above would be to tax increases in potentially administered prices. The tax could be at a flat rate or progressive; it could take effect above x per cent per annum where x might be as low as zero.[11] The details would obviously require careful thought. (e.g. to what extent might income effects of the tax counteract its substitution effects?) I am merely suggesting that if we do deem administered pricing to have serious actual or potential long-run inflationary repercussions, we ought to think realistically about least cost long-run policies to combat it.

The virtue of a tax deterrent to administered inflation is that it would interfere minimally with relative price movements. This is not to claim that it would allocate resources optimally, but simply that its misallocation costs might be lower than we would otherwise incur from inflation, unemployment or both. In neoclassical terms, the tax deterrent policy views administered inflation as a diseconomy external to the union or firm, and attempts to tax it accordingly.

A word of unconventional wisdom

There are many other lessons the inconvenient economists could teach us. The one I have just sketched out is among the least startling. I have the following closing advice for our Government: Do not be mesmerised by your economists. Do not be afraid to trust your own judgment and that of your constituents. And read the bibliography I have appended.

Notes

[1]This term was coined by Myron Sharpe to describe J.K. Galbraith, (*Challenge* magazine, Sept./Oct. 1973).

[2]It is widely believed that Joan Robinson has been payrolled by Peking since she wrote, *The Economics of Imperfect Competition*; that Kenneth Boulding lost his senses shortly after the publication of *Economic Analysis*, and that James Meade died when he finished, *The Geometry of International Trade*.

[3]The invocation was edited from the *Fortune* article, but the full transcript of the interview was later released in Ottawa (*Maclean's* magazine, September 20, 1976).

[4]The *Working Paper* acknowledges the existence of market power, "at least in the short to medium run" (p. 16). That admission is all that is necessary to initiate the process I am about to describe.

[5]Monetary expansion may be undertaken deliberately, or more commonly (since central bankers are both politically insensitive and sensibly conservative) as a byproduct of deficit fiscal finance.

There is also the technical problem that most central banks' efforts to control the monetary base are subject to serious demand pressures. The system of lagged reserve requirements in effect both here and in the U.S. allows banks to generate deposits in the current averaging period without generating current reserve requirements [ref. no. 12]. Central banks are understandably fearful of the money market consequences of forcing an expanding banking system to contract in the next averaging period, and typically validate deposits generated currently by simply supplying sufficient reserves when they come due.

A second source of demand pressures on the money supply in Canada is the Bank of Canada's tradition of targeting the excess reserve ratio. The Bank often cannot distinguish between decreases in this ratio due to its own restriction of the *supply* of reserves, and the banks' increase in *demand* for reserves due to deposit expansion. Thus in the latter case the Bank will simply fund increases in the demand for money by increasing the supply of reserves. The Bank's recent adoption of monetary growth targets is therefore an important step toward improved monetary control.

[6]The latest dismal econometric consensus is that this rate was a full 5 per cent as early as 1948 and has climbed since then to 5.5 - 6 per cent. *Fortune* magazine (Sept. 1976) cheerfully hails the news that the U.S. could sustain near-zero inflation rates at these levels of unemployment with the title, "We've Learned How to Lick Inflation!"

[7]This is not to suggest that measures to contain and diminish monopoly power — through competition, the desanctioning of government monoplies, etc. — should be eschewed. It is merely to recognize that General Motors and the like will remain powerful despite the Department of Consumer and Corporate Affairs.

[8]This is the word the French have used to describe their brand of planning. In a different context one of our "inconvenient economists," James Meade, a firm believer in the usefulness of market mechanisms, employed the term in 1970 [ref. no. 9]. Meade refers to a process designed to simulate the allocative results that would be achieved were there a comprehensive set of competitive forward markets including markets for contingency goods.

[9]In 1975, Wassily Leontief and a number of other distinguished Americans formed the Initiative Committee for National Economic Planning. It was in part responsible for the sponsorship of a bill to Congress by Senators Humphrey and Javits entitled, "The Balanced Growth and Economic Planning Act of 1975." Of course the bill did not pass. But it is not inconceivable that something similar might pass under the Carter administration. A fact often cited during the Carter campaign was that during the 1973 "oil crisis" the U.S. Government proved incapable of calculating the country's existing stocks of oil. [Editor's Note: The problem is one of some difficulty and has more to do with the nature of the supply of oil process itself than with the institutional framework. See, *Oil in the Seventies*, edited by Campbell Watkins, the Fraser Institute, 1977.]

[10]I lay this out here because not one of my professional acquaintances this side of the Atlantic has read Meade's superb *The Intelligent Radical's Guide to Economic Policy*.

[11]A similar proposal was made several years ago by Henry Wallich and another of the inconvenient economists [ref. no. 16, Chapter 6]. They proposed using adjustments in the corporate income tax to deter firms from submitting to wage inflation.

Bibliography

1. Bain, Joe S., *International Differences in Industrial Structure* (New Haven: Yale Univ. Press, 1966).

2. Baran, P.A. and P.M. Sweezy, *Monopoly Capital* (New York: Monthly Review Press, 1966).

3. Beigie, Carl E., and Gail C.A. Cook, Judith Maxwell and Caroline Pestieau, *Comments on the Federal Government's Recent Working Paper* (Montreal: C.D. Howe Research Inst. Nov. 18, 1976).

4. Boulding, K.E., *The Economics of Love and Fear* (Belmont, Calif.: Wadsworth, 1973).

5. Canada, Government of, *The Way Ahead: A Framework for Discussion*, Working Paper (Ottawa: 1976).

6. Galbraith, J.K., *Economics and the Public Purpose* (Boston: Houghton Mifflin, 1973).

7. Leontief, Wassily, and Herbert Stein, *The Economic System in an Age of Discontinuity: Long Range Planning or Market Reliance?* (New York: NYU Press, 1976).

8. Meade, James E., *The Intelligent Radical's Guide to Economic Policy* (London: Allen & Unwin, 1975).

9. Meade, James E., *The Theory of Indicative Planning* (Manchester: Manchester University Press, 1970).

10. Mishan, E.J., *The Costs of Economic Growth* (London: Staples Press, 1967).

11. Mishan, E.J., *21 Popular Economic Fallacies* (New York: Praeger, 1970).

12. Poole, William, "A Proposal for Reforming Bank Reserve Requirements in the United States", *Journal of Money, Credit and Banking* (May 1976).

13. Robinson, Joan, *Economic Heresies: Some Old-Fashioned Questions in
14. Robinson, Joan, Economics: An Awkward Corner* (London: Allen & Unwin, 1966).

15. Schumacher, E.F., *Small is Beautiful* (London: Blond & Brigges, 1973).

16. Weintraub, Sidney, with Hamid Habibagahi, Henry Wallich, and E. Roy Weintraub, *Keynes and the Monetarists, and Other Essays* (New Brunswick, N.J.: Rutgers University Press, 1973).

17. Weisskoph, Walter A., *Alienation and Economics* (New York: E.P. Dutton, 1971).

The Way Ahead
A Comment on
The Framework for Discussion

JOHN E. FLOYD

Professor, Department of Political Economy
University of Toronto

THE AUTHOR

John E. Floyd, a native of Saskatchewan, was born in 1937. He did his undergraduate work at the University of Saskatchewan, and received his Ph.D. from the University of Chicago in 1964. He previously held a post at the University of Washington, and is now a professor in the Department of Political Economy at the University of Toronto. Among his publications he has contributed "Alternative Fiscal Policies in a World of Capital Mobility" to a volume entitled *Stabilization Policies in Interdependent Economies* which was edited by Emil Claassen and Pascal Salin, and published by North Holland (Amsterdam). He is also author of "Portfolio Equilibrium and the Theory of International Capital Movements" in *International Mobility and Movement of Capital*, published by the National Bureau of Economic Research (New York) in 1972.

The Way Ahead
A Comment on
The Framework for Discussion

JOHN E. FLOYD

Professor, Department of Political Economy
University of Toronto

I. INTRODUCTION

The document *The Way Ahead: A Framework for Discussion* is an attempt to provide a focal point for the discussion of policy alternatives facing Canada when the current anti-inflationary programme terminates. Unfortunately, it is so lacking in focus and expertise that it clouds rather than clarifies the essential issues. By pandering to all points of view, regardless of merit, it adds nothing to our understanding of the problems the Canadian economy faces and the choices involved in solving them.

The substance of the report is particularly lacking in four basic areas:

1. There is no clear recognition of the fundamental cause of inflation and the government's role in the inflationary process;

2. The report does not come to grips with the fact that Canada is a small economic entity embedded in a world trade and monetary system and the hard choices this implies for future macro-economic policy;

3. The document does not face squarely the transitional problems and the technical policy choices that must be made to bring inflation under control;

4. The report is too preoccupied with issues that are extraneous to the inflation question - energy, economic growth, the competitive position of Canadian industry in world markets, pollution, etc. By dragging every major public issue across the stage, it detracts from the central issues of concern.

II. MONETARY FACTORS IN THE INFLATIONARY PROCESS: A *SINE QUA NON*

It is difficult to understand how anyone can ignore the evidence about the role of money in the inflationary process. Table 1 shows what has happened to money and prices in Canada and the United States since 1955. The period 1955-66 was one of very moderate monetary growth and very little inflation. During 1967-70, the rates of monetary expansion in the two countries increased, and so did inflation rates.

TABLE 1
MONEY AND PRICES IN CANADA AND
THE UNITED STATES 1955-1976:
AVERAGE ANNUAL PERCENTAGE RATES OF CHANGE.[1]

	CANADA			UNITED STATES		
	INCREASE IN MONEY SUPPLY		Consumer Price Index	INCREASE IN MONEY SUPPLY		Consumer Price Index
Time Period	Narrow Definition	Broad Definition		Narrow Definition	Broad Definition	
1955-1966	3.9	4.7	1.9	2.2	5.3	1.5
1967-1970	5.8	11.0	3.6	5.7	6.6	5.2
1971-1975	14.4	16.5	8.2	6.4	9.7	6.7
1976	7.9[2]	16.8[2]	6.2[3]	4.5[3]	7.4[3]	5.5[3]

[1]Year end to year end for money aggregates and year average to year average for the consumer price index.
[2]Sept. 1975 to Sept. 1976.
[3]August 1975 to August 1976.
Sources: Bank of Canada Statistical Summary
       Prices and Price Indices — Statistics Canada
       Federal Reserve Bulletin.

Monetary expansion escalated further in 1971-75 and the rates of inflation in the two countries increased dramatically. During the past year the rates of monetary growth have slackened in both Canada and the United States, and the rates of inflation have been correspondingly reduced. The picture for other industrial countries is essentially the same.

Cause and effect

To the retort that correlation does not imply causation there are two replies, one empirical and one theoretical. *First*, at the empirical level, it is almost invariably true that year to year changes in the rate of monetary expansion precede the associated changes in inflation rates. This is inconsistent with the view that monetary expansion is the consequence of inflation rather than the cause of it. *Second*, at the theoretical level, there are strong reasons for expecting that excess monetary expansion causes an increase in the price level, and not the other way around. A rise in prices implies that the purchasing power or value of money has fallen. As in the case of any commodity, the value of money depends on its supply relative to the demand for it. Rapid expansion of the money supply would therefore be expected to cause a fall in money's value in terms of goods. It might be argued that inflation could be caused by a decline in the demand for money rather than an increase in the supply. This is true, since the value of money depends on both the demand and the supply. However, the historical evidence suggests strongly that most of the sustained inflations that have occurred in the past have resulted from expansions of the money supply and not contractions in the demand for money. Certainly, the supply of money and not the demand is the obvious culprit in the recent North American inflationary experience because the money supply has grown at excessively high rates precisely when the price level has also been rising rapidly.

An opposing view and its errors

There is an opposing theoretical view that inflation is caused by industry and labour arbitrarily increasing wages and prices in order to capture larger shares of national output. This view has great popular appeal because of the obvious fact that it is firms and workers that establish prices and wages in the economy. The error in this approach is the assumption that those who perform the act of raising prices do so unilaterally, and not in response to an increase in the demand for the products and services they are selling. It is easily shown that unilateral wage and price increases by workers and firms deteriorates rather than improves their economic positions once wage and pricing policies appropriate to the economic circumstances have been established.

Even if it has a monopoly, a firm will lose if it increases prices beyond the level that will ensure maximum profit. Similarly, when a union succeeds in forcing wages up faster than warranted by the demand for labour, it prices its members out of the market and reduces available jobs in the industry. Once a union has achieved an optimum position along this trade-off between higher wages and lower employment it would have no reason to escalate wages. Thus, while the level of product prices in certain industries will be higher because of the market power of firms, and wages higher because of the market power of unions, *there is no reason to expect that these concentrations of power would lead wages and prices to increase faster and faster through time unless the monopoly power of workers and firms is also increasing faster and faster. And there is no evidence that the concentration of economic power has been increasing.*

Rational wealth-maximizing behaviour of workers and firms together with the available empirical evidence thus suggests that prices and wages increase in response to increases in the demand for commodities and labour services. Excessive monetary expansion increases these demands in excess of available supplies and causes wages and prices to rise.

Frequent price changes are costly and labour contracts are often two or three years in length. As a result, sellers of goods and labour services must set prices and wages on the basis of the expected future demand rather than the current demand for goods and labour services. The expectation of inflation, whether justified or not by future events, thus generates current wage and price increases even if current demand does not support them. When this happens, workers price themselves out of the market and unemployment results. This is why a slowdown in the rate of monetary expansion creates unemployment until workers and their unions learn that demand is not growing fast enough to justify current wage demands. It also explains why an increase in monetary expansion has a temporary favourable effect on employment as sellers of labour under-price their product until they learn that the rate of growth of demand has increased. Finally, it explains why changes in the inflation rate lag behind associated changes in the rate of monetary growth.

Expansionism not necessary

It is sometimes argued that the root causes of inflation lie deeper than the above discussion would suggest because the government, for institutional and political reasons, cannot control the money supply. While this has been true of many Latin American countries for some time, and may now be true for Britain, it is not yet, I believe, the case for Canada. Past excessive monetary expansion in both Canada and the United States appears to have resulted almost entirely from two causes: first, excessive government spending *in relation to taxes* financed by borrowing from the central bank (or, in effect, by printing money); and second, an unwillingness of central bankers, at least until quite recently, to focus on the money supply as a policy target. This combination of deficit finance and preoccupation with interest rates, credit conditions, and other non-money targets led the authorities in the late 1960's and early 1970's to believe that money was tight when it was in fact easy, and as a result they lost control over the money supply. There is no reason why these errors must be repeated. Indeed, judging from recent statements of Governor Bouey, the Bank of Canada has now recognized this problem.

Conclusions

We must conclude that a) inflation is caused by excess monetary expansion and can be eliminated only by bringing the money supply under control; b) if inflation is to be controlled the Bank of Canada must give the rate of monetary expansion precedence over all other policy targets; and c) unless the government is willing to borrow extensively from the general public, it must keep its budget under control. Recognition of these facts of life is an absolute prerequisite to sensible discussion of Canada's policy options in the post-control period.

III. CONSTRAINTS IMPOSED BY THE WORLD TRADE AND MONETARY SYSTEM

Another fact of life central to any discussion of inflation in Canada is the constraint on domestic policy imposed by our position as a small economy in a world monetary system. This is given only brief recognition in one sentence on pages 17 and 18 of the report before the discussion becomes bogged down on energy shortages, Canada's competitive position, the balance of trade, and other issues extraneous to the problem of inflation.

Effects of world demand on prices

Obvious cultural and political differences aside, Canada is a regional component of the North American and world economies in the same sense that California is. The prices of goods in California are determined by the demand by world residents, including Californians, for the goods produced in California. An increase in demand causes prices to rise. Similarly, Canadian prices depend on the demand of world residents, including Canadians, for the goods produced in Canada. A shift of world demand toward Canadian produced consumer and capital goods causes their prices to increase. The essential difference between California and Canada is that California money is international money - namely the U.S. dollar - while Canada has its own monetary unit. Thus a shift in world demand for California goods has a direct effect on the level of money prices in California, while the effect on money prices in Canada of a shift in world demand for Canadian goods depends in addition on what happens to the exchange rate between the Canadian and U.S. dollars.

An increase in world demand for Canadian goods will cause the level of prices in Canada to rise if the exchange rate is held constant. However, the authorities could allow the U.S. dollar price of the Canadian dollar to rise in response to the increase in the demand for Canadian dollars by foreigners wanting to buy Canadian goods. This appreciation of the Canadian dollar would make it unnecessary for prices in Canada to rise — the increased cost of the dollar substitutes for an increase in the cost of goods. Similarly, if there is a decline in the world demand for Canadian goods, the price level in Canada can be kept from falling if the authorities allow the value of the dollar in terms of U.S. currency to fall in the foreign exchange market — again, a fall in the cost of the Canadian dollar to foreigners reduces the relative prices of Canadian goods without requiring a fall in the levels of prices and costs in Canada.

But the Canadian authorities can cause the dollar to devalue or appreciate in the world market without any shift in the world demand for Canadian goods. Excess creation of money in Canada leads to a decline in the value of money in terms of both Canadian and foreign goods. This is represented by an increase in the level of prices in Canada and a corresponding devaluation of the Canadian dollar on the international market. The real prices of Canadian goods to foreigners are unaffected — prices in Canada have risen, but the Canadian dollar costs correspondingly less in terms of U.S. dollars. Similarly, a slowdown in the rate of monetary expansion in Canada, compared to monetary growth in the United States causes Canadian prices to rise more slowly than foreign prices and leads to an appreciation of the Canadian dollar. An observed change in the exchange rate may thus result from either of two causes:

1. a shift in world demand for Canadian goods; or

2. a difference between the monetary policies followed in Canada and the United States.

Inflation and the Canadian dollar

This has some very interesting implications for the control of inflation in Canada. Since 1965, prices have risen in both Canada and the United States by roughly 80 per cent. Had the Canadian authorities limited the growth of the money supply in Canada sufficiently to produce the same rate of inflation since 1965 as occurred between 1955 and 1965, prices would have risen only 20 per cent, and the Canadian dollar would now be worth something like $1.50 U.S.! Should the government allow an increase in the value of the Canadian dollar of this magnitude?

It might be thought at first glance that an exchange rate of $1.50 U.S. would impose an intolerable burden on domestic export and import competing industries because they would receive one-third less than American producers for goods sold on the world market. Not so!

While prices received in Canadian dollars would be one-third less than prices received in U.S. dollars, domestic costs, wage rates, and prices of non-traded goods and services would also be a third lower in Canada. The Canadian dollar would be worth half again as much as the U.S. dollar both at home and abroad. Nevertheless, it is almost inevitable that any troubles experienced by domestic export and import competing industries would be blamed, albeit falsely, on the exchange rate.

A second and politically favourable consequence of the lower inflation rate in Canada would be lower interest rates on loans and residential mortgages. If the rate of inflation in Canada since 1965 had been limited to the 2 per cent experienced between 1955 and 1965, the average interest rates on residential mortgages in the first half of the present decade would probably have been 6 or 7 percentage points lower. This is because borrowers would not have to compensate lenders for the annual deterioration in the real values of mortgages arising from the 6 or 7 per cent annual decline in the value of the dollar.

Implications of politicizing the dollar

If we assume that the "political realities" in Canada dictate that the exchange rate should not be allowed to rise above, say, $1.07 U.S. at the maximum, the best that could possibly have been achieved since 1965 is a once and for all reduction of Canadian relative to U.S. prices of perhaps 7 per cent. This means that the total increase in prices in Canada over the period could have been limited to 73 per cent instead of 80 per cent. Moreover, once this 7 per cent reduction had been achieved, the $1.07 U.S. ceiling would have prevented any further reduction in the inflation rate in Canada relative to the United States. To maintain the exchange rate within acceptable bounds the Bank of Canada is forced to expand the money supply sufficiently to permit a rate of inflation in Canada equivalent to the inflation rate in the U.S. — give or take some minor differences created by changes in the world demand for Canadian goods.

A fundamental policy choice

This issue of whether the authorities should pursue an independent policy and let the exchange rate run free, or maintain "acceptable" levels of the exchange rate and abandon any attempt to control domestic prices is the fundamental choice that must be made in the post-control period. *If the choice is for a politically-determined exchange rate, there is no need to discuss anti-inflation policy further. If the choice is for a truly flexible exchange rate and independent monetary policy, then the way is open for discussion of what that policy should be.*

Past policy choices

Figure 1 shows how this fundamental policy choice has been resolved in the past quarter century. The gray line is the ratio of prices in Canada to prices in the United States, and the orange line is the same ratio adjusted for movements in the exchange rate by converting Canadian prices into U.S. dollars. The black line is the exchange rate. To a rough approximation, the orange line gives the world market relative price of Canadian goods; an upward trend of this line implies that the world demand for Canadian goods is increasing and a downward trend implies that it is decreasing. If the exchange rate were rigidly fixed for the whole period, the black line would be horizontal and the orange and gray lines would move together — adjustments in the world demand for Canadian goods would be reflected entirely in adjustments of domestic prices.

On the other hand, if Canadian and U.S. monetary policies were the same, so that Canadian and United States price levels move together, the gray line would be horizontal, and the orange and black lines would move together — adjustments in the world demand for Canadian goods would be reflected entirely in adjustments of the price of the Canadian dollar in terms of U.S. dollars.

Finally, if there were no changes in the world demand for Canadian goods over the 25 year period, the orange line would be horizontal. In this case, the gray and black lines would also be horizontal if the monetary policies of Canada and the United States were the same. If the monetary policies in the two countries diverge, the gray and black lines would move opposite to each other — excess monetary expansion in Canada relative to the United States would result in a relative increase in the Canadian price level and an upward trend in the gray line, together with a decline in the exchange rate and a downward trend in the black line.

It is evident from Figure 1 that the gray line has moved relatively little over the 25 year period while the orange and black lines have varied substantially and tended to move together. This implies that the Canadian authorities have managed the domestic money supply so as to produce a rate of domestic inflation roughly equivalent to the inflation rate

Figure 1 — Relative Price Levels and the Exchange Rate, Canada and the United States, 1950-1976*

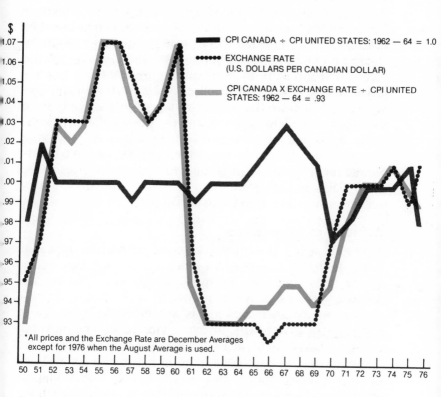

CPI CANADA ÷ CPI UNITED STATES: 1962 — 64 = 1.0

EXCHANGE RATE (U.S. DOLLARS PER CANADIAN DOLLAR)

CPI CANADA X EXCHANGE RATE ÷ CPI UNITED STATES: 1962 — 64 = .93

*All prices and the Exchange Rate are December Averages except for 1976 when the August Average is used.

abroad, and let the exchange rate adjust to accommodate the shifts that occurred in the world demand for Canadian goods. Had the exchange rate been rigidly fixed over the whole period the ratio of Canadian to U.S. prices would have behaved like the orange line. Prices in Canada would have increased by somewhat more than 10 per cent relative to U.S. prices during the 1950's, fallen by a similar amount in the first half of the 1960's, and then increased again by about 5 per cent since the late 1960's. These price movements were prevented by allowing the exchange rate to adjust.

251

Although exchange rate variations have thus been important, their role has been primarily a supporting one. While the rate has been allowed to respond to shifts in real demand conditions for Canadian goods, it has not been subjected to the pressure of a divergent monetary policy in Canada. This has probably been because the Bank of Canada has historically regarded its purpose as the maintenance of stable and orderly credit conditions. In practice this has meant that the Bank maintained money market conditions in Canada consistent with those in the United States. This accounts for both the very similar price movements in Canada and the United States and the observed adjustments in the exchange rate. Had the adjustments in the exchange rate not been allowed to occur, the Bank would have had to pursue relatively more inflationary monetary policies in the early 1950's and late 1960's and relatively more deflationary policies in the late 1950's and early 1960's.

Attempts at independence

There are a few instances where the authorities appear to have attempted to pursue an independent monetary policy. These cases are evidenced in the graph where the ratio of prices and the exchange rate move in opposite directions — that is, where a devaluation is accompanied by a rise in Canadian relative to U.S. prices or vice versa. The most important case occurred in 1970 when the appreciation of the dollar appears to have gone hand in hand with a slowdown in the inflation rate. One suspects that the Canadian authorities, realizing that inflation was out of control in the U.S., may have tried briefly to "go it alone." The gains in terms of a reduced rate of inflation were soon lost, however, as the Bank of Canada resumed its preoccupation with interest rates and credit conditions.

Recent statements of Governor Bouey suggest that the Bank's policy has now shifted to one of maintaining a steady and gradually declining rate of monetary growth until inflation has been eliminated. Unless a similar policy is followed in the U.S., this will eventually result in a divergence between the rates of inflation in the two countries and a secular movement of the exchange rate.

IV. THE PROBLEM OF TRANSITION TO LOWER INFLATION RATES

Although it is obvious that the way to cure inflation is to appropriately limit the rate of monetary growth, the problem is much more difficult than it might at first seem. Since wages are set on the basis of expected rather than actual demand conditions, a slackening of the rate of monetary expansion in the face of unabated inflationary expectations reduces the demand for labour without a corresponding reduction in the rate of inflation of wages. Workers price themselves out of the market and a temporary period of unemployment results. It is, in fact, virtually impossible to find a case where the authorities successfully reduced or eliminated an ongoing inflation without temporarily creating unemployment. Another hard choice therefore arises. Are we willing to pay the price required in terms of unemployment to reduce or eliminate inflation?

The typical response of government to this question is to try to avoid facing up to it. One way of doing this is to deny that excess monetary expansion is the cause of inflation and that control over monetary growth is the only cure, and to try to legislate the problem away by imposing direct controls on wages and prices. As a cure for inflation, however, this is strictly a "head in the sand" approach; the evidence about the relationship between money and prices, and the theory which supports it, is simply too strong to justify the view of inflation implied by this policy. One cannot cure the disease by suppressing its symptoms.

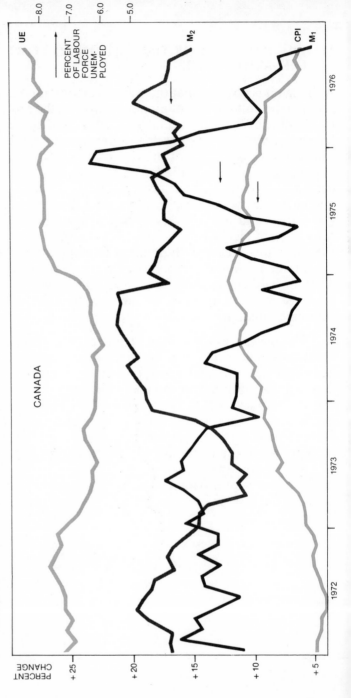

Figure 2 — Money, Prices and Unemployment, Canada and the United States, 1972-1976

CPI = CONSUMER PRICE INDEX; M1 = NARROWLY DEFINED MONEY STOCK;
M2 = BROADLY DEFINED MONEY STOCK; UE = PERCENT OF LABOUR FORCE
UNEMPLOYED;

CPI, M1 and M2 ARE PERCENTAGE INCREASES CALCULATED
FROM THE SAME MONTH IN THE PRECEDING YEAR.

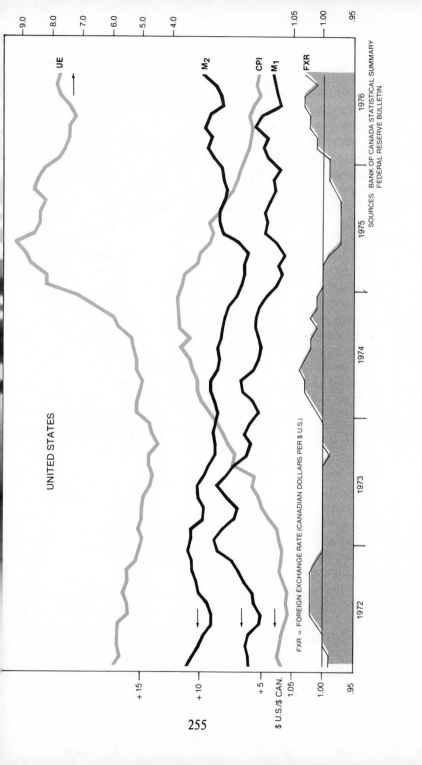

UNITED STATES

UE

M₂

CPI

M₁

FXR

FXR = FOREIGN EXCHANGE RATE (CANADIAN DOLLARS PER $ U.S.)

$ U.S./$ CAN.

SOURCES: BANK OF CANADA STATISTICAL SUMMARY
FEDERAL RESERVE BULLETIN

255

The effects of controls

Nevertheless, there is a theoretical possibility that temporary controls on wages and prices *could* reduce unemployment in the transition period when the inflation rate is being brought down. By limiting wage increases to those consistent with actual rather than anticipated market conditions, it is possible to prevent workers from temporarily pricing themselves out of the market. To be effective, of course, the policy must be accompanied by an appropriate reduction in the rate of monetary growth, and eliminated as soon as expectations about inflation have fallen into line with the new rate of monetary growth.

Figure 2 presents evidence about the extent to which wage and price controls have contributed to the recent reduction in the inflation rate in Canada. The chart gives for both Canada and the United States the percentage growth of money and prices from a particular month of the previous year to the same month of the current or designated year, together with the level of the exchange rate (U.S. dollar price of the Canadian dollar) and the percentage of the labour force unemployed. For example, the level of the line marked CPI in August 1975 gives the percentage growth of the consumer price index from August 1974 to August 1975. The exchange rate and unemployment for each designated month are the average levels for that month.

Inflation falling before controls

It is clear from the chart that the rates of growth of consumer prices in both Canada and the United States began to turn down late in 1974. Since wage and price controls were not imposed until October of 1975, they cannot claim any credit for turning inflation around in Canada. The turnaround in both countries can be interpreted as a lagged response to gradual declines in the rates of monetary expansion that had been taking place for at least a year previously. In the United States, the rate of expansion of the narrow definition of money fell gradually and somewhat intermittently from about 9 per cent in June 1973 to about 4 per cent in January 1975, while the rate of expansion of the broader definition fell from around 10 per cent in June 1973 to about 6.5 per cent in January 1975.

In Canada, the rate of growth of the narrow definition of money is highly variable. But its trend is clearly downward from mid-1972 to early 1975. The rate of growth of the broad definition of money declined from mid-1972 to mid-1973, then rose markedly between mid-1973 and mid-1974, finally turning down just before the turnaround in the inflation rate. The behaviour of the broad definition of money suggests quite strongly that money was not as tight in Canada as in the U.S. right before the inflation rates turned down.

Unemployment not affected by controls

As expected, the turnaround in the inflation rate was accompanied by an increase in the unemployment rate in both countries — from 5 to 9 per cent in the U.S. and 5 to 7 per cent in Canada between June 1974 and June 1975. Since the major change in the unemployment rates occurred before the establishment of wage and price controls in Canada, the smaller growth of Canadian unemployment could not be attributed to the controls. Rather, it would appear to be the result of the relatively easier monetary policy in Canada prior to the turnaround in inflation. This is consistent with the fact that the Canadian dollar was depreciating in terms of the U.S. dollar throughout the period in which unemployment rates in both countries were experiencing most of their increase. It is also consistent with the slower decline in the inflation rate in Canada between late 1974 and late 1975.

Controls had some effect

The rates of expansion of both definitions of money increased gradually and somewhat intermittently in the U.S. from early 1975 to August 1976. The data on the narrow definition of money in Canada is useless for this period because the postal strike of late 1975 and the resulting failure of cheques to clear led to a large and spurious increase in the observed rate of monetary growth. The rate of growth of the broad definition of money in Canada, though it is somewhat variable, exhibits no discernible trend between early 1975 and August 1976. This apparent easing of monetary expansion in the U.S. relative to Canada is consistent with the slower decline in the U.S. inflation rate and the appreciation of the Canadian dollar in terms of the U.S. dollar between late 1975 and August 1976. It is also consistent with the fact that unemployment declined in the United States and increased in Canada during the same period. Although the slightly more rapid decline in the Canadian inflation rate is consistent with the view that controls had some effect on prices in Canada, the increase in unemployment in Canada would not have occurred had controls been entirely responsible for the observed behaviour of Canadian prices relative to U.S. prices. A view that attributes the greater decline in the inflation rate in Canada to relatively tighter money is necessary to explain the relative increase in the Canadian unemployment rate.

V. *THE WAY AHEAD*

Unfortunately, the document does not address any of the technical policy questions that must be faced in the post-control period.

● *Should wage and price controls be eliminated completely?*

● *What stance should monetary policy take?*

● *What about fiscal policy?*

● *Unemployment?*

It is evident from Figure 2 that the battle against inflation in Canada is now about half won. We have absorbed at most an extra 2 per cent unemployment since January 1975 and in return have managed to reduce the inflation rate from about 12 per cent to 6 per cent per year. The remaining 6 per cent will probably be somewhat easier to eliminate because inflationary expectations will become less and less tenable and wage demands more and more realistic as the evidence of declining inflation unfolds. Since we have come so far it would appear to be unwise for the government to make any move that could signal a weakening of its resolve to effect a complete cure.

Thus, it would seem inappropriate for the Bank of Canada to ease the rate of monetary growth at this time even if our monetary policy turns out to be quite tight in relation to U.S. policy and the exchange rate appreciates considerably. If the United States succeeds in bringing its inflation rate down close to zero, it may eventually be worthwhile for Canada to go back to the *orderly markets* approach to monetary policy that was followed in the 1950's and 1960's. However, any move in this direction should be held off until the Carter Administration's approach to monetary policy becomes clear. This would maintain our option of pursuing monetary independence if inappropriate policies in the U.S. should make it desirable.

Meanwhile, in order to attempt to reduce unemployment a dose of fiscal policy would seem appropriate. This should take the form of public works and other employment subsidy policies fully financed by taxes. Any additional government deficits could lead to increased expenditure on domestic goods and thereby interfere with an orderly reduction in the actual and expected rates of domestic inflation. Since wage and price controls have done and will do nothing to control either inflation or unemployment, it makes no sense for the government to absorb the political costs and the taxpayers the financial costs of maintaining and administering them. They should be promptly terminated.

VI. FACTORS EXTRANEOUS TO THE INFLATIONARY PROCESS

In completing this review, it is worthwhile to explain why many issues which the working paper dwells on at great length are tangential to the problem of controlling inflation. Three issues merit brief consideration: energy and raw material shortages; economic growth; and Canada's competitive position in world markets.

Energy and raw material shortages

Energy and raw material shortages have two monetary effects. First, they tend to limit to some extent the rate of growth of output and with it the rate of growth of money demanded for making transactions. Second, they raise costs in

259

certain industries. These get passed on initially in the form of higher prices, which increase the amount of money needed to make transactions. Whether the shortages lead to expansion or contraction of the aggregate demand for goods and the level of employment depends on the relative strengths of these two forces. In any event, unless the government counters with an appropriate reduction in the rate of monetary expansion, it is likely that the level of prices would increase to some extent and that, as a result, there could be a temporary increase in the rate of inflation. However, these effects would certainly be minute in comparison to the 80 per cent inflation experienced since 1965. It is possible that the timing and sharpness of the turnaround in the inflation rate in the fall of 1974 could have been affected to some extent by these forces. Nevertheless, the rate of inflation was increasing before the energy crisis, and would be declining now had the energy crisis not occurred. To give energy and raw material shortages anything more than a passing nod in the analysis of inflation is to vastly overstate their significance.

Economic growth

It is asserted in the report that high rates of economic growth have created inflation by exacerbating inequities of income distribution and causing a "restless quarrel over shares" (p. 18) and continued escalation of wage and price demands. I have already shown that this theory òf inflation makes no sense and is not supported by the evidence. Indeed, the muddleheadedness of not only this view but the entire document is illustrated by the assertion just two pages earlier that slower rates of growth could create inflation for essentially the same reasons. There is some theoretical support for the view that a slowdown in the rate of growth will tend to increase inflation. Slower growth means a slower increase in the demand for money which implies, other things being equal, a faster decline in the value of money. However, the available evidence about the effect of growth on the demand for money suggests that the growth rate would probably have to fall by a full percentage point in order to bring about a one per cent increase in the inflation rate. Given the degree of inflation we have been experiencing this problem might be worth worrying about when we get the inflation rate down to one per cent per year.

The Canadian competitive position

Finally, there is the concern that inflation will deteriorate the competitive position of Canadian industry in world markets. This simply reflects a lack of understanding of the inflationary process. If all countries inflate at the same rate, costs of production rise equally in Canada and abroad and there is no deterioration of our relative position. If Canada inflates more rapidly than other countries, the Canadian dollar must devalue in world markets by the difference between the Canadian inflation rate and the inflation rates of our major trading partners. This devaluation of the dollar will exactly compensate for the excess increase in Canadian relative to foreign costs and the competitive position of Canadian firms will again be unaffected.

Final comment

The document *The Way Ahead* was collectively written, I am told, by a number of senior civil servants and advisors and passed on and modified by Cabinet. The lack of insight and expertise, indeed competence, of this report is strong and unfortunate support for the view that government's role in managing the economy should be kept to an absolute minimum.

Making Realistic Choices on *The Way Ahead*

HERBERT G. GRUBEL

Professor of Economics
Simon Fraser University

THE AUTHOR

Herbert G. Grubel was born in Germany in 1934 and educated at Rutgers University and at Yale, where he received his Ph.D. in 1962. He has been at Simon Fraser University since 1972, where he is now a Professor in the Department of Economics and Commerce. He specializes in international trade and finance. Professor Grubel has held academic posts at Stanford University, the University of Chicago and the University of Pennsylvania. He was a visiting Research Fellow, 1974-75, at Nuffield College, Oxford, and during 1970-71 he was a Senior Policy Analyst for the U.S. Treasury Department in Washington D.C.

Professor Grubel's latest books are *Intra-Industry Trade* (Macmillan, 1976), *International Economics* (Irwin-Dorsey, 1977), and, with Richard W. Schwindt, *The Real Cost of the B.C. Milk Board: A Case Study in Canadian Agricultural Policy*, published by the Fraser Institute, 1977. He is a member of the Editorial Advisory Board of the Fraser Institute.

Making Realistic Choices on *The Way Ahead*

HERBERT G. GRUBEL

Professor of Economics
Simon Fraser University

I. INTRODUCTION

The authors of the Canadian Government's Working Paper *The Way Ahead: A Framework for Discussion*, criticize the past performance of the Canadian economy on four grounds: inflation, unemployment, income distribution and growth. They appear to acknowledge the fact that the trade-off between inflation and unemployment, once believed to exist, does not, in fact, provide a solution to what they believe to be the most important shortcoming of the economy, namely high and growing average levels of unemployment over the business cycle. As a result, the critical economic problem of our time appears to be the design of policies to lower the average rate of unemployment by some other mechanism. The Working Paper hints ominously at the need for a change in the basic system of free enterprise if such policies cannot be devised within the existing institutional framework.

The main theme of my comments in this paper is that the high and growing average unemployment rate in recent times has been caused by government efforts to achieve greater income equality in Canada and that this unemployment is a necessary cost of these policies. I present the economic analysis in defence of this proposition in Section III, after presenting in Section II the argument that market power, contrary to the views expressed in the Working Paper, does not cause inflation or unemployment.†

A second theme of this paper presented in Section IV is that social welfare legislation and the provision of public goods have the further undesirable side-effect of lowering economic growth. In Section V, I argue that the conclusion from my analysis is that the Canadian people should be informed about the inevitable trade-off between policies to equalize incomes and provide public goods on the one hand, and higher average unemployment and slower growth, on the other. Failure to do so will lead to economic and social policies which, like in totalitarian regimes, cannot remove the trade-off, but hide it through the suppression of personal liberty and freedom of expression.

II. MARKET POWER DOES NOT CAUSE INFLATION OR UNEMPLOYMENT

Before introducing the explanation of how social policies for income equality cause unemployment, it is important to deal with the view presented in the Working Paper that market power by producers and labour unions causes unemployment. To do so, it is useful first to deal briefly with the issue of whether market power causes inflation, as is suggested in some parts of the Working Paper.

It is a fundamental theoretical proposition verified by easily-observable facts that firms, unions and marketing boards cannot raise their prices and incomes without limit. At any given moment in time and with a given strength of their power they always face the threat that their attempts to raise the prices of their products and their incomes will have the opposite effect. Consumers have the option to switch to substitute products, firms can use more capital in place of labour, move abroad or go out of business and so on. Given these constraints and the limited power to influence them, there is always one price or wage rate which represents the

---

†Editor's Note: This theme arises in several papers in this volume, notably those of Professor Lipsey and Professor Dean.

maximum obtainable. There is good reason for believing that firms and unions, alleged to be very selfish maximizers, can usually be found charging the highest prices or exacting the highest wages that the market will bear. As long as constraints and power are unchanged, prices and wages will not rise, though they tend to be at a higher level than they would have been in the absence of the market power.

Government policy encouraged use of power

Wages and prices in industries with market power rise only if the constraints or the degree of power are changed. In recent years in Canada the level of market power appears to have grown only very little and by an insufficient amount to explain the actual inflation. The main causes of the observed inflation have been changes in the constraints on the exercise of the power itself. These changes in constraints took the form of lower probabilities of undesirable response from the market: from the point of view of the firm, the fear that competitive substitutes would undermine the sales of goods whose prices were raised; for unions, the fear that firms would go out of business or substitute capital for labour when wages were raised. These changes were brought about by the excess demand created by the Canadian government through expansionary monetary and fiscal policies aimed at lowering the average unemployment rate.

The result of these changes in constraints on the exercise of power led to the inflation which is now an historic fact. However, it is interesting to note that the inflation following the excess demand creation would have taken place even if the Canadian economy had been perfectly competitive because even in such an environment small firms and individual workers have some power, albeit a limited amount. When constraints on this power are changed it leads to inflation just as in the case where power is more concentrated. In concluding this analysis of the causes of inflation it is worth pointing out that the exploitation of market power following changes in constraints cannot raise incomes permanently because general inflation soon erodes the gains made by individual groups in the economy. Yet, the initial achievement of higher incomes

267

makes the subsequent loss psychologically hard to take and has led to the sense of frustration and anger felt by many Canadians in recent years.

Power and unemployment

While the preceding analysis may be known and accepted by an increasing number of people in Canada, the proposition that market power also does not cause unemployment is known and accepted much less. To understand the validity of this last proposition, consider what happens if a firm is unionized and wages are raised. The firm introduces labour-saving capital, it is forced to reduce its output, or both. In either case, the unionized high-wage firm has fewer workers than does the non-unionized low-wage firm. The workers who have become unemployed or failed to have been hired as the firm grows are forced to join the supply of labour in the non-unionized sector. There is no reason that in the absence of any social assistance programmes, workers in need could not find some sort of employment in this sector. The rate of pay and working conditions might be considered unjust by modern standards and found unacceptable to those able to draw on current welfare programmes, but the fact is indisputable that those who want to work always could find some job if the only other alternative was starvation. It should be noted that under these conditions, as a result of the activities of unions, the wage rates in the non-unionized sector are lower than in the unionized sector and lower than they would have been in the absence of unions.†

By analogy, if an industry newly turned oligopolistic raises the price of its output above that prevailing when the industry was competitive, fewer goods are sold and labour demand is less. But the resultant lay-off of workers (or failure to hire workers in a growing environment) only adds

---

†Editor's Note: If, as Professor Grubel discusses later, there is a minimum wage law or if the level of support available from social welfare agencies is at a level higher than the market determined wage in the non-unionized sector then the net result of union activity may create the circumstances for higher rates of unemployment in the non-union sector.

to the supply of labour in the competitive sector of the economy, causing wage rates to be lower and output and employment to be higher there than they were before the creation of the market power. All of the effects of market power noted may be undesirable and, in fact, constitute the economic case against oligopolies and unions, but unemployment is not one of the effects of such power.

III. THE SOCIAL POLICIES CAUSING UNEMPLOYMENT

The average rate of unemployment in Canada during periods of cyclical expansion and pause has risen in each successive cycle in the post-war years (*The Way Ahead*, p. 11). It is the main purpose of my comments to identify, as the cause of this rise in unemployment, the social policies aimed at the equalization of incomes in Canada. The following analysis should not be interpreted as an argument against the use of these policies. Its aim is to show that these policies have the undesirable and largely ignored but unavoidable side-effects of raising unemployment.

Minimum wage legislation

The first of the policies designed to equalize incomes is the minimum wage legislation. This legislation does not and cannot force employers to hire the low-skilled teenagers, minorities and handicapped the value of whose productivity is below the legislated minimum wage. As a result, these workers cannot find jobs and join the ranks of the unemployed. One of the results of this, especially in the case of teenagers, has been to deprive new entrants into the labour market the opportunity to acquire work disciplines and skills through learning by doing in low-paid jobs. When these youngsters grow up they are more likely to have low productivity and continue to be unemployed than they would have otherwise. The problem of unemployment among these workers is increased by the activities of unions which increase the supply of workers in the non-unionized sector in which the minimum wage legislation is effective.[1]

Unemployment insurance

The second major social legislative programme causing unemployment is the unemployment insurance programme.[2] Designed to equalize incomes between those working and unemployed, it has the undesirable side-effect of inducing workers to prolong job-search, to change jobs more frequently, to join the work-force temporarily, to hold seasonal jobs and even, in some instances, to enjoy genuine vacations. The responses of workers to the subsidization of these activities through unemployment benefits is entirely rational and has nothing to do with cheating.

Knowing that quitting a job leads to only a relatively small reduction in income after taxes and expenses, some workers dissatisfied with the jobs they are holding quit them while in the absence of the benefits they would stay on. The benefits enable these workers and others who have lost their jobs for the usual reasons of cyclical downturn in demand or technical change, to be more selective in their search for a new job. They can afford to reject employment, which otherwise they would have accepted, because of a job's distance from home, the need to learn new skills, the low pay or any other of many possible reasons. The search for new employment opportunities can be less intensive and, in the case of some individuals without financial commitments or family responsibilities, can be mixed with spells at leisure activities.† The benefits permit workers to engage in the luxury of working in seasonal industries, such as gardening and fishing, for which they may have a great preference but which they would be forced to abandon in the absence of the insurance programme. Housewives and pensioners are induced to enter the labour force to become eligible for

---

†Editor's Note: An extension in the length of time taken to find a new job can have a startling effect on the unemployment rate. For example, if 16 per cent of the labour force changes jobs each year and normally takes 3 months to find a new job, (the average duration of unemployment is currently 3 months) this alone would yield an unemployment rate of 4 per cent. If the time taken to find a new job increased by one month to four months, the unemployment rate would, on this account alone, rise to 5.3 per cent.

benefits and then quit or get themselves fired. By setting very high standards of acceptability on new jobs, such persons often succeed in remaining unemployed until benefits cease legally. Their behaviour has brought them an implicit hourly working wage much in excess of that paid by the employer.

This sort of behaviour induced by unemployment benefits can only be mitigated, not eliminated, by more stringent enforcement of eligibility rules by bureaucrats. There simply is no way of establishing eligibility rules suitable for catching most abusers without causing undue hardship and inefficiencies for many others.

Welfare programmes

Analogous arguments can be made about the way in which the availability of general welfare programmes induces unemployment. Genuine and honest differences among observers about the proper interpretation of eligibility rules are responsible for the widely differing estimates about the level of "cheating" among welfare recipients which sweep the media periodically. As in the case of unemployment benefits, there is no doubt that the availability of welfare benefits induces some people to set higher standards on the acceptability of jobs and to reduce their willingness to enter and get through retraining and rehabilitation programmes than they would otherwise. The result of this induced behaviour is an increased rate of measured unemployment.

IV. SOCIAL POLICIES AND ECONOMIC GROWTH

In the past, economic growth due to greater productivity has been considered to be an acceptable and relatively painless way of alleviating the ills of market economies conceived by critics of the system. Thus, growth raises the absolute levels of incomes of the poor, permits the increased provision of public goods and allows progressive income taxes to reduce after-tax income inequalities without forcing the higher income groups into a painful absolute reduction of their living standards.

Unfortunately, in recent years the growth of the Canadian economy due to increased productivity has slowed considerably. It is my conviction that this slowdown is permanent and will become more severe, because of the social programmes of the government aimed at increasing income equality and providing public goods.

The minimum wage laws and unemployment and welfare programmes discussed above, by causing increased unemployment, reduce productivity for two reasons. *First*, unemployed workers produce nothing and the statistics of output of the labour-force show lower overall productivity. *Second*, the taxes imposed on those working in order to finance the benefits induce inefficiencies. Taxes on income create incentives to consume more leisure, to take jobs whose non-taxed pecuniary benefits are great and to buy consumer rather than investment goods. The latter incentive may be illustrated by considering someone who has a net worth of $50,000. Investment in productive resources such as the ownership of a small business may yield 10 per cent per year, or $2,500 after taxes at the 50 per cent marginal rate. The purchase of a luxury car with a price tag of $50,000 therefore costs only $2,500 per year in foregone income (ignoring depreciation), not the $5,000 implied by the 10 per cent yield on capital. As a result of these tax distortions many luxury cars and other items of consumption are bought every year in Canada with money which otherwise would have gone into the capital market to be used to equip workers with productivity-raising machines.

The general effect of taxes just sketched works with special force on upper income earners faced with high marginal tax rates. The resultant, visible and increased consumption of luxury goods by these income groups adds to the resentment of low income earners.

The government programmes aimed at raising the incomes of retired people and the sick through public pension funds and health care programmes increase consumption by the community as a whole and therefore lead to reduced capital formation and productivity increases. The increased consumption is brought about by the fact that, in the absence of these programmes, people used to be forced to set

272

aside savings during their working years for their retirement and, while they were healthy, for medical contingencies. As a result, in a growing economy, the savings of those working and healthy exceeded the dis-savings of the retired and sick and total capital formation was higher than it is in the presence of these programmes.

Under the current system, the taxes paid for these programmes only just pay for their current costs, and typically do not result in net capital formation, so that the growth of productivity in Canada is reduced below what it would have been under the old system.[3]

Programmes to raise the incomes of farmers through the operation of marketing boards, of fishermen through many kinds of subsidies, of workers in textile and other industries through restrictions on imports and of many other interest groups in the economy have the side-effect of creating incentives to keep resources employed in uses where their productivity is lower than it would be in others not needing such government supports. As a result, the level and growth of Canadian productivity are reduced.

In recent years, the Canadian government has also embarked on the provision of public goods, which has caused a lowering of the level and growth of productivity. Thus, the supply of a public good in the form of national, cultural and economic independence was increased through legislation which requires the screening of foreign take-over bids. Other legislation of the same ilk was recently responsible for the demise of the Canadian edition of *Time* magazine. This sort of legislation has the effect of reducing the inflow of foreign capital and therefore of reducing the growth in Canadian productivity. The provision of public goods in the form of a cleaner environment has led to the installation of expensive pollution control equipment by industry. The capital used for this purpose is not available for increasing the productivity of the Canadian economy measured in the conventional way.

V. IMPLICATIONS FOR THE WAY AHEAD

The preceding analysis of the effects of recent government programmes on unemployment and productivity does not constitute an argument against the programmes. Greater income equality, more public goods and increased protection against the uncertainties of the world may well be worth their price in terms of higher measured unemployment and lower income in terms of the private consumption of real goods and services. Galbraith in his early writings may well have been correct in his judgment that Western societies in the past have spent too little on these public programmes. Or, alternatively it could be argued that in recent years private incomes generally have increased so much that the consumption of private goods has run into diminishing returns and it is rational for the public to demand more public goods.

Furthermore, the analysis does not imply a support of market power. While market power does not cause inflation or unemployment, it does create an undesirable income distribution, leads to the concentration of political influence and lower productivity. Attack on such market power is most desirable and should be pursued through the elimination or modification of legislation which created much of it, such as agricultural marketing boards, the Bank Act and import restrictions. It should also be attacked through the enforcement of existing anti-combines legislation aimed at both business and labour.

The main conclusion to be drawn from the preceding analysis is that the trade-off between income equality and public goods on the one hand, and unemployment and growth on the other, is an unpleasant but unavoidable fact of life. This fact needs to be explained to the people of Canada and responsible politicians of all parties must refrain from promising to deliver the impossible. The public and political debate should shift instead to the discussion of the nature of the trade-off and how far the people of Canada want to go on it. No one can predict the outcome of such a discussion, but it is conceivable that it could lead to the recommendation that politicians tolerate greater income inequality, provide fewer public goods and reduce economic power. The

Working Paper suggests that the mood of the Canadian people points in this direction generally.

There are some observers who believe that the trade-off between income equality, public goods and unemployment and growth is not inevitable and that it can be eliminated or reduced by innovative government policies. The world has seen a long list of such innovative policies suggested and tried. In Canada, the latest has been the wage and price control programme. Eventually, all of these programmes have failed and they will fail in the future because in a free society the responses of people in their infinite variety cause the government control programmes to be circumvented and finally turned into inequitable and inefficient instruments of oppression of a minority of the public too weak to avoid them.

Totalitarian regimes of the world appear to have solved the problem of trade-off through the suppression of personal freedoms. Cuba has an anti-loafing law, China needs periodic and costly upheavals, such as the Cultural Revolution, to prevent the development of income inequalities accompanying the growth of an elite. The people of the Soviet Union and East European countries suffer from low productivity, shabby goods and the threat of confinement to concentration camps and insane asylums. Because these societies suppress free public debate it is difficult to be certain about what is happening in them. But, what little we know about income equality, public goods and economic growth in these countries (the latter properly adjusted for the nations' natural resource base and the sacrifices of consumption for rapid capital accumulation), suggests that these societies have not succeeded in eliminating the trade-off. They have only prevented it from becoming an issue for public debate.

In my judgment, and that of the authors of the Working Paper, complete government control and totalitarianism are not the solution for the trade-off problem for Canada. Policies for the creation of a better society must assume that the Canadian people remain free. I can only hope that this expression of principles is more than just rhetoric and that the ominous references to the need for a possible fundamental change in the system remain just a threat. The recognition by politicians and the people of Canada of the inevitable trade-off between income equality, public goods and unemployment and growth is a necessary condition to safeguard against the future use of wage and price controls and other such measures which by a slow but unavoidable process would lead to undesirable changes in the present economic and social system in Canada.

Notes

[1]For a discussion of the evidence on the effects of minimum wage legislation on unemployment see Jacob Mincer, "Unemployment Effects of Minimum Wages," *Journal of Political Economy*, 84, 4, Part 2, August 1976.

[2]The evidence on the effects of unemployment insurance on the rate of unemployment is reviewed in R. Bodkin and A. Cournoyer "Legislation and the Labour Market: A Selective Review of Canadian Studies," presented at the Conference on Unemployment Insurance held by the Fraser Institute in Vancouver, B.C., Sept. 1-4, 1976. This, paper, together with a number of others reviewing evidence from other countries is to be published, H. Grubel, editor.

[3]M. Feldstein "Seven Principles of Social Insurance," *Challenge*, November/December 1976, reviews the evidence on the effect of social insurance programmes on savings.

The Way Ahead:
Small if not Beautiful

JOHN F. HELLIWELL

Professor of Economics
University of British Columbia

THE AUTHOR

John F. Helliwell is currently Professor of Economics at the University of British Columbia. Born in Vancouver in 1937, he was educated at the University of British Columbia and at Oxford University, where he was a Rhodes Scholar. He received his D.Phil. (Economics) degree in 1966. Professor Helliwell has held research positions with the Royal Commission on Banking and Finance, 1962-63, and the Royal Commission on Taxation, 1963-64. He has been an econometric consultant to the Research Department of the Bank of Canada since 1965, where he has been a major contributor to the Bank's quarterly forecasting models of the Canadian economy. He is a Fellow of the Royal Society of Canada.

Professor Helliwell is the author of more than 60 scholarly articles, studies, reviews and books. Among them are: *Public Policies and Private Investment*, published by the Clarendon Press (Oxford) in 1968; *The Structure of RDX2* (with others), Bank of Canada Staff Research Study No. 7, 1971; "Monetary Interdependence of Canada and the United States Under Alternative Exchange Rate Systems" (with T. Maxwell) in *National Monetary Policies and the International System*, R.Z. Aliber, editor, published by the University of Chicago Press in 1974; "Economic Consequences of Developing Canada's Arctic Gas," in *The Energy Question: Failures of Multinational Policies*, edited by E. Erickson and L. Waverman, published by the University of Toronto Press in 1974; *Aggregate Investment*, published by Penguin Books in 1976.

The Way Ahead:
Small if not Beautiful

JOHN F. HELLIWELL

*Professor of Economics
University of British Columbia*

I. INTRODUCTION

The Way Ahead is a more important document than it first appears in its masquerade as a paper explaining the causes of inflation. It soon becomes apparent that inflation is not the fundamental problem being described, but is only the result of unsuccessful attempts to deal with more basic problems. *Anyone can explain inflation, and can tell you how to get rid of it — cut the money supply in half, with a flexible exchange rate, and prices will eventually follow.* The paper seems at times to blur this point by some discussion of ratchet effects and similar relatively transient influences, but the answer is still there. If the solution is not adopted, then inflation itself is obviously not the central problem.

The real problem, as the paper points out in well-guarded civil service prose, is that we are collectively unable to get along happily on what we collectively produce. We are all inclined to demand more, but the supply is not so easily forthcoming. If we do not get what we think we deserve, we may take our labour or capital elsewhere, where we expect to be better treated. Or we may simply sit on our hands. In either case, the immediate effects are to lower output and

279

employment without lowering claims on real income. *The Way Ahead* argues that these problems are likely to get worse rather than better in Canada and in the world; that governments have contributed to the problems by encouraging rising expectations and deferring necessary adjustments; and that there are positive steps that governments can take in the future. I shall comment first on the state of the world, and then on the proposals for the future.

II. THE STATE OF THE WORLD

There are valid reasons why the future rate of growth of perceived real incomes for Canadians is very likely to be less than over the past twenty years. Real resource limitations are showing up wherever we look.† Even as low-cost energy becomes more scarce, British Columbians are starting to attach higher values to unspoiled and undammed river valleys. Even as the forest industry is working into timber lands of ever-decreasing productivity, British Columbians are attaching ever-higher values to alternative uses of the remaining undeveloped timber lands. And the very population growth that increases the demand for food forces out of agricultural use the land required to produce local foodstuffs.

In Canada, nature's restrictions have in the past been mainly climatic, and these have been sufficient to limit most other pressures on resources. Even now, there are frontiers left, but everyone is starting to grasp that there is no longer a seemingly endless supply of lands beyond the mountains. To get more output from any of our natural resources it will be necessary to put more resources in, to an extent apparently much greater than over the past seventy-five years.

It does not do to exaggerate the extent to which real costs must rise and real incomes fall below past trends. It is possible that costs elsewhere in the world could rise even

---

†Editor's Note: In a forthcoming Fraser Institute book, *Oil in the Seventies*, Professor E. Berndt of the University of British Columbia, specifically considers the question of energy and economic growth and it is his conclusion that while production may become less "energy-using" in the future this in itself does not mean slower growth.

faster than in Canada, and thus re-establish our rentier position even though our deposits are of ever-diminishing quality. And it is a commonplace that technological change has helped to permit profitable development of resources that previously had no commercial value. Nevertheless, if one is to find a single feature of our present economy that signals trouble for the way ahead, it is the inability of our current technologies or 'ways of doing things' to adequately overcome the physical and environmental limitations on our ability to produce better standards of living for present and future generations of the world's peoples.

III. PROPOSALS FOR THE FUTURE

The Way Ahead notes that the initial reaction of all groups affected by physical and environmental limitations is to demand that 'something be done about it,' and governments are inevitably the parties receiving the demands. When canvassing alternatives for the future, the document recommends increasing reliance on the market system and a more pragmatic realization of what governments can and cannot do. The paper notes that government policy must do more to make labour markets work better, and to concentrate relatively less on simple income replacement. The specific proposals are for the use of unemployment insurance funds in job creation (but not in competition with the private sector). Yes, but how is it to be done?

In terms of social policies, the paper argues that the necessary price adjustments in the 1980's will only be feasible if the parties most adversely affected can be given adjustment relief that does not jeopardize the adjustment process itself. I suspect that energy prices were chiefly in the authors' minds; and their analysis would have carried more weight if they had been more forthcoming about what sort of policies would do the trick.

For labour-management relations, the paper wants more cooperative and less adversarial procedures. Don't we all? But how do we get there from here?

Next, in seeming response to the reader's impatient cries for more explicit solutions, the paper turns the issue around and states the obvious (obviously unacceptable?): "if we truly want our governments to do less — for us, and to us — we as individuals and in our private institutions will have to do more — for each other." The implied role for the government, in helping us to do more for each other, is to make sure that government services, at least, are priced to reveal their social costs; and to facilitate the creation and operation of institutions with cooperative goals.

After flirting briefly with decentralization (without offering to turn Ottawa back to E.B. Eddy) the paper returns to the economic issues of growth and investment. After noting the pressures on resources, the paper argues that the probability of attaining satisfactory economic growth in the 1980's will be greater if the structure of growth is changed. The plea, essentially, is to recognize future scarcities when making plans for the future; for example, to invest in energy conservation and small-scale renewable sources instead of merely upping the ante and charging into ever more expensive and ever-further diminishing deposits of non-renewable energy sources. One of the accompanying advantages of the small scale, of course, is that it encourages decentralization and reduces the pressures for more government control.

It is easy to demand more of a policy document, and of government policies. It would be easy to respond in such a vein to *The Way Ahead.* But this would be to deny *the important and revolutionary message in the document: that many of the problems of the 1980's, including the problems caused by governments, can best be met by individuals and groups increasing their own abilities to help themselves and others. If individuals are bothered by big governments, big business, big unions, and big everything else, then they should demand less from big institutions and supply more to small ones.*

Comments on the Working Paper: *The Way Ahead: A Framework for Discussion*

STEPHAN F. KALISKI

Professor of Economics
Queen's University

THE AUTHOR

Stephan F. Kaliski is a Professor of Economics at Queen's University. He was born in Warsaw in 1928, and was educated at the University of British Columbia and the University of Toronto. He received his Ph.D. from Cambridge University in 1959. He has also done research at Manchester University, the University of California at Berkeley, and Harvard University. He was a research supervisor for the Royal Commission on Taxation, 1963-64. Currently, he is the Managing Editor of the *Canadian Journal of Economics*.

Among his publications Professor Kaliski has written: *The Tradeoff Between Inflation and Unemployment, Some Explorations of Recent Evidence for Canada*, published under the auspices of the Economic Council of Canada, 1972; "People, Jobs, and the New Unemployment," *Canadian Public Policy*, Vol. II, no. 3, Summer 1976; "Unemployment and Unemployment Insurance — Testing Some Corollaries," *Canadian Journal of Economics*, Vol. IX, no. 4, November 1976.

Comments on the Working Paper: *The Way Ahead: A Framework for Discussion*

STEPHAN F. KALISKI

Professor of Economics
Queen's University

I. HISTORICAL PERSPECTIVE BLURRED

One can as easily be too critical as not critical enough of this document: on first reading, one tends to bristle at the partial, tendentious, and self-serving version of recent economic history it puts forward, for instance. Yet, a sober second reading, coloured by the realization that it is foolish to seek here a serious essay in economic history and that it is almost certainly too early for a *definitive* history of the 1970's inflation, leaves one calmer. One remains uneasy, however, about the impact on the public's economic literacy of pretending, in the document as elsewhere, that since inflation slowed down after the "Anti-Inflation Programme" was introduced it is obvious that it is the Programme that slowed down inflation. But perhaps the public is by now beyond the reach of quite so crude a claim.

II. NOT A FRAMEWORK FOR DISCUSSION

To stick then to the essentials, the most basic criticism one might level at the document is that it neither provides a "framework for discussion" — whether by "framework" one means a body of analysis, or a set of institutional assumptions or of political or moral imperatives, or a more general economic setting within the confines of which the discussion is to take place — nor even specifies what is to be discussed.[1] Everything seems to be up for debate: not only the control of inflation, to which most of the working paper is devoted, but also growth and the environment, the proper sphere of government and the characteristics of a good society, competition and commercial policies and industrial strategy, unemployment and manpower policies, and interpersonal, interregional and international distribution of income and wealth, to name only the major subjects.

Now, one need not be a doctrinaire adherent of either the classical dichotomy between real and monetary economics or the more modern trichotomy that divides functions of government into allocation, distribution, and stabilization to feel that this may not be the most fruitful way to proceed. Even if the economy, or the policy for that matter, turns out to be so interrelated that policies to attain all objectives have ultimately to be jointly determined, it is simplistic, to use a favourite expression of the document, to believe that intelligent informal discussion can be conducted in so wholistic a manner. It is a positive disservice to discuss a number of issues, each potentially more important than inflation itself, under the head of "Sources of Inflationary Pressure."

III. MY COMMENTS

As a result, one imagines, of this unfortunate methodology there is virtually no sustained discussion of the problems of containing inflation, or of any other problems. Instead, the working paper contains many scattered observations that strike one as intelligent, insightful, or provocative. The comments that follow are perforce equally scattered; the alternative was to ignore the document and launch on an essay of one's own.

---

[1] This point has also been made by the C.D. Howe Research Institute, "Comments on the Federal Government's Recent Working Paper," November 18, 1976.

1. Self-interest the key

There is much confusion between non-market, or even extra-economic, considerations on the one hand and market failure on the other. The market is inherently incapable of resolving problems of equity, freedom, or good government or of providing public goods. It can and should allocate resources with reasonable efficiency. If it fails to do so, as it will if there are differences between private and social costs and benefits, the most effective solution is likely to be to remove the obstacles to efficiency by altering the legal environment within which the market operates. This is not always easy to do, or to do well and quickly; but it is likely to produce better and more lasting effects than the call to consult, or to be more sensitive to the needs of others, or to practice "voluntary restraint" in the name of "social responsibility," and "sharing, compassion, tolerance, and responsibility towards others." For better or for worse, it still is our fellow citizens' self-interest that we must normally rely on, not their benevolence.†

2. Choices not reconciliations

There are real (and hard) choices to be made between current consumption on the one hand and investment, including conservation, on the other. There are also similar choices between consumption of private and public goods, between one's own consumption and others', and among different objects of investment. There is no point in seeking "mechanisms" to reconcile or "balance" these objectives, unless one means by that mechanisms for eliciting, influencing and giving effect to individual and societal preferences.

---

†Editor's Note: This rings a two hundred year old bell. "It is not from the benevolence of the butcher, the brewer or the baker that we expect our dinner, but from their regard to their own interests..." Adam Smith, *The Wealth of Nations* 1776.

3. Public sector pay

The working paper refers repeatedly to the role of "market power," and "administered pricing" in the inflationary process. But aside from general references to price rigidity and demand-shift and supply-shift inflation, it gives only one convincing example: the process of determination of compensation in the public sector. This important source of difficulty is given far too brief a discussion. Surely here, if anywhere, there is a crying need for "mechanisms" and "structures" to be put in place before the present controls expire and a particular responsibility upon governments to develop them! Here, too, there may well be need for extensive consultations, including ones among the various authorities and levels of government involved.

4. Competitiveness, politics and vulnerability

Finally, the working paper suggests three important areas for research although none of them is outlined in any detail:

a. What does it mean to say, as the working paper repeatedly does, that a country (as distinguished from a firm or an industry) may become internationally *uncompetitive* as a result of general inflation, lagging productivity growth, taxation, etc.? Are there limits upon the magnitudes of exchange rate adjustments or of changes in real income, or do such alterations react back in an unstable fashion on inflation and productivity? Is it capital flows or items in the current account that present problems? Or is one really talking not about *general* uncompetitiveness, but about the adjustments forced upon particular sectors of the economy and the costs they impose? What are the solutions to such problems as one might identify?

b. To what extent are governments endogenous, i.e. unable to make and carry out desirable policy decisions because of political, legal, social, or economic constraints? Are the limitations imposed by such endogenity equally serious for various types of policy, e.g.

traditional macropolicy, tax and other incentives, direct controls, moral suasion? How can limitations of this sort best be minimized? Or should one welcome and strengthen them instead?

c. What is the relative importance of the various sources of current and recent inflation? How "inflation-prone" are modern economies, and why? How can their vulnerability be reduced to a more satisfactory level, and what level of vulnerability (or of inflation, for that matter) is satisfactory?

These three areas constitute ample initial agenda for a discussion of how to handle inflation after the controls lapse. Many of the other issues touched upon in the working paper richly deserve separate discussions.

the way ahead:
a framework for discussion
Government of Canada
october 1976

WORKING PAPER

THE WAY AHEAD:

A FRAMEWORK FOR DISCUSSION

GOVERNMENT OF CANADA

CONTENTS

PREFACE

In October of 1975 the government introduced a temporary program of direct controls of income and prices. Since that time, the successful implementation of the Anti-Inflation Program has been the most urgent priority of the government.

It is not enough to dampen current inflationary expectations. The root causes of inflation—the conditions which led the government to impose controls in the first place—must also be assessed and solutions found. Towards that end, the government has been involved in a fundamental examination of the major structural components of our economy and our society.

This review has not been restricted to Ministers and senior officials alone. The consultation effort has been widespread. Within the Liberal Party, informal policy groups have been active. Caucus has held special meetings to assess post-control problems. Parliament has debated economic issues on many occasions and the government has listened with care to the views presented by members from all parties. Over the past several months, Ministers have met often with representatives of labour organizations, business associations, farmers' groups, fishermen, representatives of consumer and other public interest groups.

These discussions have been useful. But in order to better focus future consultations and to aid national understanding, many groups and individuals have asked for a general paper outlining the economic and social directions the government intends to take after controls end. This Working Paper outlines these principles and strategies and provides a context for further consultation. It sets new directions for the application of liberal philosophy in the light of the economic and social conditions of our time. Some measures, consistent with these new directions, will be announced in the Speech from the Throne. Other measures, as the paper makes clear, require further consultation with all segments of Canadian society. The government will actively pursue such consultation before proposing further measures to Parliament.

Canada's economic prospects are excellent. The talent of our people and the richness of our resources assure us of a bright future. How best to utilize these talents and resources in a manner that will promote national unity, assure balanced growth without inflation, and enhance individual freedom and opportunity, is one of the pressing issues of our time. The government hopes that this Working Paper will assist Canadians in understanding both the economic and social challenges which all of us must face and the principles and strategies which this Liberal Government advocates to meet them.

THE WAY AHEAD: A FRAMEWORK FOR DISCUSSION

I. INTRODUCTION

In October of 1975, the federal government introduced a temporary program of direct controls on incomes and prices. It did so only after a sustained effort to arrive at a voluntary consensus had broken down: It was becoming apparent that rapidly rising expectations with respect to future levels of inflation posed grave threats to the stability of the Canadian economic and social system. A period of restraint on the part of labour and business, together with government restraint in spending, was and is essential in order to reduce the rate of inflation to the point where it would no longer threaten the continued well-being of Canadians.

The program is working. The rate of inflation is coming down. But inflation is still Canada's greatest problem and the uncertainty it has created about the future, and about the future role of government in the period beyond controls, persists.

Controls will lapse in 1978. The government will remove them sooner if conditions allow. Shortly after the Anti-Inflation Program was introduced the government began a search for the conditions and policy directions that would be necessary for the removal of the controls program and for the post-control period. Policies were sought that would assure necessary economic growth, consistent with the full use of our human resources, a continued increase in the quality of living conditions, and freedom from inflation.

The principles and strategies that have emerged from this process amount to a statement about the role that the federal government will play in Canada's future. These strategies, and the principles that have shaped them, are presented in this paper. The central principles are a continued pursuit of liberal ideals, consistent with fiscal responsibility, and continued and reinforced reliance on the market economy. Strategies required to give effect to those principles entail a search for policies that will improve the workings of the market system and stand against pressures for rapid increases in government expenditure and the size of bureaucracies.

This government has no intention of lessening its commitment to its fundamental social goals. It reaffirms its commitment to a society in which all Canadians can develop their potential to the fullest degree possible, a society in which justice, compassion, tolerance and understanding lead to a strong and united Canada, a society based upon individual initiative and marked by personal freedom. However, the government believes that the preservation and enhancement of individual freedoms and opportunities depend critically on our ability, not only as a government but as a society, to control inflation.

New means must be sought to achieve our goals and new policies will be required. Important aspects of these policies must be not only their capacity to serve individual well-being but their capacity to convey to all Canadians a sense of living responsibly in a responsible society. An important dimension of the task to be

7

accomplished is to achieve a shared appreciation of how the economy works and how governments and individuals can best work together to serve individual and collective economic and social goals.

Canadians will recall that one advantage of the controls program is that it provides a "breathing space" to reflect on the economic directions that would be appropriate after controls are removed. This statement presents the government's assessment of where we are and the directions in which we must move. It outlines strategies designed to ensure the efficient, effective and equitable performance of Canada's social and economic system. The first policy measures in the implementation of these strategies will be presented in the Speech from the Throne. These specific actions flow from principles that the government has adopted.

These principles, and the further policies that they suggest must be pursued, could ultimately reshape the nature of government's role in our society. Most critical in this process is the need for close and continuing consultation with all segments of the Canadian public. A common understanding of our future prospects and the challenges that confront us is essential if we are to act, as governments and individuals, in ways that serve our longer-term interests and objectives. The policy directions that are set out in this paper can be viewed as an agenda for further consultation. The government seeks the active participation and advice of all Canadians in the modification or further elaboration of these policies.

II. THE INFLATIONARY PROCESS

A search for future directions must begin with an understanding of current economic conditions and, in particular, the inflationary process. Simplistic explanations of inflation are bound to be incomplete and misleading. Inflation is a complex economic, social and political phenomenon, both in its origins and in its effects. One of the characteristics of a period of continuing, rapid inflation is that expectations that prices will continue to escalate become deeply entrenched. Groups with market power demand higher wages and prices in order to offset not only past inflation but anticipated future price increases. Those individuals and groups who cannot 'keep up' in this process—those with fixed incomes, those who cannot work or cannot find work, and many who simply lack market power—suffer a loss of real purchasing power. This leads to increased demands on governments to redress the inequities bred by inflation. Increased government spending can lead to higher prices if the government simply prints the money or if additional taxes levied to finance these expenditures are passed on to others through higher wages and prices. Excessively high wage settlements and pricing decisions impose higher levels of cost, leading directly to higher prices. Expectations escalate and inflation continues to feed upon itself.

The debilitating effects of inflation extend beyond economic considerations to threaten the very nature of our institutions and traditions. The problems that unrestricted inflation creates were spelled out in the Budget Speech of June 23, 1975:

> ...inflation ultimately inflicts grievous damage to the fabric of society. It lowers the living standards of those on fixed incomes, including pensioners. It

8

leaves people without reliable, understandable guideposts by which to arrange their economic affairs. It injects grave uncertainty into decisions on family budgets, housing, savings and provision for old age. It provokes deep frustration, social tension and mistrust of private and public institutions. Collective bargaining is embittered. Industrial relations are damaged. We in Canada are already beginning to live some of these experiences.

There is a real sense in which the stability and endurance of our economic system and the social and cultural traditions on which it is based will be measured by our ability to respond to the challenge of inflation.

Inflation is not just a recent phenomenon. Escalating prices, and concern about their impacts on the economy and society have been with us for at least the past thirty years. For a large part of this period inflation was fairly moderate, though slowly increasing. It was widely, if reluctantly, accepted as a necessary and fairly tolerable cost of maintaining adequate levels of employment. Only in the late 1960's and early 1970's, when inflation began to accelerate rapidly in Canada and in other countries, were its dangers clearly perceived.

There have been many reasons advanced as to why industrialized countries appear to be increasingly vulnerable to inflation. At one extreme, inflation is seen as a purely monetary phenomenon that can be eliminated by controlling the supply of money. Others argue that governments' monetary and fiscal policies must be viewed together, and assert that excessive government spending in pursuit of social goals together with a government commitment to full employment create inevitable inflationary pressures. There are those, as well, who would argue that even if governments do not incur deficits, increasing levels of taxation required to fund growing expenditures lead to the erosion of incentives, a shift of income from investors to consumers and a consequent reduction in available output that is accompanied by rising prices.

There is a further view that asserts that inflationary forces are deeply embedded in the very structure of our society. A rapid shift of employment to the service industries and declining rates of productivity growth, as well as broad differences in income and wealth and the ability of powerful groups to protect too narrow interests, are factors which are said to lead inevitably to continuously rising prices. In this view, the market system as we know it does not always allocate resources efficiently and cannot provide a socially acceptable distribution of the fruits of growth.

In addition, there are those who point to the worldwide inflationary experience, in part a result of the rapid expansion of international liquidity, and to the sudden and severe increases in food and energy prices. They argue that Canada, as a trading nation, is extremely vulnerable to imported inflation.

There is a real sense in which the growth experience of the past thirty years has, itself, been seen as a basic factor in the inflationary process. Since World War II, cyclical slowdowns that occurred were short and quickly reversed by expansionary government policies. One of the legacies of this period, fundamental to an understanding of inflation, is a deeply rooted expectation that real growth will continue at past rates and an increasing willingness on the part of both individuals and governments to borrow against anticipated future income to support higher current living standards.

There is no single cause of inflation. Not all observers would rank the importance of the factors noted above in a similar way. There would nonetheless be general agreement with the following conclusions:

1. Industrialized economies for the last three decades, but more particularly since the mid-1960's, have become increasingly vulnerable to a long-run, continuing increase in measured inflation rates.

2. Continuing inflation creates short-term problems—internal inequities and a possible reduction in the ability to compete in world markets. These, together with the longer-term disruptions that accompany behaviour modified to anticipate inflation, exacerbate the inflationary process.

3. Once inflationary expectations have become entrenched, corrective policy measures can be offset—particularly in an economy as dependent on world trade as Canada's—by price increases that the government may not be able to control. The eradication of inflation can therefore be a long and painful process.

4. Continuing inflation, particularly in North America, has been accompanied by an increase in measured unemployment rates. Over the long term, continuing inflation is inconsistent with the maintenance of full employment. Fiscal and monetary policies directed at the control of inflation, unless associated with other measures, will have increasingly costly and socially disruptive unemployment consequences before they have a significant effect on inflation rates.

5. Continuing inflation inevitably results in greater public demand for government intervention in the economy, to offset the structural disabilities and inequities bred by the inflationary process. It is therefore imperative that inflation be controlled if governments are to be free, in responding to and serving social and economic objectives, to opt for less rather than more intervention in the economy.

III. CANADIAN ECONOMIC PERFORMANCE: RETROSPECT AND PROSPECT

The force of these conclusions is that a careful and critical assessment of the sources of the inflationary process is essential. This assessment demands an understanding of the growth we have experienced and our prospects for further growth.

The period following World War II has been as sustained a period of real growth as the industrial world has ever known. In most industrialized countries real after-tax income per person almost doubled through this period. Industrialized economies were characterized by the continued substitution of relatively cheap capital and energy for increasingly expensive labour in primary and secondary manufacturing processes, leading to rapidly increasing output per person employed. This was an important factor in sustaining and enhancing economic growth, which increased employment opportunities.

This growth process, through the broad rise in real incomes and living standards it provided, greatly expanded the opportunities and increased the well-being of all Canadians. In Canada, real after-tax income per person more than doubled in the thirty years following World War II. Our population almost doubled. New houses were built and jobs were created for the fastest growing labour force in any of the industrialized countries. Working and living conditions improved dramatically and the opportunities for individual Canadians to choose—where they wanted to live and how they wanted to live—continued to expand.

Sustained growth, and the benefits it brought, were in substantial part attributable to the successful economic management policies of the governments of industrialized democracies. Internationally, new economic institutions contributed to economic stability and the rapid expansion of trade and prosperity. Domestically, a collective determination that the widespread suffering of the Great Depression must not occur again led to government commitments to supplement the market system with policies to enhance job creation and minimize unemployment.

At the same time, rising incomes led to increasing government tax revenues. In Canada, these revenues were used to provide programs designed to equalize opportunity, through the construction and operation of schools, hospitals and transportation facilities and through the extended provision of direct income assistance. The introduction or strengthening of such programs as unemployment insurance, family allowance, public pension plans, and hospital and medical care sought to assure that the fruits of growth were distributed to all Canadians in a just and equitable manner. Through this period the growth in federal government expenditure as a proportion of Gross National Product was almost entirely related to increasing transfer payments—to individuals and to provincial governments. The goods and services provided directly by the federal government grew at roughly the same rate as the national economy, although growing transfer payments increased access by all Canadians to a growing array of goods and services financed by tax dollars rather than private after-tax incomes.

However by the late 1960's and early 1970's—even before the rapid escalation of inflation accompanied by recession and high unemployment recently experienced—several disturbing features of the post-war growth period had begun to become apparent. Not only in Canada, but in other countries as well, disquiet was increasing over the ability to manage the economy with traditional policies alone.

Of primary concern was the growing evidence, particularly marked since the early 1960's, that periods of cyclical expansion were taking off from successively higher plateaus of inflation. As well, successively higher rates of unemployment in cyclical pauses were associated with substantial and continuing price increases. There was an increasing apprehension that the growth process itself was unbalanced, creating the very pressures which threatened its continuation.

From an international perspective, continued growth had been of disproportionate benefit to the industrialized world. Despite increasing demands for the raw materials of the developing countries, income and wealth disparities between the developed and much of the developing world continued to widen. The result was a number of attempts by export-dependent developing countries to force a more rapid redistribution of income and wealth by acting in concert to restrict the supply of their export commodities and so drive up the price. Attempts to form effective export cartels generally met with failure until, in the fall of 1973, the Organization of Petroleum Exporting Countries was able to quadruple the price of oil. The immediate success of OPEC has led to renewed efforts by other countries to accelerate a redistribution of income and wealth.

From a domestic perspective, as well, the growth process has produced, along with its obvious and tangible benefits, increasing social and economic pressures:

1. Although the proportion of people living below the poverty line decreased, the gap between the rich and the poor showed little evidence of narrowing. This has led to claims that growth did not adequately serve social goals. It must be recognized, however, that a comparison of relative living standards must take into account, as well as incomes, the increased availability of publicly provided goods and services such as low-cost medical care and post-secondary education. To the degree that these are low-cost because they have been financed by taxpayers as a whole, a substantial extension of a common standard of basic protection for the individual within our society has taken place. It has occurred, however, together with and as a direct result of an increasing responsibility assumed by governments at all levels for the direct provision of goods and services.

2. This growing role of governments, in response to real needs for social assistance and legitimate desires for equality of access to basic necessities, was essentially financed through the 1960's by the increased government revenues that accompanied rapid growth. By the late 1960's, and through the early 1970's, however, as the pace of economic growth slowed, the net financing requirements of governments became quite large. As a result there was an increase in borrowing against expected future income in order to finance existing programs and this, together with an accommodating monetary policy, reinforced inflationary pressures. As inflation increased, so did the pressures on government to redress the inequities that were created, and the cycle threatened to intensify.

3. A further concern about the nature of the growth process is reflected in a heightened awareness of the adverse effects on the natural environment—and in some instances the health and safety of individuals. Continued growth presses further against the natural constraints that are imposed by the capability of air, water and land to support industrial, agricultural and urban activity. Increasingly, concerns are expressed that growth, as we know it, is less responsive than it might be to our collective demands for adequate health and safety standards and a decent environment.

4. Finally, the size, power and complexity of institutions and organizations have increased. This has been accompanied by a growing sense of alienation from, and mistrust of, big corporations, big labour organizations and big government.

The explosion into double-digit inflation in 1974-75, in Canada and in the rest of the world, must be viewed against this general background. The demands created by the rapid growth experienced in most industrial countries were beginning to press severely against available international supplies. These inflationary effects were compounded by the quadrupling of oil prices and the resulting rise in other energy prices, and by drought and crop failures, leading to widespread food shortages. These inflationary forces, through the real income losses they imposed on oil and food importers and through the constraining actions of governments which they made necessary, forced a severe cyclical contraction on most of the world economy through 1974 and 1975. However, while real production declined in other industrial countries, it continued to advance moderately in Canada. This relatively healthy economic performance, combined with continuing labour settlements that contained not only elements of 'catch-up' but anticipated inflation as well, threatened to prolong and to intensify inflation in Canada which would erode further Canada's competitive position in the international trading economy.

Prior to the summer of 1975, it appeared that the rapid international inflation would run its course as the industrial economies adjusted to much higher price levels for basic commodities and for energy. Indeed, the rate of inflation in most of our major trading partners had begun to ease considerably. In the United States, the annual rate of inflation had fallen from 12.2% at the end of 1974 to 7.8% by September 1975. In Canada, however, the annual rate of inflation was still over 10.5% in September of 1975. Inflationary expectations had become deeply entrenched and there were indications that they were about to increase to extraordinary levels. In late summer and early fall of 1975, it was not unusual to read of demands for wage and professional income increases in the range of 30%-60%. The risks were great that Canada would effectively price itself out of international markets. While the rest of the world shared in economic recovery Canadians would suffer a continuously deepening recession, until the rate of unemployment rose high enough to restrain price and wage increases to a range that would restore our ability to compete. The government viewed such a prospect as intolerable.

It was in this context, and only after a sustained effort to achieve a consensus on voluntary restraint had failed, that the government took its decision, in October of 1975, to impose controls and to adopt a posture of fiscal and monetary restraint. The immediate target of the government's Anti-Inflation Program was to reduce inflation below 8% by the fall of 1976. It is now clear that this target will be achieved. The target for the coming year is 6%. To support these objectives the government will limit the rate of growth of government expenditures to no more than the rate of growth in GNP. The Bank of Canada has also adopted targets for managing the money supply that are consistent with the overall objectives of the program. The government's Anti-Inflation Program is working. The process of economic recovery is underway and inflation has been decreasing to a rate that is more tolerable, if not yet acceptable.

There is still a long way to go. The annual rate of inflation in Canada has decreased from 11.1% in August of 1975 to 6.2% in August of 1976. Some deterioration in this performance can be anticipated through the next two months resulting from higher oil prices and municipal property taxes. In addition, our inflation rate remains higher than the inflation rates of certain of our important trading partners. Continuing high wage settlements, together with relatively poor productivity performance, threaten the competitive position of Canadian exports. The deficit in the current account of our balance of international payments increased to record levels in 1975 and was financed by record borrowings from other countries. In large measure, this deficit arose because Canadian growth was greater than that of our trading partners. Our exports declined while our imports remained high. As worldwide economic recovery proceeds the demand for Canadian exports is strengthening. But to take full advantage of this opportunity it will be necessary to ensure that the competitive position of Canada's export industries is not only safeguarded but improved. Cost increases must be constrained and, most important, expectations that prices and costs will continue to rise must be further reduced.

Continued determination, and the development and implementation of new policies, are needed to guard against a repetition of the experience of previous economic recoveries. By mid-1976, resumed growth in industrialized countries was widespread. The early strength of the recovery and strengthening prices for natural resources and food raised concerns that another inflationary spiral might begin, this time taking off from a plateau much higher than the last. These concerns were heightened by continuing levels of wage settlements that were inconsistent with future reductions in the rate of price increase.

The Government of Canada—like other governments—is determined to prevent a renewed outbreak of inflation. However, the high rate of growth of the Canadian labour force will continue through the remainder of the 1970's. This, together with the need to carefully manage the economic recovery and the controls program, and the necessity to further reduce inflation, means that new strategies must be found if currently high unemployment rates are to drop significantly before the end of the decade.

Looking beyond this decade to the 1980's, Canada's economic prospects are excellent. Indeed, they are matched by few other industrialized countries. Canada's opportunities for continued real growth lie in its relative wealth of resources, its abundant food-producing potential, its technology, and of course, its highly skilled and educated population. They lie, not least, in Canadians' capacity for enterprise. But to take advantage of these opportunities, to ensure that our substantial potential is indeed attained, Canadians and their governments will have to meet a number of major challenges.

The international economy is likely to be marked by strong competition for productive resources and markets. Continued growth will lead to increasing demands for food, energy and mineral resources, all of which will become increasingly more expensive. As their prices rise, competition for the financing, equipment and skilled labour necessary to produce them will increase. Such increases in the prices of scarce commodities must be accepted in order to provide the incentives and the conditions necessary to increase production, lead to more efficient use and stimulate the development of substitutes. It is this dynamic process of adjustment that leads to innovation and growth. It is imperative, however, that price adjustments for particular commodities not be allowed to feed a general inflationary process, to the detriment of all.

In Canada, the rate of growth of the labour force will slow during the 1980's. Continuing economic growth may lead to tighter labour markets, together with problems of adjusting to new economic opportunities. Estimates of our energy requirements, even with much lower rates of growth in demand, indicate that a substantially higher proportion of our total resources will be allocated to the development or importation of higher cost energy in the future than has traditionally been the case. Additional investment requirements and opportunities—in minerals, transportation, manufacturing—suggest that conflicting demands will have to be carefully reconciled if shortages in the supply of equipment or skilled labour are not to result in renewed inflation.

In addition to the necessity to avoid overloading the economy, a number of other potential problems must be addressed:

—Anticipated demands for Canada's resources by other countries, together with rapidly increasing investment requirements, raise the issue of foreign investment in the Canadian economy. It will be necessary to reconcile Canadians' desires to develop their potential to the fullest with objectives to increase the ownership and participation of Canadians in the Canadian economy. In effect, Canadians must recognize that this can only be achieved by increasing even more our already high rates of saving.

—Similarly, it will be necessary to balance the need for increased competitiveness in the international economy, and the large-scale organizations that may imply, with the continuing objective of more balanced economic and population growth within and among the regions of Canada.

—It will, as well, be increasingly important to rationalize Canada's trade and industrial strategies with the growing demands of the developing world. Particularly in secondary manufacturing, Canada will face an increasingly competitive international environment and a continuing shift in comparative advantage towards the developing world for some labour-intensive industries. Canada must respond to this challenge positively and constructively. However, the adjustment problems created for Canadian industries, communities and individuals could be considerable and must be eased.

Canadians have always faced challenges and it would be naive to assume that we will not continue to do so. Recognizing their existence is not cause for pessimism, but necessary in order to face them realistically and resolve them successfully. The coming decades offer tremendous opportunities to Canada and to Canadians. To seize these opportunities, however, requires a shared appreciation of the nature of the prospects and problems confronting us.

IV. SOURCES OF INFLATIONARY PRESSURE

The gravest threat to our ability to meet these challenges would lie in our incapacity to arrest inflationary pressures. The 1980's promise to be an environment in which such pressures will be continuously latent. Our ability to resist them requires an appreciation of the forces that produce them, an appreciation that transcends narrow economic considerations and examines inflationary pressures in the context of Canadian society, its existing institutions and economic prospects.

The notion that inflation results from excessive government spending is a popular one and, indeed, there may be instances where governments must bear a large share of the responsibility for inflation. To diagnose the inflationary spiral we have recently experienced as largely attributable to a profligate government, however, is simplistic to the point that it is misleading. Such a diagnosis ignores the fact that the recent acceleration of inflation was a worldwide phenomenon. It ignores the fact that all industrialized democracies have experienced gradually increasing inflation for at least the last three decades. Most fundamentally, it ignores the institutions that make up the Canadian economy and the complex relationships that define Canadian society.

To understand the inflationary process, and the issues surrounding the role that governments play in that process, it is necessary to examine those aspects of our social and economic structure that lead to inflation directly or indirectly through demands on government—to spend money and to intervene in the economic system. The existence of market power, declining productivity growth and rising expectations, Canada's role in the world economy, economic growth itself and the issues it raises, all contribute to the nature of the role that government plays in the economy and the responsibility that the government bears for inflation.

Freedom from inflation in the post-control period demands an understanding of these issues so that effective policies can be developed to deal with the basic pressures they produce.

A. Market Power

The market system is a continuously evolving set of relationships. The notion that private markets are characterized, always and everywhere, by competition that leads to flexible prices is patently a stereotype that ignores the evolution of private and public institutions over hundreds of years. At the same time, the view that all markets are dominated by powerful groups is no less a stereotype. A balanced view must acknowledge that in some markets, at least in the short to medium term, organizations and institutions exist that have substantial economic power, including the power to set wages and prices in a way that may bear little relation to supply and demand.

Although the ability to set prices in this way may not be a critical source of inflation, the use of market power to "administer" prices can pass on and hence aggravate inflation originating from excess aggregate demand or from specific price increases. "Administered" prices frequently embody inflationary expectations as well. Powerful economic groups, on the assumption that inflation will continue and acting to protect themselves, create cost pressures that in fact lead to higher prices, the realization of their own expectations and a continuing process of self-fulfilling prophecy. This is particularly the case when governments and monetary authorities act permissively out of a concern to avoid unemployment and to protect those affected by inflation.

Such prices are typically rigid in a downward direction; they are not lowered when demand falls. When overall demand is not excessive, but prices are rising in some sectors, this rigidity can create an inflationary bias even in the presence of substantial unemployment. Instances of employees accepting reduced wages or of industries reducing prices in order to sustain output and employment are becoming rare in today's environment.

A particularly serious consequence of widespread market power is that increases in the prices of goods or services that are relatively scarce tend to be interpreted as an increase in inflation generally. Wages increase, labour costs increase and prices of other goods and services increase as well. The price "signals" that result in efficient markets are impaired and the market system fails to work as effectively as it should.

Although one typically thinks of market power as characterizing the private sector, a serious administered pricing problem also exists in the public sector, where governments must often provide essential services that are widely considered to be "vital at any cost", and where labour does not feel there is any danger of "driving the company bankrupt" by asking for substantial increases. The development of collective bargaining in the public sector has served to remove many of the inequities which existed between public and private sectors in the past. But the process has nonetheless directly contributed to higher spending by governments and can indirectly increase inflationary pressures by providing high-profile settlements which give other workers an inflationary target to aim at. It is important that public service collective bargaining not be allowed to overshoot and go beyond what is fair. Modifications in public sector employer/employee relations are an essential element in a broad anti-inflation strategy, along with improved labour-management relations in the private sector and policies to sustain and enhance competition.

B. Declining Productivity Growth and Rising Expectations

Demographic trends will reduce the rate at which the Canadian labour force will grow in the 1980's. A continuing shift of employment to the service sector, together with some evidence that the productivity of capital goods may be declining, implies a future in which average productivity may grow less rapidly than it has over the past thirty years. Lower rates of productivity increase and slower rates of growth in the labour force would result in a potential for growth that would be lower in the future than it has been in the past. The confrontation that may occur between lower rates of future growth and increasing income expectations of Canadians could create new inflationary forces.

The amount and type of goods and services that can be produced will have to be reconciled with Canadians' expectations of higher levels of real consumption, as well as with the large and growing requirements for investment. This reconciliation is likely to be difficult. It will ultimately be dictated by the interplay of market forces. In the process, however, frustrated expectations can lead to concerted attempts to maintain relative positions. In an international context, the structural adjustments that will be called for may be exacerbated by continuing short supplies of energy and food and increasing demands by the developing world for a better distribution of wealth.

Policies will have to be developed to ensure that these necessary adjustments occur with the least possible disruption and do not lead to a renewed outbreak of inflation. An important component of such policies will be to establish measures to increase productivity. New investment will obviously be required, as will the capability to develop new and improved technologies, entrepreneurial skills and organizational structures.

C. Canada in the World Economy

Exports account for about a quarter of Canada's gross national product. Similarly, about a quarter of all the goods and services that Canadians consume is imported. This relatively large dependence on international trade raises concerns, not only about the capacity of the Canadian economy to compete internationally and the need to resist internal inflationary forces, but also with regard to Canada's vulnerability to inflationary forces originating abroad. While a flexible exchange rate can accommodate modest deviations in relative rates of inflation, it cannot cope easily with large discordant swings in price levels and has little role to play in periods of world-wide and coincidental price increases.

The broad prospects for the world economic community should favour Canada's trading interests. The rise in relative prices for natural resources which can be anticipated through the 1980's will benefit Canada as a seller. They will be, however, a mixed blessing. Not only are there commodities, such as oil, for which Canada's net dependency will increase but rising resource prices in general could result in inflationary income adjustments in an attempt to offset them.

In addition to the direct concerns arising from the impact of inflation, whether domestically or foreign induced, on Canada's trading prospects, there exists a more fundamental concern. Severe inflation breeds recession, and periods of high unemployment and low growth such as the one we have recently experienced, typically lead to pressure by nations to limit imports and expand exports through measures such as tariffs, quotas, and export subsidies. Such rounds of national self-protection would not only harm Canada's ability to compete but in the longer run would also present the gravest threat to an expanding and stable world trading community—a community on which Canada as a major trading nation greatly depends. The process of trade restriction must be resisted.

A further serious element in our prospects is the recent marked deterioration in Canada's balance-of-trade. Traditionally, Canadian merchandise exports have exceeded imports and the balance has been adequate to service the foreign debt we have incurred. In 1975, however, mainly because Canada continued to grow while other countries experienced a severe recession, merchandise imports exceeded exports, putting Canada in a position of borrowing abroad to make up the balance as well as to pay the interest and dividend charges on previous borrowings. To the extent that such borrowing is used to finance consumption rather than investment it lowers the rate of future growth and thus shifts some of the burden of supporting current living standards to future generations.

As the world recovery proceeds and resource prices firm, demand for Canadian exports will increase and our merchandise balance should again become positive and continue to increase. This general prospect is endangered, however, by the declining rates of productivity growth referred to above and recent, high levels of wage settlements which together have resulted in increases in the unit labour cost of production that seriously threaten our competitive position.

The government will continue to seek broader and mutually beneficial trading relationships with the European Community, Japan and our other trading partners, and to preserve and intensify our already substantial trade relationship with the United States. It will be necessary, as well, to seek measures that will increase the productivity of the export sector and ensure that cost increases do not erode its ability to compete.

D. Growth and Growth-Related Issues

Growth itself has been a contributing factor to inflation. While growth has brought about a substantial increase in average levels of economic well-being, the inequity of the distribution of its benefits both within and among nations has been a principal source of a restless quarrel over shares that has seriously escalated over the past few years. The very success of the growth process has created firmly embedded expectations of the continuing capacity of the economic system to deliver a continously increasing array of goods and services.

The debate over growth has shifted from the earlier issues of whether continued growth was desirable, or indeed, sustainable to a more meaningful discussion of "quality of growth" concerns. There are a number of pressing problems that must be the legitimate concern of governments.

Earlier concerns that absolute limits to growth might exist are being recast in a more sophisticated, but no less disturbing, form. It is increasingly recognized that, as resources become depleted, prices will rise to reflect scarcity and that higher prices will lead to more efficient use of existing resources, development of less accessible and more costly resources, and concerted efforts to develop substitutes. This process of adjustment, however, raises questions about the ability of high consumption societies to generate the savings necessary to finance the higher investments required for the extraction of less accessible resources and for the development of substitutes. The necessary adjustments will require further shifts in relative prices to provide the signals essential to the successful operation of a market economy. All of these price shifts must be accomplished without renewing the inflationary process.

In addition, concern is increasing about the continued environmental degradation associated with high energy using and high resource extractive activities. This is a particular manifestation of a general concern that continued growth imposes increasing "social costs", because of the incapacity of the market system, as it currently functions, to provide balanced growth. It is particularly important to understand the relationship between the growth process we have experienced, the social costs that this process has generated, and the increased direct role of government in the economic system.

The market economy, and the price system on which it rests, is the most efficient allocative mechanism available. The billions of daily decisions that are freely taken by individuals and together comprise a viable, functioning economy make it obvious that any alternative to the market system would require a massive bureaucracy to administer with the unacceptable result of diminution in individual freedom of action and choice.

Our belief that the market system provides the greatest efficiency and growth rests on the presumption that prices direct scarce resources to their most valuable use, that the price charged for a commodity reflects both the incremental cost of producing it and the incremental benefits that accrue through its purchase. There are obvious cases, however, where prices measure private cost and benefit but fail to reflect the costs and benefits to society as a whole. In such cases resources will not be put to their most appropriate social uses.

For example, the presumption that air and water are "free" has led to production processes and consumer decisions in which the costs of polluting the air and fouling the water are not reflected in the prices of the products produced and consumed. This leads to greater demands for, and increased use of, such products than would occur if individuals had to pay to protect the environment. At the same time, it leads to growing demands for government expenditures to redress the damage done to the natural environment. The provision of individual commodities demanded by some is, therefore, subsidized by all consumers in their role as taxpayers. Industrial pollution is a popular example, but consumers also pollute. Garbage disposal, automobile exhausts, non-returnable bottles are all examples of consumer decisions that impose a social cost, leading to increased demands on governments to intervene in the economy to provide environmental protection or abatement—to try to "balance" the growth process.

One view is that these social costs should be charged more directly to the recognized production costs of business so that they are reflected in the prices consumers pay. On the other hand, it is clear that forcing Canadian producers to absorb costs that their competitors in other countries do not reflect would increase their competitive disadvantage. It is important, however, to be clear about the issue. Social costs can be ignored: rivers can be polluted, urban congestion can worsen, transportation systems can deteriorate, the quality of working life can be impaired. The real costs will, in the end, be borne by society as a whole and often by future generations. Ultimately the accumulation of such costs leads to intense social pressure to have them alleviated. They become a claim on governments, as "spenders of last resort", and are met by general tax measures. We are paying now to redress the social costs of previous actions.

Meeting social costs leads to a reduction in real disposable incomes, through higher prices, lower wages and profits, or higher taxes required to defray the real costs. The simple fact is that we cannot protect the quality of our life unless we are willing to pay for it. The issue is who pays. To the degree that such costs are charged directly to the private sector, Canadian prices would rise further, or wages and dividends would be lower, in those industries most affected than they would under a more generalized and dispersed tax burden. But it is precisely these relative price changes—in a healthy market system—that will stimulate a search for new methods of production and new technologies that will be less wasteful of natural resources and less damaging to the environment, providing healthier and better balanced growth. Through such measures as the Canada Water Act, the Clean Air Act and the Arctic Waters Pollution Prevention Act, the government has taken steps which have this effect and seek to assure that the quality of our natural environment is protected and enhanced.

As well as concerns raised by depleting resource availability and increasing social costs, the question of who should pay for publicly provided goods and services is becoming increasingly important. Governments have traditionally provided goods and services that are, in large part, financed by all taxpayers—parks, educational facilities, transportation systems, and many others. There are obviously instances where such subsidization is appropriate and necessary to provide broad access and equality of opportunity. In many instances, however, the true costs are inadequately perceived and this may result in levels of demand that increase government expenditure to the point where the capacity of the economy to support their provision can become strained. Better information about how the costs of publicly provided goods and services are met is required to provide an increased understanding of the process and to facilitate a determination of the appropriate sharing of costs between users and all taxpayers.

Finally, there is mounting social concern that the economies and efficiencies of large-scale operation have led to the creation of corporate conglomerates and growth in labour organizations and government. Increasing scale has led to centralist forces that have created conflicts with objectives of regional and demographic dispersion and have contributed to the present unease with "bigness" and the remoteness of decision-making processes. There is also a view that increasing concentration and scale result in a vulnerability of systems to sudden and severe shocks. In the context of a future which is likely to be characterized by continued economic tension in the international economy, with the possibility of serious and sudden economic disturbances, it will be necessary, as we develop policies to deal with the period beyond controls, to consider carefully the resilience of our economy and our society.

E. The Responsibility of Governments

The issues that are in dispute about the responsibility that governments bear for inflation can be clarified by distinguishing three basic views as to the role of government in the social and economic system.

(i) A Minimal Role for Government

In economic terms, this view asserts that the market system allocates resources most efficiently resulting in the highest possible production and growth. It is this growth and only this growth that enables the government, through the tax system, to raise the revenues necessary to pay for public goods or serve social purposes. Intervention or interference in the operation of the market system impairs this efficiency and leads to rigidities that threaten growth. Adherents of this view would admit that imperfections in the price system exist and that the distribution of income that results may be socially unacceptable. They would emphasize, however, that the "benefits" to be gained by government intervention—whether through regulation, taxation or direct expenditures—are short-term and outweighed by the longer-run "costs" of lost efficiency and output, and higher inflation.

Philosophically, this view sometimes acknowledges a public responsibility to provide "equality of opportunity". But it is characterized by the belief that government intervention in pursuit of "equity of outcomes" has led to the loss of individual freedom and initiative—and could undermine the market system, which it sees as the best guarantor of a better life for all.

In this view, governments play a central role in the inflationary process through

—levels of taxation that erode incentive;

—social assistance payments that bias production in favour of consumption and against investment;

—regulations that reduce enterprise; and

—adherence to full employment policies that bias the economic system in the direction of excess aggregate demand and enhance inflationary pressures.

(ii) A Continually Expanding Government Role

This view emphasizes governments' responsibility to support economic growth, equity, the public provision of goods and services, and intervention in the working of the market system to ensure socially acceptable outcomes. In this view inflation is seen not merely as an economic phenomenon but rather as a result of a complex interplay of economic, social and political forces. The ultimate sources of inflation are to be found both in market "failures" and in the incapacity of the market system to serve social goals, with a consequent need for increasing government intervention. These "failures" and incapacities would include:

—the fact that market economies cannot assure a socially acceptable distribution of incomes, both among persons and between wages and profits;

—the inability to recognize the increasing demands put upon public authorities arising as a result of private decisions, for example the provision of social capital such as transportation systems, roads, sewers;

—the failure to account properly for social costs, which leads to demands on governments to remedy pollution, urban congestion, and to correct for resource misallocation generally; and

—the failure to provide all persons equal access to a growing range of perceived necessities such as education and health care, leading governments to undertake the provision of such goods and services either directly or through the subsidization of private production and consumption.

To a considerable degree, therefore, this view would assert that the growing role of government has been thrust upon it by the incapacity of the private market economy to serve social goals. Many adherents of this view would go further to argue that social direction of production is imperative if a socially optimal array of goods and services is to be assured.

(iii) *A Middle Road*

There is a middle view that resists both of the more extreme views outlined above. This view would not accept the social costs of a minimal role for governments. It would not deny the legitimacy of the goals that governments have generally pursued. It would assert that the principal sources of expanding government expenditure have derived from the pursuit of greater equity in income distribution, wider access to basic goods and services, and the necessity to offset or repair the social costs that result from the operation of the market system as it has evolved.

This view, however, would acknowledge that at any point in time it is indeed possible for governments, in pursuit of social and economic goals, to damage the engine of economic growth, contribute to excess aggregate demand, and hence originate or exacerbate inflationary pressures. In this view, it is entirely possible for governments to:

—establish commitments to a range and volume of expenditure goals that either demand a tax structure beyond the community's ready acceptance or lead to recurring deficits which in turn are financed by borrowing from Canadians and non-Canadians or by selling government debt instruments to the central bank, thus increasing the supply of money;

—contribute to "rising expectations", either by underwriting the costs of unemployment or by a series of accessions to public demands that cause the public at large to lose sight of economic constraints;

—intervene excessively in pursuit of social goals and better social performance of the economic system, with a consequent erosion of incentives, initiative and personal freedoms and responsibilities.

There is an emerging middle view that essentially argues that the inflationary consequences of government actions reside less in the ends that governments have sought to pursue than in a choice of means, including timing, that may not always have been most appropriate.

Those who hold this view would not deny that the pursuit of social goals can damage the economic fabric. They would emphasize, however, that the pursuit of narrow economic goals can as easily damage vital social fabrics, which are just as important. Rather than relent in the pursuit of social goals, they would seek new and effective means to pursue them, and recognize that all segments of society must work together in this pursuit. They would seek a rationalization and simplification of the vast array of government programs. They would argue that it is both possible and desirable to seek a substantial reduction in the rate of growth of government expenditure and direct government intervention, and to search for alternative strategies—less expenditure-oriented—to serve the legitimate social concerns of government, and in fact to better serve society.

It is this emerging middle view that has been adhered to by the present government in its search for appropriate policies for the post-control period and for the principles that will shape the role that the government will play in this period.

V. THE ROLE OF GOVERNMENT IN THE POST-CONTROL PERIOD

Current government policies of controls and determined restraint in fiscal and monetary policy are appropriate if the inflationary forces unleashed by the events of 1973-75 are to be wound down. Looking beyond the period of controls it is clear that the posture of fiscal and monetary restraint must be sustained. If these policies are to be supported, however, it is critical that the deeper structural issues in the inflationary process which contribute to inflation directly, or indirectly through their expenditure pressures on governments, be addressed. Some clear directions have been noted in the discussion of particular sources of inflationary pressure. The government has concluded, however, that what is ultimately required to meet the challenges of the future goes beyond the introduction of new policy measures to a basic and fundamental reassessment of the role of government itself.

An essential theme emerging from this reassessment is the necessity to increase both the reliance on and the effectiveness of the market system. The role of government policy should not be to direct and manage the economy in detail. The interplay of dynamic forces that results from the market system and has led to continuing economic growth must be encouraged. It is not only growth that is at issue. Governments can become too pervasive and oppressive actors in the daily lives of Canadians.

At the same time, however, it must be recognized—certainly by those who wish to strengthen the market system—that market-directed economic growth has not fully served the social goals and aspirations of Canadians. This government has no intention of reducing its deep commitment to liberal ideals of individual freedom, equality of opportunity and social justice. It does not intend to participate in, or to allow, a dismantling of the socially progressive society Canadians have built in this country. Indeed, the preservation and improvement of this society is a paramount reason for the government's determination to control inflation. It will therefore be necessary to seek and to implement a broad range of supportive public policies that will enable improved operation of the market economy. Such supportive policies must be developed and managed in a way that allows governments to fulfill their legitimate responsibilities, but to do so with less, rather than more, direct intervention in the economic system. Such policies must provide effective alternatives to increasing expenditures and expanding bureaucracies.

A number of policy initiatives have been identified as consistent with the above themes and necessary to the successful functioning of the Canadian social and economic system in the period beyond controls. Some directions have already been indicated and specific policies will be announced to Parliament in the Speech from the Throne. Necessary as these policies are, they will not in themselves be adequate to ensure the elimination of inflationary pressures and to produce the balanced growth necessary to provide continuing increases in the quality as well as the standard of our living conditions. It will be essential to pursue additional strategies. These strategies must serve effectively the government's social concerns—and certainly its commitment to enhance the welfare of the individual—in those areas which most seriously threaten the government's resolve to restrain its own growth. The government is committed to the strategies. The precise policy implications are clearer for some than others. The government looks to the processes of consultation to lead to further elaboration of policies consistent with these strategies.

A. Employment Policies

Continued high rates of unemployment impose enormous costs on individual Canadians and heighten disparities among the regions of Canada. The high level of unemployment currently prevailing and the prospect that the unemployment rate may be reduced only gradually over the balance of the 1970's pose the greatest threat to the government's determination to exercise fiscal restraint.

Social policies, and particularly unemployment insurance, have enormously reduced the element of 'hardship' accompanying unemployment and have been a major factor in sustaining total demand. A prolonged period of severe unemployment, however, imposes a significant expenditure strain on the government, a strain that has no direct counterpart in productive employment.

The average government payment to unemployed Canadians, through programs such as unemployment insurance, welfare and retraining, currently exceeds 75% of the average industrial wage. The total cost of unemployment is even greater if one considers the indirect costs as well. Not only does the cost of unemployment to society remain high in this sense, but there is also abundant evidence that the true cost to the unemployed individual, despite the maintenance of his income, is also high. All evidence available indicates that the vast majority of Canadians prefer wages in reward for work to transfer income. Periods of prolonged unemployment are a disaster for the individual, eroding moral strength and personal dignity. This is particularly the case when unemployment rates are high, as they are now, among young entrants to the work force and in particular regions. In addition, the most rapid erosion of poverty and the most significant narrowing of income disparities occur in periods of high employment, and not through income transfer policies. New employment policies, that increase productive work and reduce all of the appalling costs associated with unemployment, are clearly called for. Such policies must be implemented within the general framework of monetary and fiscal policies of government but must supplement these policies by focussing on specific employment problems and particular regions, in ways that do not increase inflationary pressures.

Excessive tightness in job markets, as in any market, can be an inflationary force. The unemployment problems we may experience through the remainder of this decade may slowly transform themselves into problems of shortages of workers and workers with particular skills in the early 1980's, particularly in certain regions. During this decade a number of changes in the structure of our economy will be both necessary and desirable. As the nature of economic activity shifts so will the nature of employment opportunities. Government employment policies must help match people with jobs, both in occupational categories and in different regions of the country, and thus avoid inflationary pressures created by shortages in the supply of skilled labour. This will require the reexamination and intensification of manpower training and mobility programs. But government neither can nor should play this role alone; industry and labour organizations must assume a greater share of the responsibility for ensuring that job markets function efficiently and effectively.

While enhanced labour mobility and training are essential elements of a viable employment policy for the future, there will continue to exist unemployed persons who are actively seeking productive work but not able to find employment. From any point of view—enhancing the welfare of individuals, reducing the total cost to society, providing valuable services that the market system does not now offer—it is both appropriate and desirable to introduce programs of direct job creation. Imaginative programs of direct job creation, community employment schemes, and the developing experiments in the use of unemployment insurance funds to support job creation will be indispensable elements of the government's commitment to sustain a fuller employment society consistent with fiscal restraint and an anti-inflation objective.

These programs will be designed to ensure that the job opportunities created will not be in competition with the private sector. At the same time, the government is anxious to confer with private employers on means to sustain private employment when industries or firms experience short-term reductions in the demand for their products.

B. Social Policies

The government's commitment is to a society in which incomes from productive and satisfying employment, rather than from government transfers, sustain the dignity and the income requirements of most individuals of working age. However, programs to assure minimum levels of income to those who cannot work, or whose work income is inadequate, and to provide greater access to basic services for all Canadians are a continuing commitment of the government. Over the past decade the number, scope and scale of such programs have expanded greatly, providing real benefit to millions of Canadians. The rapid and continuing growth of these programs, however, creates potential conflicts with the need to restrain government expenditures to responsible levels. Excessive demands upon government to equalize opportunities and to protect the disadvantaged could create formidable pressures to depart from fiscal restraint.

An additional dimension of these potential pressures arises from the fact that a large number of government programs have multiple objectives, one of which is frequently a social concern. For example, food and energy policies have in the past been shaped by a desire to intervene directly in pricing decisions in order to protect the interest of particular regions or to ease adjustment problems for individuals most seriously affected. It is anticipated that the decade of the 1980's will be a period of important structural price changes. If the necessary adjustments that these price changes call for are to occur in an orderly manner, it is imperative that the price changes themselves neither give rise to, nor reinforce, a general inflationary process. Successful management of the economy in a way that will facilitate balanced growth and freedom from inflation will depend upon the ability of individuals and institutions to react to these market forces. At the same time, however, the government must develop an enhanced ability to provide adequate relief to those Canadians affected most adversely by particular price changes and to do this in a manner that does not compromise the operation of the market system by directly controlling prices.

It is in the context of these concerns that the government has undertaken to redesign social programs, with an emphasis on focussing assistance more directly towards those in need through greater integration of existing programs and an enhanced reliance on programs that encourage self-help. The rationalization, simplification and redesign of programs in the social policy area will provide governments with instruments that are more flexible, efficient, and capable of serving government objectives more compassionately—instruments that can effectively constrain rapidly expanding expenditures, increasing bureaucracies and the direct manipulation of strategic prices to serve social policy goals. What is required is not less commitment, but greater efficiency together with delivery systems that protect the dignity of individuals in need. To accomplish this, it will be necessary to pursue an examination of the integration of income transfers with the tax system. The results for those who need it will be more help, not less.

C. Labour-Management Relations

The government remains committed to the collective bargaining system as the fairest and most publicly acceptable method of determining wages and working conditions, in both the private and public sectors. However, the collective bargaining system is, in many instances, not working as equitably or effectively as it should. The increasing number of working days lost through strikes is not only a burden for all involved, but severely threatens the satisfactory performance of the economy. In some cases, strikes have imposed particular hardships on the general public, especially in the public sector where essential services have been withdrawn.

The collective bargaining process has been seriously strained by the inflationary experience of the past few years. Escalation of the quarrel over relative shares and growing pressures to protect against expected future inflation have resulted in increasing confrontation between labour and management. To the degree that the Anti-Inflation Program is successful in constraining the increase in living costs to tolerable levels, it will itself reduce the tension surrounding labour-management relations. But, if social and economic strains are to be minimized, new directions in which labour-management relations can continue to evolve through the post-control period, becoming more cooperative and less adversarial, are necessary—in both the private and public sectors.

Closely related to concerns about the collective bargaining process are deep concerns about the productivity performance of Canadian industry. Low rates of productivity increase, together with continued high levels of wage settlements, threaten the international competitive position of our existing industries and reduce the attractiveness of Canada as a location for new industries.

Governments have a responsibility to develop a framework that will encourage a continuing search for productivity increases. But within this general framework, the major initiatives that can improve Canada's productivity performance should, and indeed must, be taken at the level of the individual plant or industry.

It will be necessary for labour, management and governments to seek measures that can broaden the scope of labour-management relations and the collective bargaining process in both the private and public sectors. Employers must become more responsive to demands for high standards of industrial health and safety and more sensitive to the overall quality of the working environment. Employees must become more aware that continued employment opportunities depend upon the continuing viability and profitability of the enterprise. Over the longer term sustained increases in real labour income can be supported only by advances in productivity. Both employers and employees must become more responsive to the interests of the general public in settling disputes.

D. Social Responsibility

This paper has discussed a number of difficult challenges to *government's* social responsibility. That matter is far easier to discuss than the subject of the social responsibility of individuals and institutions. No theme sounds more utopian—yet none is more crucial if Canadians are to fulfill themselves, as individuals and as a society, without expanding government spending and bureaucracy; without giving free rein to the inflationary pressures that have threatened our economy in the recent past; without abridging personal freedoms; and without retreating to the social dark ages of the 1930's. It is a constant theme of this paper that if we truly want governments to do less—for us, and to us—we as individuals and in our private institutions will have to do more—for each other.

The question of social responsibility is becoming both more important and more difficult. The increasing size and complexity of the economy make it difficult for any institution or individual to perceive the social, as opposed to the private, consequences of economic behaviour. The result has been a heightened concern about issues of common interest that affect all Canadians but are the responsibility of no single individual or institution. Ultimately, the government becomes a focus for such concerns.

The capacity of the individual to perceive how the economy is working can be significantly improved through the establishment of better information and public and private accounting practices which make social costs more visible. Other countries, particularly the United States, are moving towards the establishment of such practices within businesses and the development of social accounting measures as a counterpart to the gross national product. More information on the way in which the economic system functions—its benefits as well as its social costs—cannot but help encourage both better understanding of the sources of claims upon governments and more socially responsible decisions by the private sector.

The government has spoken often about the need for voluntary restraint as the alternative to restraint by government. What is needed is a reaffirmation of values which embrace a greater sense of sharing, compassion, tolerance and responsibility towards others, values which reflect a sense of Canadian cooperation and common direction. Individual values cannot—and indeed should not—be imposed by governments. It is nevertheless clear that as social responsibility has shifted from individuals to their governments, the direct role of government in the economy has increased.

Experience confirms that Canadians, when made aware of the challenges we face and the nature of the choices open to us, act responsibly and in their own long-term interest. The government will therefore act to improve the information available to Canadians on the manner in which the economic system operates, its opportunities and its constraints, and to develop appropriate forums in which such information can be critically discussed.

Beyond the development and distribution of such information, the following areas merit further consultation and consideration:

1. Ways and means to encourage the recognition of social costs and to lead to their being taken into account by private companies and individual consumers so that they do not become the expenditure responsibility of governments. For example, taxes might be placed on production or consumption decisions that breed social obligations and costs (as road use and automobile weight are now taxed) or on polluters generally. Another area that deserves further scrutiny is the more realistic pricing of publicly provided goods and services. For example, the user's price of an airline ticket might reflect more—and the public's tax bill reflect less—of its true cost.

2. Mechanisms to encourage a broader recognition and acceptance of social responsibility by both corporations and labour organizations, as well as an understanding of that responsibility by the general public. Such mechanisms might include the increased participation of employees in plant management and profit sharing, and heightened corporate responsibility for training, job maintenance and the quality of the working environment.

3. Mechanisms to encourage the further development of cooperatives and voluntary organizations.

4. The possibility of the private sector providing goods or services that are now provided through government enterprises and programs.

The appropriate balance between the public and private sectors with regard to how social costs should be met will depend on particular circumstances. The development and implementation of appropriate measures will require extensive consultation with those organizations and individuals that will be most affected. Any changes that might be introduced must be carefully considered and phased over a time period sufficiently long to allow the necessary adjustments to take place with a minimum amount of disruption.

E. Decentralization

One change that could foster greater social responsibility in the private and public sectors is greater decentralization. The openness of the Canadian economy, the dependence on exports and the competitive world trading environment foreseen for the 1980's, all create a continuing need to sustain and improve Canadian competitive capacity. In some instances this will require the reorganization and rationalization of Canadian industry in order to gain the economic advantages of large scale production. The increasing scale of organizations, however, has resulted in major centralist tendencies in the economy. These have conflicted with government objectives to promote regional balance. They have also led to a heightened sense of individual alienation from decision-making processes and have contributed to the increased direct intervention of government in the economic system.

The capacity of any single trading nation, and particularly one so dependent on international trade as Canada, to stand against centralizing forces is extremely limited. In many cases the economies of scale are real and important and outweigh the social costs that "bigness" might entail. Nevertheless, there is a growing appreciation in many countries that "bigger is not necessarily better". In many cases the efficiencies of scale may be overestimated, and when the resulting social costs are considered, may indeed be non-existent. While objectives of economic efficiency and decentralization must be carefully balanced, opportunities may arise where it is possible and desirable to lean against centralizing forces.

One such opportunity that the government intends actively to pursue is the elaboration of a consistent and comprehensive small firm development strategy that will preserve and enlarge the role of small businesses—most of them owner-managed—in our economy. While much public attention is devoted to corporate giants, small to medium-sized business forms the life-blood of most Canadian communities. To the degree that it is necessary to devise further policies to ensure that this continues to be the case, the government intends to do so. No theme is more consistent with the government's objectives to maintain a healthy and regionally diverse economy and to enhance individual opportunity and enterprise.

The government will pursue vigorously its own decentralization program, to bring the delivery of government services closer to those they serve, and to resist needless centralism. It is eager to pursue consultations with the private corporate sector on the capacity of that sector to sustain maximum regional diversification consistent with efficient and competitive operations.

Decentralizing policies can make an important contribution to a regionally diverse and equitable economy. Assurance of regional equity will, however, continue to depend either upon the capacity of the federal government to assist less advantaged regions or upon decisions of the private sector to do so. While the federal government will restrain its growth, it cannot and will not forsake its capacity to sustain and deepen the sense of national unity flowing from its regional equalization and development policies.

A further opportunity, and indeed obligation, that must be pursued is the continuing search for a more productive and constructive basis for federal-provincial relations. No attempt has been made in this paper to continuously note issues and directions in which federal-provincial collaboration will be essential. The principal policy directions outlined above will, of course, require intensive federal-provincial cooperation in their implementation. Without such cooperation, success can only be limited. The government will actively seek more effective federal-provincial consultative mechanisms, to discuss the sharing of responsibility and capability for public programs and to ensure that such programs are efficiently implemented.

F. Growth

Continuing real economic growth is essential to the health of the economy and the well-being of Canadians. But unbalanced growth imposes "costs" on society. If these costs cannot be accommodated within the growth process itself, they will lead to increasing public demands for direct government intervention. Concerns have focussed particularly on issues of environmental degradation and continuing high rates of resource use.

It has been suggested that the 1980's may be a period of severe strain on world resources—labour and equipment as well as investment capital. The investment requirements foreseen for energy in Canada, though feasible with careful management, may be only one component of a severely stretched economy. It is in this context that policies that can provide more balanced growth, by increasing social responsibility and by serving the objectives of decentralization and smaller scale, take on added importance. Government policy can increase the range of choices and provide the information that can allow Canadians to be more selective about growth.

There are a number of policy directions that offer the potential to ease the adjustment problems of the 1980's, to enhance our ability to avoid inflationary pressures and, generally, to assure that the growth process results in an improved quality of life. Energy conservation programs, for example, are a least-cost, least-risk direction for Canadian energy policies and a critical contributor to the reduction of inflationary pressures. Such programs must be intensified and expanded.

In this same regard, the capital intensity and large scale of present energy supply alternatives, together with their adverse environmental implications, strongly suggest that urgent attention be given to less capital intensive, more decentralized, renewable energy alternatives. Solar space heating, for example, even in a Canadian climate may become economically competitive well within the next decade. This, and other renewable energy options, offer substantial potential that needs to be carefully assessed and, where appropriate, vigorously developed.

Finally, there are a number of other areas where government may have a role to play in ensuring that our limited resources are utilized for the greatest benefit. The advantages of recycling increasingly scarce and expensive mineral resources, the increasing concerns expressed that some forms of advertising serve little social purpose, and the growing resistance to wasteful, built-in obsolescence that seems to characterize growth as we know it, are all areas that merit further consideration.

G. Investment

One of the major challenges posed by increasing capital requirements will be the need to generate sufficient domestic savings. Over the past few years the government has introduced a number of measures to increase the incentives for Canadians to save—for housing, for their own retirement, and to facilitate more investment by Canadian industry.

Large investments will be required over the coming decades—for energy and other resources, for transportation, and to improve the productivity and competitive performance of Canada's secondary industries. Satisfying these capital demands may lead to structural adjustments in the economy that could, if not carefully managed, result in a renewed outbreak of inflation.

It is imperative that these investments occur in order to produce the range of goods and services and the quality of life that future generations of Canadians will demand. Fostering a climate in which Canadians and others will invest with confidence in the future of this country is a primary objective of this government. For the shorter term, the Anti-Inflation Guidelines have been revised to encourage investment. In the longer run, our continuing capacity to provide attractive opportunities for new investment will be measured by our ability to control inflation and to pursue the responsible implementation of the policies required to sustain balanced growth.

VI. CONCLUSION: THE NEED FOR CONSULTATION IN THE DECISION-MAKING PROCESS

Inflationary forces are deeply embedded in industrial economies. There is no simple source of the problem nor any simple solution. Bringing inflation under control will be a long and painful process. There will be a continuing threat of renewed inflationary pressures both internally and from world-wide forces beyond Canada's control. The growth of government expenditure must bear some of the burden of responsibility for inflation. It is clear, however, that the pressure on governments to continue to grow rapidly and to increase areas of intervention will be intense unless inflation can be arrested and unless inflationary pressures arising in the market economy can be allayed.

The imposition of controls, the commitment to fiscal restraint and the adoption of monetary targets were, and are, the appropriate short-term responses to the current Canadian inflation. The policy proposals that will shortly be announced in the Speech from the Throne form a broad and consistent package addressed to a further reduction in the sources of inflationary pressure. Though each is necessary, they are not likely, alone or as a package, to provide a sufficient solution to the longer-run inflationary problem. A fully developed strategy for the continuing reduction of inflation requires both an examination of the sources of increasing government expenditure and the articulation of a role for government which might reduce expenditure and interventionist pressures.

In establishing its priorities in the summer of 1974, the government highlighted five themes:

—a more just, tolerant Canadian society

—with greater balance in the distribution of people and in the creation and distribution of wealth between and within regions

—which makes more rational use of resources and is sensitive to the natural and human environment

—accepting new international responsibilities particularly with regard to assisting developing countries

—with an evolving federal state capable of effective national policies as well as sensitive, responsive and competent government at all levels.

The government remains committed to these priorities. They are essential if we are to create a strong and united Canada.

It is clear, therefore, that principles of fiscal responsibility, less direct intervention, and increased reliance on the market economy demand, for consistency policies which will both reduce pressures upon governments arising from 'imperfections' of the market economy and which will permit the government's priorities to be served in a less expenditure-oriented and interventionist manner. Ne strategies for pursuing employment and social goals, improving labour-management relations, promoting social responsibility, and encouraging decentralization, balance growth and investment, are all necessary avenues for further pursuit.

Underlying many of the themes developed in this paper is the central role that broader public understanding of the Canadian economic system, its opportunities and its problems, can play in the development of appropriate policies for the post-control period. Indeed, it is a basic assumption of this paper that Canadians—when presented with the information necessary to assess our future options and opportunities to discuss the directions in which we should be moving—will make their choices in a manner that is both responsible and in accordance with their longer-term interests. The concept of a new sharing of social and economic responsibility is fundamental to the search for new directions that will assure balanced growth without inflation.

The further elaboration of these new directions cannot and should not take place without a focussed public dialogue. What is at issue is nothing less than the nature of Canada's social and economic future and the role that government will play in that future. The government believes that a concerted and coordinated process of responsible consultation with all segments of Canadian society will enhance our understanding of the options available to us and the directions in which we must move. In the final analysis, the responsibility for the decisions that must be taken and the policies that must be implemented will rest with the government and with Parliament. In the process of formulating those policies, however, the government seeks the advice and views of all Canadians.

The government will initiate a formal process of discussion, dialogue and consultation with all elements of Canadian society: provincial governments, representatives of business, labour and consumer organizations, other special interes groups, and individual Canadians. This paper represents a major step in such a process.

OCTOBER, 197

To: The Secretary,
    The Fraser Institute,
    626 Bute Street,
    Vancouver, British Columbia. V6E 3M1
    Canada.

PUBLICATION ORDER FORM

Please send me:

_____ copies of _____

_____ copies of _____

_____ copies of _____

Enclosed is payment in full of $_____ or
credit card no.: Chargex # _____
Mastercharge # _____

Signature: _____

Name: _____

(please print)

Organization: _____

Address: _____

_____

MEMBERSHIP REQUEST FORM

Dear Sir:

Please send me information on how I can become a
member of the Fraser Institute.

Name: _____

Title: _____

Organization: _____

Address: _____

_____

To: The Secretary,
     The Fraser Institute,
     626 Bute Street,
     Vancouver, British Columbia. V6E 3M1
     Canada.

PUBLICATION ORDER FORM

Please send me:

_____ copies of _____
_____ copies of _____
_____ copies of _____

Enclosed is payment in full of $_____ or credit card no.: Chargex # _____
Mastercharge # _____

Signature: _____

Name: _____
                    (please print)

Organization: _____

Address: _____

_____

--✂

MEMBERSHIP REQUEST FORM

Dear Sir:

   Please send me information on how I can become a member of the Fraser Institute.

Name: _____

Title: _____

Organization: _____

Address: _____

_____